GIBBON

AND HIS

ROMAN
EMPIRE

This attitude [tapping his snuff-box while talking] continued to be characteristic of Mr. Gibbon. The engraving in the frontispiece of the Memoirs is taken from the figure of Mr. Gibbon cut with scissars [*sic*] by Mrs. Brown thirty years [1794] after the date of this letter. The extraordinary talents of this lady have furnished as complete a likeness of Mr. Gibbon, as to person, face, and manner, as can be conceived; yet it was done in his absence.

—LORD SHEFFIELD

The utter incongruity of those combining elements produced this masterpiece—the gigantic ruin of Europe through a thousand years, mirrored in the mind of an eighteenth-century English gentleman.

—LYTTON STRACHEY

GIBBON
AND HIS
ROMAN
EMPIRE

David P. Jordan

University of Illinois Press
URBANA   CHICAGO   LONDON

FOR MY FATHER AND MOTHER

ACKNOWLEDGMENTS

THIS BOOK began life as a doctoral dissertation and still carries the scars of the birth. But some of the pain was eased by skillful midwifery, and hence I have several pleasant debts of gratitude to discharge. I hope my teachers and friends who were kind enough to read this manuscript and give me the benefit of their suggestions will understand if I merely list their names. They will also, I trust, not be offended that I have not always taken their suggestions.

Of my teachers at Yale University I am particularly grateful for the kindness shown me by my dissertation director, Lewis P. Curtis, and also by my mentor in Roman history, the late C. Bradford Welles. Professors Franklin L. Baumer, Yale University; A. C. Jefferson, University of Massachusetts, Boston; Leonard Krieger, Columbia University; Stephen J. Tonsor, University of Michigan; W. K. Wimsatt, Jr., Yale University; and John B. Wolf, University of Illinois at Chicago Circle, read all or part of this work in various forms and at various stages, gave me encouragement and showed me friendship. It is a pleasure to thank these scholars in print.

Two friends who read the manuscript a couple of times and engaged me in discussion on countless evenings can hardly be adequately thanked here. Jonathan L. Marwil and my colleague Professor Peter R. McKeon, University of Illinois at Chicago Circle, both know the importance to me of their friendship, and will perhaps accept this formal expression of my feelings.

I share many of Gibbon's attitudes toward universities, but alas, I do not share his eloquence. I will only say that all the work on this book, including the drudgery of making a first draft into a manuscript fit for publication, was done by me. No academic body, no institution dedicated to the promotion of historical studies, lightened my burden in the form of financial aid or other assistance. This fact only deepens my gratitude to my friends.

Paris
September, 1970

CONTENTS

INTRODUCTION

"Studies on Gibbon and the *Decline and Fall*" might be a more accurate title for this book. It is a work of dissection, and each chapter focuses on a single problem. Only in the final chapter are the pieces put back together and Gibbon's *History* considered as a whole.

This deliberate arrangement is more than methodological. Almost all the studies of Gibbon and his *History* see either more unity in Gibbon's work than I do, or else a different principle of unity. Those who see more unity tend to follow closely the historian's *Memoirs*, and the smooth contours and carefully controlled logic of that masterpiece of self-advertisement color their view of the man and his monument. Those who see a different principle of unity in the *Decline and Fall* tend to fix their attention on the first half and neglect Gibbon's development as a historian and an artist. Neither of these views is false. They are, in fact, accurate reflections of Gibbon's perceptions of himself and his work.

I do not think Gibbon's *Memoirs* are deliberately misleading, nor do I reject the commonplace that a man's work is best understood through a study of his life. But the *Memoirs* are the work of a literary artist, a very self-conscious artist. Gibbon has memorialized "the historian of the Roman empire," a *persona* he first created and then became. And the motives of "the historian of the Roman empire" are sometimes different from those of the man. "The historian of the Roman empire" becomes, especially in the final volumes of the *Decline and Fall* and in the *Memoirs*, a subject worthy of study. And as Gibbon becomes self-consciously "the historian of the Roman empire," his view of himself becomes increasingly objective. I have tried in these essays to get at the subjective reality behind the *persona*.

The unity of the *Decline and Fall* is the mind of the creator. It is Gibbon's Roman empire we admire, that unique creation of a remarkable mind. The *Decline and Fall*, despite its formal rhetoric and its elevated, perhaps even oracular, tone, is the most personal of histories. The character and temperament of the man, and the creative intelligence of "the historian of the Roman empire," are evident on every page. Gibbon is a great Cicerone, conducting us carefully through a thousand years of history. All the complexities of a thousand years of history are sifted through his mind, and the *Decline and Fall* is a sumptuous feast of all that Gibbon finds interesting, memorable, or instructive in the past. In each of the seventy-one chapters the logic controlling the whole is dimly perceived, if at all. Yet the final impact is of a perfectly proportioned work, a faithful and wonderful realization of the architect's design. It is the cumulative effect of the *Decline and Fall* that is extraordinary, and the controlling intelligence of the creator, "the historian of the Roman empire," is everywhere apparent.

It is the mind of the historian that is the central concern of this study. To understand how Gibbon created his Roman empire, I have looked at the mind from several angles. It would be presumptuous if not downright stupid to ask the reader to see some similarity between these essays and Gibbon's *History*. But I have tried to write about Gibbon as he wrote about Rome. The cumulative effect of these essays will, hopefully, give a convincing picture of the historian's mind. And just as Gibbon returned regularly to the city of Rome, no matter how far afield he wandered, so too will the mind of the historian be the focal point of this study.

My thesis, then, is that Gibbon created the Roman empire, *his* Roman empire, out of the materials available to him—his own genius, and his vision of Rome. The *Decline and Fall* occupied him for twenty years, and in this time his ideas and his craft matured. I have selected seven vantage points from which to view Gibbon's mind and have given to each of them a separate chapter.

I have not followed a chronological or biographical arrangement. Gibbon's life is neither intrinsically exciting nor interesting. In his own words his was "a private and litterary life." Much will be said about the events of Gibbon's life, and about the *Memoirs*, but only the first chapter is biographical. I am interested in explaining Gibbon's development from his first book, the *Essai sur l'étude de la litterature* (1761), and the first volume of the *Decline and Fall* (1776). In the fifteen years separating these works, Gibbon the historian developed.

In 1761 Gibbon was a talented, somewhat confused young man, whose ambitions reached no higher than those of an *érudit*. By 1770, or 1772 at the latest, he was working on the *Decline and Fall*. His own explanation of this development, in the *Memoirs*, stresses the overwhelming importance of his conversion to pagan Rome, experienced on the Capitoline in 1764. This dramatic event, if it really happened, does not adequately explain Gibbon's development. I argue here that it is his father's death and the resulting untangling of the family finances that freed Gibbon for his life's work, giving his talents direction and his frustrations a creative outlet.

The second chapter considers Gibbon the scholar. I have concentrated particularly on his debt to the seventeenth-century authorities for Roman history. Gibbon's familiarity with the sources and his genius as a student of antiquity has been acknowledged since the appearance of the first volume of the *Decline and Fall*. But his use of secondary authorities has received less attention.

Gibbon was fortunate, as he himself often said, in the moment of his birth and the circumstances of his life. Had he been born a generation earlier, his genius no doubt would have been consecrated to antiquarian studies. Had he lived a generation later, even his massive powers of assimilation might have been inadequate for the task. But he came to maturity at a time when a single man could absorb almost everything that was known about Rome. And, most important for "the historian of the Roman empire," he inherited a reliable set of the sources of ancient history, carefully edited and annotated, by generations of French and Italian scholars. Gibbon himself did not increase our knowledge of Roman history, but he synthesized all that European civilization knew of her ancient past.

This treasure of materials made the *Decline and Fall* possible, and the Enlightenment tradition, which Gibbon shared and partially shaped, gave him a great creative vision of how Europe emerged out of the ruins of Rome. The third chapter, then, considers Gibbon's relationship to the traditions of the European Enlightenment. Gibbon was no *philosophe*. He often repeats the arguments of his French contemporaries, but with little enthusiasm. He was, like all men, a child of his age. Yet his attachment to the seventeenth century and to Rome tempered his views. When such Enlightenment concerns as the idea of progress or the irrationality of religion are examined in Gibbon's work, he sharply diverges from the *philosophes*. Gibbon was nourished by the Enlightenment tradition, but his enlightenment is as unique as his Roman empire.

From these general chapters the study then moves to a more specific consideration of the place of enlightenment and erudition in the *Decline and Fall*. Chapter four is a study of Gibbon's debt to the great seventeenth-century Jansenist historian, Sébastien LeNain de Tillemont, whose twenty-two folios on the history of the early church were his favorite guides. But Tillemont was for Gibbon something more than a reliable guide; he was also the representative of a diametrical view of history and of Rome. Tillemont worked strictly within the Augustinian tradition. Gibbon used Tillemont, and used him well, but he also sought to destroy the Augustinian view of Rome's fall. One of the ways he did this was through his mastery of irony. Irony, even on subjects of "Ecclesiastical solemnity," is a hallmark of Gibbon's style and of his mind; he learned to wield this weapon from another Jansenist, Blaise Pascal. Pascal, like Tillemont, is temperamentally opposed to Gibbon, yet his debt to these two Jansenists is enormous.

Chapter five deals with the problem of influences, that most tricky problem for the intellectual historian. Much of life—artistic and intellectual life as well as daily behavior—is imitative. From Gibbon's journals and from the *Decline and Fall* itself, we can find abundant evidence of intellectual influence. Gibbon was scrupulous in discharging his intellectual debts, and from those who are often cited in the *Decline and Fall*, or memorialized in the *Memoirs*, or discussed in the journals, I have selected three men who were important in the development of "the historian of the Roman empire"—Pierre Bayle, Montesquieu, and Tacitus. They are not the only thinkers who might have been singled out, but they are, respectively, Gibbon's favorite philosopher, his favorite "philosophic" historian, and his favorite historian. Gibbon read all three when he was forming his ideas about history and the historian, and their influence is palpable throughout the *Decline and Fall*.

Chapter six begins the reconstruction of the *Decline and Fall*. The several aspects of Gibbon's mind which have been isolated for analysis are put back into context. To do this I have analyzed a large section of the *Decline and Fall*, the chapters on the Age of Constantine. Almost any sizeable section of Gibbon's *History* could be subjected to this kind of treatment, since almost any section would demonstrate how Gibbon solved the problem of constructing a narrative out of the elements of Roman history. The chapters on Constantine and his times have, however, a particular advantage. Not only do these chapters include all the problems which confronted "the historian of the Roman empire," but we know that Gibbon was especially careful in their composition. And he was especially careful because the Age of Constantine is, for him, central to any consideration of Rome's fall, and of Christianity.

The final chapter views the *Decline and Fall* as a whole, thus completing the Renaissance logic of this study and the logic of the *Decline and Fall* itself, building the whole out of its parts. Gibbon's *History* is about the destruction of a great civilization, and not to put the book back together, not to consider his explanation of Rome's fall, would have done violence to Gibbon's thought and his *History*. It would have been to leave the building unfinished, the architect's vision unfulfilled, and the materials scattered.

The genius of the *Decline and Fall* is its architecture. Gibbon's great achievement is that the utter incongruity of the elements of Roman history are so combined by the "historian of the Roman empire" and so masterfully balanced that "the gigantic ruin of Europe through a thousand years . . . [is] . . . mirrored in the mind of an eighteenth-century English gentleman."

GIBBON
AND HIS
ROMAN
EMPIRE

CUE TITLES

All references to the *Decline and Fall of the Roman Empire* are to J. B. Bury's revised edition (5th ed., 7 vols., London, 1909). The roman numerals indicate the chapter number, the arabic numerals the page number, and the footnotes are indicated by the letter n. followed by the number. All references to Gibbon's journals or his letters include the date of entry or letter (and the recipient) only when this was considered important to the argument.

Memoirs Edward Gibbon, *Memoirs of My Life*, edited from the manuscripts by Georges A. Bonnard (London, 1966).

Misc. Gibb. *Miscellanea Gibboniana*, ed. G. R. de Beer, Georges A. Bonnard, L. Junod (Lausanne, 1952).

Jour. A. *Gibbon's Journal to January 28th, 1763: My Journal, I, II, & III and Ephemerides*, ed. D. M. Low (New York, 1929).

Jour. B. *Le Journal de Gibbon à Lausanne*, ed. Georges A. Bonnard (Lausanne, 1945).

Jour. C. *Gibbon's Journey from Geneva to Rome: His Journal from 20 April to 2 October 1764*, ed. Georges A. Bonnard (London, 1961).

Letters *The Letters of Edward Gibbon*, ed. J. E. Norton (3 vols., New York, 1956).

MW *The Miscellaneous Works of Edward Gibbon, Esq.*, ed. John, Lord Sheffield (2nd ed., 5 vols., London, 1814).

Essai Edward Gibbon, *Essai sur l'étude de la littérature* (1761), reprinted in *MW*, IV, 1-93.

Low D. M. Low, *Edward Gibbon, 1737-1794* (London, 1937).

Young G. M. Young, *Gibbon* (New York, 1933).

CHAPTER I

GIBBON BECOMES "THE HISTORIAN OF THE ROMAN EMPIRE"

"Without engaging in a metaphysical or rather verbal dispute, I know by experience that from my early youth, I aspired to the character of an historian."

THE HISTORY OF THE DECLINE AND FALL OF THE ROMAN EMPIRE, Volume the First, by Edward Gibbon, Esq., appeared on February 17, 1776. Horace Walpole, that "elegant trifler" whose gossip attains the level of art and who is one of the most faithful mirrors of his age and his class, dashed off a letter to William Mason. "Lo," he wrote, "there is just appeared a truly classic work." And not satisfied with unalloyed praise, he sketched for Mason the character of the author: "he is the son of a foolish alderman, is a member of Parliament and called a whimsical because he votes variously as his opinion leads him. I know him a little, never suspected the extent of his talents, he is perfectly modest."

There is nothing remarkable about Walpole's judgment. The *Decline and Fall* was immediately recognized as "a truly classic work." Walpole expressed the enthusiasm of his age for Gibbon, and he also expressed the surprise of his age at the unsuspected

3

genius of Gibbon. The little that Walpole was able to tell Mason about the author of the *Decline and Fall* was as much as any but Gibbon's closest friends knew. A more hostile critic might have added that Gibbon was physically unattractive, had a taste for extravagant dress, and was vain. But beyond these few details Gibbon had made little impression on London society. Certainly he had given no indication of his genius before 1776; and no one outside his immediate family and close friends knew he was writing the *Decline and Fall*.

Walpole's surprise and delight at Gibbon's "truly classic work" raises a question that has troubled admirers of the *Decline and Fall* to the present day. How did Gibbon become the "historian of the Roman empire," and perhaps more to the point, how and why did he create this *persona* which conceals his real development? The answer lies in Gibbon's personal history from 1761 to 1776. The materials for biography are abundant: Gibbon's *Memoirs*, which describe his life until the year before his death; three journals, running almost without interruption, from August 24, 1761, to October 2, 1764;[1] 333 letters from this early period; and his miscellaneous writings collected by Lord Sheffield. Yet these materials are not easy to interpret. Much that we should like to know Gibbon has deliberately hidden. The elegant *Memoirs* are sometimes misleading, and Gibbon reveals only a part of himself. The *Memoirs* are a history of "the historian of the Roman empire" rather than an autobiography of Edward Gibbon.

It is the dual nature of the problem, Edward Gibbon and his artistic *persona*, that causes difficulties. Gibbon created "the historian of the Roman empire" while he was creating the Roman empire in his *History*. In chapter XXXVII of the *Decline and Fall*—exactly halfway through his *History*—Gibbon first refers to himself as "the historian of the Roman empire." From this point until the end of his life this *persona* conceals Gibbon.

---

[1] The full titles are: *Gibbon's Journal to January 28th, 1763*, ed. D. M. Low (New York, 1929); *Miscellanea Gibboniana*, ed. G. R. de Beer, Georges Bonnard, L. Junod (Lausanne, 1952), which contains his Paris Journal; *Le journal de Gibbon à Lausanne, 17 Août 1763 à 19 Avril 1764* (Lausanne, 1945); and *Gibbon's Journey from Geneva to Rome: His Journal from 20 April to 2 October 1764*, ed. Georges Bonnard (London, 1961).

As he worked at the *Decline and Fall* Gibbon became convinced that the true character of men was so complex and elusive that it could be only tentatively described. Men are known—whether contemporaries or historical characters—only through their actions and the circumstances of their lives. The problem is especially vexing for a historian whose major task, as Gibbon saw it, was to explain human motivation in the past. He expressed his melancholy realization when he summed up Muhammad's character:

> At the conclusion of the life of Mahomet, it may perhaps be expected that I should balance his faults and virtues, that I should decide whether the title of enthusiast or imposter more properly belongs to that extraordinary man. Had I been intimately conversant with the son of Abdallah, the task would still be difficult, and the success uncertain: at the distance of twelve centuries, I darkly contemplate his shade through a cloud of religious incense; and, could I truly delineate the portrait of an hour, the fleeting resemblance would not equally apply to the solitary of mount Hera, to the preacher of Mecca, and to the conqueror of Arabia.[2]

If even a contemporary could not unravel the complexities of character, what can the historian hope for? Indeed, Gibbon becomes increasingly reticent about judging character and motivation. And he extended this attitude toward character to all history and even to himself. Gibbon presents history as "pre-eminently a construction, a literary work with aesthetic rather than systematic order and coherence."[3] And the pattern perceived by "the historian of the Roman empire" is not inherent in the material itself, but rather is imposed by a single, perceptive individual.[4] As the *Decline and Fall* moves on, the presence of the ordering intelligence, the historian, becomes more and more palpable. It is but a short step from this view of history as an enclosed object created by the historian to the *persona* "the historian of the Roman empire."

Gibbon becomes more and more convinced of the personal

<hr>

[2] Low, L., p. 375.
[3] Leo B. Braudy, *Narrative Form in History and Fiction: Hume, Fielding and Gibbon* (Princeton, 1970), p. 214. Hereafter cited as Braudy.
[4] Braudy, p. 214.

and tentative nature of his *History*. As he moves away from the more optimistic assumptions of the early volumes he comes to see himself not so much as Edward Gibbon, but as that other *persona*. The work of ordering, of assorting, of varying, of qualifying the past become the work of "the historian of the Roman empire." This *persona*, the direct outgrowth of Gibbon's maturity as a historian, obscures from view Edward Gibbon the man. When he came to write his *Memoirs* it is "the historian of the Roman empire" who appears important, and Gibbon is incapable of remembering that time before he was "the historian of the Roman empire." It appeared natural to him that he had always been the *persona*, and that his life had moved, logically, imperceptibly, and inevitably, toward this end.

The creation of "the historian of the Roman empire"—the creator of the Roman empire itself—is the final expression of Gibbon's philosophy of history. And this view of history Gibbon extended to his own life. In the *Memoirs* Gibbon becomes the historian of his *persona*. All the events of his life are made to flow in a single direction, all the false starts are either eliminated or minimized. His explanations of his own motivation are not tentative, but they are certainly open to question. The reader is asked, in the *Memoirs*, to contemplate the development of "the historian of the Roman empire," but on closer examination this history, too, is found to be a creation of the historian. From those writings which antedate "the historian of the Roman empire" must be extracted how Gibbon in fact came to write Rome's history, and then the creation of "the historian of the Roman empire" can be explained. But before setting out this dual story, a word should be said about the *Memoirs*.[5]

[5] For an account of the writing of the *Memoirs* see Georges Bonnard's excellent preface to his edition of the manuscripts, *Edward Gibbon: Memoirs of My Life* (London, 1966). Other accounts are: Dero A. Saunders, "Six-and-a-half Autobiographies of Edward Gibbon," *History*, III (1960), 143-153; and the same author's edition of the *Memoirs* (New York, 1963). There are several editions of the "official" autobiography, as edited by John, Lord Sheffield, and that in the World's Classics series (London, 1959) is perhaps the most easily available, and contains an introduction by J. B. Bury. The manuscripts were first published without cuts by John Murray, *The Autobiographies of Edward Gibbon, Printed Verbatim from Hitherto Unpublished MSS.* (London, 1896).

Gibbon's *Memoirs*—he preferred this title to "autobiography"—have had a curious history. Gibbon left six and a half "versions" of his life when he died in 1794. These were edited, or rather manipulated, by Lord Sheffield, into the "official" *Autobiography*, first published in 1796. Sheffield's edition has been considerably modified by the opening of the Gibbon papers in 1894 and the publication of the complete manuscript. But whether read in Sheffield's edition or in the more accurate and scholarly reconstruction, Gibbon's *Memoirs* are remarkable. Nowhere does he display more art, more richness of language and concept. He is here the master of practically every tone of expression, from playfulness to the studied eloquence fit for great occasions. The *Memoirs* are a masterpiece of elegance, but it is informal elegance.

This is part of the problem. The *Memoirs* are a perfect example of the seductive powers of art. They present a contrived, and sometimes misleading, account of Gibbon's life. There are errors of fact, errors of judgment, vague recollections presented as truths. All of these faults are common to the genre. Also common to the genre is the overall pattern, rhythm, and tone which Gibbon imposed on his life.

The *Memoirs* were left unfinished at Gibbon's death, and it is not known what changes revision would have brought. But it is instructive that the man who experienced no difficulty in writing six volumes on Roman history, the man who could turn out a volume of history in less than three years, should have been unable to finish a short book about himself. Gibbon experienced less difficulty in organizing a thousand years of Roman history than he did in writing the history of his own life. The major problem was his inability to settle the proportions and set the tone of the work. The several manuscript versions of his life are a case study in the failure of a supreme artist to find a satisfactory form for his materials.

The six sketches left by Gibbon have been designated Versions A through F. Version A is the earliest draft and the roughest of the six. It was probably intended as no more than a literary exercise. It covers the family history down to the generation preceding Gibbon's own. Version B covers the family background and Gibbon's childhood quite concisely, and it is much more ample for the period from his banishment to Lausanne (June, 1753) to a point just before the Italian journey (April, 1764). Version C extends to the period soon after the death of his father (1770). Version D is so short—only twenty-five pages—that it resembles an outline more than a draft. Version E is the only one covering the years of his maturity, when he was working on the *Decline and Fall*. Version F was probably intended as a final draft, but its ninety-five pages cover only the first seventeen years of his life, to his departure from Oxford.

What led Gibbon to abandon one draft and start another, or what led him to deal with specific episodes in several drafts and in different ways, can only be conjectured. But there is good reason to use the *Memoirs* with caution, and to test them, whenever possible, against his other writings.

The misleading statements in the *Memoirs* result from three different urges: the literary artist imposing on his life aesthetically satisfying patterns, the mature man perhaps anxious to forget or distort the experiences of an unhappy and even traumatic childhood, and the blurrings in the author's mind between himself and his *persona*, "the historian of the Roman empire." These three motives for distortion are not always distinct in the *Memoirs*. That is, they are operative at the same time and often on a single episode. But the result is the same. The Gibbon of the *Memoirs* is not always the same Gibbon discernible in his letters, his journals, or his other writings. Some examples are in order.

In a famous passage, picked up and repeated by many biographers, Gibbon says: "So feeble was my constitution, so precarious my life, that, in the baptism of each of my brothers, my father's prudence successively repeated my Christian name of Edward, that in case of the departure of the eldest son, this patronymic might be still perpetuated in the family." [6] The passage intensifies Gibbon's picture of a sickly childhood—and he was certainly a sickly child—and reinforces his melancholy notion that his survival was a matter of chance. In fact, the statement is not strictly true.

[6] *Memoirs*, p. 28.

Gibbon had four brothers who died in infancy, but only one (who died on Boxing Day, 1740) was baptized Edward. Two were called James, and another Stanier. Gibbon's parents were apparently more concerned about keeping the Porten family names alive.[7]

Gibbon is equally uncertain about the chronology of his early life. In the *Memoirs* he says his mother died in December, 1747;[8] in fact, she died in December, 1746. He says his grandfather's financial ruin was in 1748;[9] in fact, it was in 1747. He says he entered Westminster school in 1749;[10] in fact, it was in January, 1748. These are not serious errors, but they do indicate a kind of informality that Gibbon would not have permitted himself in the *Decline and Fall*. They also reveal a man careless of the unhappy events of his childhood.

More serious is his lax treatment of episodes which profoundly influenced his life. Gibbon's conversion to Roman Catholicism is a celebrated episode in his life. In the *Memoirs* Gibbon builds up a careful and moving picture of a serious youth, sent to Oxford by the capricious whim of his father, who arrived there "with a stock of erudition that might have puzzled a Doctor, and a degree of ignorance of which a school boy would have been ashamed." There, his vanity flattered by "the velvet Cap and silk gown" of a gentleman commoner, and his appetite whetted by "more money than a school-boy had ever seen," he became disgusted with his tutors and the lazy irresponsibility of the institution. He came upon some controversial literature, became "bewildered in the maze of controversy," and converted to Catholicism. But it was not his fault; he was but a boy and the university failed to look after him:

According to the statutes of the University, every student, before he is matriculated, must subscribe his assent to the thirty nine articles of the Church of England, which are signed by more than read, and read by more than believe them. My insufficient age excused me however from the immediate performance of this legal ceremony and the Vice-Chancellor directed me to return, so soon as I should have accomplished my fifteenth year; recommending

[7] See Low, p. 24. He examined the Putney registers.
[8] *Memoirs*, p. 34.   [9] *Memoirs*, p. 36.   [10] *Memoirs*, p. 37.

me in the mean while to the instruction of my College. My College
forgot to instruct: I forgot to return, and was myself forgotten by
the first Magistrate of the University.[11]

But the guile of the university is less than Gibbon imagined: his
signature to the thirty-nine articles (on April 4, 1752) is in the
university archives.[12]

Gibbon always viewed his conversion with shame and embarrassment, and in the *Memoirs* he tried to shift the burden of guilt to
Oxford. The smooth, almost inevitable movement toward Catholicism, encouraged by an inept and irresponsible college, is not
strictly true. Gibbon was not totally neglected; and if Oxford did
not compel him to be punctilious as an Anglican, it certainly did
not drive him into Catholicism. It is Gibbon's urge to see himself
in the best possible light—a not uncommon desire—and his artistic
urge to give unity to his life, that led him to blur the outlines of
his conversion.

Perhaps one more example is useful. Gibbon left two statements
about how long it took him to write his *Essai sur l'étude de la
littérature*: one in the *Memoirs* [13] and the other in his *Journal à
Lausanne*.[14] In the former he says he wrote the *Essai* in six weeks;
in the latter he says two months (and the *Journal* account was
written only two years after publication of the *Essai*). In fact, it
took him more time than either account indicates. Between March
8 and 15, 1758, he wrote fifteen of the eighty-three chapters. Another thirty-three were written in about six weeks, in the following
summer; another seven chapters in February, 1759, and the remainder at the end of April, 1761. All told, he spent about three
months on the *Essai*, spread over a three-year period. The error is
instructive. Gibbon considered the *Essai* a minor work. This probably led him to diminish the time it took to write (and the actual
writing time was doubtless preceded by some days, if not weeks,
of worry and thought). Gibbon thought the *Essai* a commendable
performance for a young man, but hardly worthy of "the historian of the Roman empire." He was easily led to see the *Essai*
as a piece dashed off in a couple of months. The very alacrity of

[11] *Memoirs*, pp. 57-58.   [12] Low, p. 40.   [13] *Memoirs*, p. 99.
[14] *Jour. B.*, p. 169 (December 7, 1763).

composition gave the work even more of a flavor of brilliance than it legitimately deserved.

Gibbon's retrospective view of his life is a careful and deliberate creation, and caution should be used in accepting it literally. Like all autobiographers he wanted to be well thought of; he also wanted to be thought of as "the historian of the Roman empire." It would be foolish to disregard Gibbon's testimony about himself, but it is important to provide the perspective he himself could not have. In order to distinguish Gibbon from his *persona* it is necessary to trace his development from the *Essai* (1761) till the *Decline and Fall* (1776).

Gibbon returned to England on May 4, 1758. He had been exiled in Lausanne since 1753, sent there by his father after his conversion to Roman Catholicism. "The whole term of my first absence from England," he wrote, "was four years, ten months, and fifteen days." The story of the making of "the historian of the Roman empire" begins with his return.

Gibbon returned to England "good protestant & . . . extremely glad of it." He saw his return as a new beginning. These years, before the publication of the *Decline and Fall*, were to be the most eventful in Gibbon's life. It is also one of the few periods when Gibbon the man, as distinguished from "the historian of the Roman empire," can be seen. After 1776 Gibbon and his book become a single entity: the man and the book become so perfectly identified that they cannot be separated. But for the years before 1776 the life of the man and the growth of the historian can be followed.

Gibbon returned to England with trepidation and foreboding. He had been an exile—thus did he refer to himself—for almost five years. His father's letters had been hardly friendly, and he vividly remembered the mean circumstances of Pavillard's house, his meager allowance, and the petty deprivations inexplicably forced on him by his father. In addition to these unpleasant experiences, Gibbon had recently learned, from a country neighbor, that his father had remarried. In a word, Gibbon had no idea of what reception he might expect. His first impulse on reaching London was to rush into the arms of his Aunt Porten, "the affectionate guardian of my tender years." Only after an "evening . . . spent in the effusions of joy and confidence" was he ready to face his father—"not without some awe and apprehension." But all went well. Gibbon was received "as a man and a friend."

His first act as an Englishman once again was to agree to the breaking of the entail on his father's estates: "The time of my recall had been so nicely computed that I arrived in London three days before I was of age: the priests and the altar had been prepared, and the victim was unconscious of the impending stroke." [15] This was Gibbon's first introduction to the crazy world of financial incompetence created by his father. He would ultimately come to know all the details of the story. For the time being an annuity was settled on him, and he spent his summers at Beriton with his family, and his winters in London. But if his father needed Gibbon's approval to extract himself from financial difficulties, Gibbon needed his father's approval for his proposed marriage to Suzanne Curchod. When he finally worked up his courage, he told his father of the engagement. Gibbon senior "would not hear of this strange alliance" and "after a painful struggle I yielded to my fate." Or as he said in a more famous phrase: "I sighed as a lover: I obeyed as a son." On February 23, 1759, he wrote a letter of renunciation to Suzanne.[16]

His life in these years immediately after his return was tranquil enough. Gibbon continued on amiable terms with his father and his stepmother. Living at home was sometimes irksome, but Gibbon had no other plans for the moment. He wanted to make his way in the world of society and letters, but he had no desire for a career or profession, and no desire to change the pleasant round of London, country life, and desultory study. The library at Beriton, "stuffed with much trash of the last age, with much High-church Divinity and politics" yet "contained some valuable Editions of the Classics and the fathers," and this room was soon considered Gibbon's "peculiar domain." [17] His placid life continued uninterrupted until May 10, 1760, when Gibbon and his father

[15] *Memoirs*, p. 90.   [16] *Letters*, I, 119-122.   [17] *Memoirs*, pp. 95-97.

were called up with the militia. The years in the militia (1760-62) are recorded by Gibbon in his *Journal to January 28th 1763*. There Captain Gibbon is followed through the routine of the camp and the parade, snatching an hour here and there from business and debauchery for his beloved reading. He often sighed "for my true situation of a private gentleman and a man of letters," yet he managed to complete and publish his first work, the *Essai sur l'étude de la littérature*. It appeared on July 7, 1761.

The circumstances of publication and composition are interesting. Gibbon's father—and this is a pattern for all Gibbon's decisions in these years—urged completion and publication of the *Essai*. Gibbon lost his "litterary maidenhead" to satisfy his father and gratify his own inclinations. Peace negotiations were in the offing, and his father, whose plans for his son were those common to a country squire, thought a favorable reception of the French essay would win Gibbon a diplomatic position. Gibbon "yielded to the authority of a parent" but no diplomatic post was forthcoming. Earlier in the same year, again yielding to "the authority of a parent," he had stood as a Parliamentary candidate for Petersfield. He withdrew before the election, and would not be a "senator" until October, 1774.

With the disbanding of the militia Gibbon returned to a favorite plan: the Grand Tour of the Continent. He convinced his father of the usefulness of the project, and "only thirty six days after the disbanding of the Milita," on January 28, 1763, he arrived in Paris. He remained there until May, 1763, and "heard more conversation worth remembering, & . . . [saw] more men of letters amongst the people of fashion, than I had done in two or three winters in London." [18] Then, to prepare for the pilgrimage to pagan Rome and to save money, he retired to Lausanne. Here he stayed until April, 1764,[19] frolicking with old friends and enjoying enormously his triumphal return to his place of exile. He had

[18] To Dorothea Gibbon, *Letters*, I, 133 (dated Paris, February 12, 1763).
[19] For a study of Gibbon's intellectual work in Lausanne see Georges A. Bonnard, "L'importance du deuxième séjour de Gibbon à Lausanne dans la formation de l'historien," in *Mélanges d'historie et de littérature offerts à M. Charles Gilliard* (Lausanne, 1944), pp. 401-420.

been preceded by his *Essai,* and was pleased both by its reception and by his new role as an English gentleman visiting a foreign country. He also read profoundly in Roman history, and on April 19, 1764, set off for Italy.[20] He stayed in Italy until May, 1765, then returned home, arriving in England in June, 1765.

In Rome, according to the *Memoirs,* he experienced the one lasting conversion of his life, on October 15, 1764, "as I sat musing in the Church of the Zoccolanti or Franciscan fryars." But despite this dramatic conversion "some years elapsed, and several avocations intervened before I was seriously engaged in the execution of that laborious work."[21] On his return to England Gibbon resumed his customary life, dividing his time between London and Beriton. But he was now twenty-eight years old and no longer satisfied with an aimless, yet comfortable, life. He began, actively, to seek literary recognition. In 1767 he started, and then abandoned, his first historical work, the *Histoire générale de la république des Suisses.* He also corresponded with and then met David Hume, his first important mentor. After he dropped the Swiss history, perhaps because of Hume's suggestions, he and his friend, Georges Deyverdun, collaborated on the *Mémoires littéraires de la Grande Bretagne.* Only two issues appeared, in April, 1768, and early in 1769.

At the end of 1768 the most trying, and in many ways important, period of Gibbon's life began. His father's finances, always confused and sometimes desperate, finally collapsed. Gibbon was given the difficult, frustrating, and thankless job of straightening out the situation, for his father's health was failing at the same time. The first of many letters dealing exclusively with the family finances is dated December 12, 1768. From this date until 1772 Gibbon's letters are almost exclusively taken up with money difficulties. He is revealed in this correspondence as a responsible, capable, kind, and remarkably patient man. In the midst of the crisis he published his first English work, the curious *Critical Observations on the Sixth Book of the Aeneid* (1770). His father, declining rapidly since 1768, finally died on November 12, 1770.

---

[20] The Italian tour can be followed in *Jour. C.* This is the least interesting of Gibbon's journals for a study of his intellectual development.

[21] *Memoirs,* pp. 136-137.

It was not until October, 1772, that Gibbon was able to let Beriton, and not until December of that year that he settled his stepmother in Bath. In February he moved into 7 Bentinck Street; and on September 10, 1773, the first direct reference to the *Decline and Fall* appears in his letters. From 1773 until his retirement to Lausanne, in 1783, Gibbon's life is crowded with society, politics, and his *History*. In 1774 he joined The Club and attended meetings regularly: far more regularly than did either Dr. Johnson or Boswell. In October of the same year he was elected Member of Parliament for Liskeard. In 1775 he was presented at Court and dined with Lord North. In July, 1775, the printing of the first volume of the *Decline and Fall* began, and on February 17, 1776, that remarkable volume appeared.

A survey of what Gibbon wrote during these years will fill out this brief sketch. In addition to his three published works, there are a number of miscellaneous writings of varying degrees of interest and importance. Much of what Gibbon wrote in these years was for his own amusement or his own instruction and improvement. He received almost no formal education, and his study habits came from personal experiment. Gibbon early developed the habit of making abstracts and observations on his reading, and these brief essays make up the bulk of the miscellaneous writings. "An Inquiry Whether a Catalogue of the Armies Sent into the Field Is an Essential Part of an Epic Poem"; "An Examination of the Catalogue of Silius Italicus"; "A Minute Examination of Horace's Journey to Brindisium and of Cicero's Journey into Cilicia"; "On the Fasti of Ovid"; "On the Triumphs of the Romans"; "On the Triumphal Shows and Ceremonies": these are but some of Gibbon's essays. Of the papers published by Lord Sheffield and attributed to the years between 1758 and 1776, sixteen are on classical topics, seven on modern topics (since the Renaissance), and two on general historical problems.

Side by side with these occasional essays are more substantial works, perhaps not intended for publication, but extensive, serious dissertations. In 1759, for example, Gibbon embarked on a serious study of numismatics, and in two works of that year can be seen his considerable scholarship, his accustomed thoroughness, and his high tolerance for dull but useful books. His "Principes des poids, des monnoies, et des mesures des anciens, avec des tables construites sur ces principes," and his "Dissertation sur les anciennes mesures, &c. du bas empire jusqu'à la prise de Constantinople par les Turcs" are serious works (running to fifty-four and forty-nine printed pages, respectively) and indicate how early Gibbon laid down the foundations of his exceptional erudition.

At least one of these essays, which swelled into 170 printed pages, was possibly meant for publication. In 1763 and 1764, in preparation for the Italian trip, Gibbon wrote a comprehensive historical geography of Italy, the "Nomina gentesque antiquae Italiae." Intended for his own use, Gibbon nevertheless contemplated publication, and mentioned the project to his stepmother: "I should not even despair, but that this mixture of study and observation properly digested upon my return to England, might produce something not entirely unworthy the eye of the Public, on a subject, upon which we have no regular or compleat treatise." [22] The "Nomina" forms an interesting contrast to the *Essai*, written several years earlier. In the former Gibbon is not striving for the memorable apothegm, he is not striving to express "perhaps a common idea with sententious and oracular brevity." The "Nomina" is not belletristic, and is certainly not in the manner of Montesquieu, which marked and perhaps marred the earlier work. The *Essai* was Gibbon's bid for a place in French literature. The "Nomina" is his bid for a more modest place in the world of scholarship. In the "Nomina" Gibbon is seen taking a place among the *érudits* whom he defended in the *Essai*. Indeed, he saw himself, in 1764, as nothing more than an *érudit:* the role of "historian of the Roman empire" was perhaps not even a favorite fantasy at this time.

The most important of these miscellaneous writings, however, is the unfinished Swiss history. It is a work of more than scholarship. Indeed the evidence of profound scholarship in the Swiss history is not impressive. It is Gibbon's first attempt at a narrative

---

[22] To Dorothea Gibbon, *Letters*, I, 154 (dated August 6, 1763). The project is again mentioned to Dorothea in a letter from Florence, dated June 20, 1764 (*Letters*, I, 181).

history on a great theme—the history of Swiss liberty—and its failures are instructive and will be considered in chapter three.

In the *Memoirs* Gibbon viewed his life, from the *Essai*, or rather from his return to England in 1758, until the *Decline and Fall*, as relatively calm. He saw in retrospect only three important events: his break with Suzanne Curchod, his father's death, and his conversion to pagan Rome. The first two are quickly passed over in the *Memoirs*: the conversion is memorably and poetically celebrated. In what follows Gibbon will be distinguished from his *persona*, and his development from the *Essai* to the *Decline and Fall* will be based largely on writings other than the *Memoirs*. Like the master himself we return to the "fountainhead"—the sources—to tell the story.

Few travelers, either in the eighteenth century or at any other time, have been more prepared to visit Rome than was Gibbon. Ten years of his life had been devoted to a study of the classics, and especially Roman history. The months immediately preceding his departure for Italy had been devoted to writing a detailed historical geography of the country in antiquity. Gibbon crossed the Alps with high expectations, which were not disappointed when he entered Rome at the beginning of October, 1764: "But at the distance of twenty five years I can neither forget nor express the strong emotions which agitated my mind as I first approached and entered the *eternal City*. After a sleepless night I trod with a lofty step the ruins of the Forum; each memorable spot where Romulus *stood*, or Tully spoke, or Caesar fell was at once present to my eye; and several days of intoxication were lost or enjoyed before I could descend to a cool and minute investigation." [23]
After this burst of enthusiasm—and there is much enthusiasm in Gibbon—he employed an antiquary, a Mr. Byers, and began a detailed study of ancient Rome.[24] It is in the course of this study, says Gibbon in the *Memoirs*, that he first conceived the *Decline and Fall*. From this point (October 15, 1764), so memorably and

[23] *Memoirs*, p. 134.
[24] For an account of Gibbon in Rome, and a description of the physical Rome he saw, see J. J. Saunders, "Gibbon in Rome, 1764," *History Today*, XIV (1964), 608-615.

beautifully recorded, Gibbon fixes the decisive moment for "the historian of the Roman empire."

The episode is famous and important. Only in recent years has Gibbon's accuracy or memory been questioned. And rightly so, for there are several difficulties in accepting the master's account. Gibbon left, in his autobiographical manuscripts, three versions of this decisive moment, and it is useful here to provide the texts for analysis.

> In my Journal the place and moment of conception are recorded; the fifteenth of October 1764, in the close of evening, as I sat musing in the Church of the Zoccolanti or Franciscan fryars, while they were singing Vespers in the Temple of Jupiter on the ruins of the Capitol.[25]

> It was on the fifteenth of October, in the gloom of evening, as I sat musing on the Capitol, while the barefooted fryars were chanting their litanies in the temple of Jupiter, that I conceived the first thought of my history.[26]

> It was at Rome, on the fifteenth of October, 1764, as I sat musing amidst the ruins of the Capitol while the barefooted fryars were singing Vespers in the temple of Jupiter, that the idea of writing the decline and fall of the city first started to my mind.[27]

These three versions of the same event, written over a period of several months, raise a number of questions and introduce an important problem in all Gibbon's work: the tensions between the historian and the literary artist.

The manuscript of the *Decline and Fall* has not survived, and except for some marginal notes in Gibbon's hand on the first volume, and his own testimony in the *Memoirs*, there is no evidence of how he achieved his literary magic and how literary art

[25] *Memoirs*, p. 136. This account is from Version C, composed in January, 1790, and the first of the three versions to be written.

[26] *Memoirs*, p. 304. This account is from Version D, written some months after Version C.

[27] *Memoirs*, p. 305. This account is from Version E, the last of the autobiographical fragments to be written by Gibbon. It is the version that Lord Sheffield selected for his "official" *Autobiography* of 1796. The others became known only in 1894 when the Gibbon papers were made public.

influenced the historian. The manuscripts of the *Memoirs*, however, are instructive. Here, and only here, the artist at work can be seen. These three sentences, quoted in sequence according to time of composition, are a good case in point. The first is circumstantial and direct. Gibbon was obviously displeased with it, for some months later he wrote the second version. This, too, was unsatisfactory, and the third version is probably his final one. It is interesting to note that in the first version there is one obvious error of fact. There is nothing in Gibbon's journal about this moment of conception.[28] The journal speaks only of arriving in Rome and has none of the poetry of even the first, tentative, version: "Nous sommes arrivès à ROME à cinq heurs du soir. Depuis le Pons Milvius j'ai etè dans un songe d'antiquitè qui n'a etè interrompu que par les Commis de la Douane Gens très modernes qui nous ont forcè d'aller à pied chercher un logement, car il n'y a point d'auberges, pendant qu'ils conduisoient notre Chaise de poste à la Douane. L'Abord de Rome n'est pas gracieux." The following two pages of the manuscript journal (numbered 156 and 157) were left blank. Perhaps Gibbon intended to set down his impressions of Rome, and perhaps when he wrote the *Memoirs* he remembered having done so. In fact he did not.

At any rate, in the second version, he suppressed this reference to his journal, and proceeded to work his literary magic on the sentence. "Musing in the Church of the Zoccolanti" becomes "musing on the Capitol," which is a difference in fact. The reason for this was probably to eliminate any confusion in the reader's mind whether or not the church and the Temple of Jupiter were one and the same place. Then he inverted the order of the sentence to increase its dramatic effect. And he replaced the matter-of-fact "close of the evening" with the more emotional "gloom of the evening."

Still he was not satisfied, and a few weeks later he rewrote the sentence. This time he was careful that the contrast between the church services and the "ruins of the Capitol" should be clear. The power of the sentence comes from the melancholy contrast

[28] See *Jour. C.*, p. 235. Gibbon's French spelling and accents have been retained.

between Christianity, symbolized by the chanting friars, and Roman civilization, symbolized by the ruins—the victor innocently walking on the grave of the vanquished. This deliberate contrast is a favorite device in the *Decline and Fall*. Gibbon never lets pass an opportunity to juxtapose the triumph of Christianity and the vanished civilization of Rome. In the final version Gibbon achieved the proper balance and tone, and he could drop the emotional word "gloom." The contrast itself was enough: the artist was satisfied. Gibbon had thus achieved the desired effect. He was never a writer who resorted to obvious devices.

From a literary point of view the final version is certainly superior to the other two. This is the version Lord Sheffield selected for his "official" edition of the *Memoirs*. It is consequently the most familiar of the three. Yet the process of refinement leads one to question the entire episode. The urge of the artist to make this important passage as dramatic and significant as possible may have led him to disregard facts, or even to create a memory which did not exist. Georges Bonnard, Gibbon's most recent and best editor, thus questions the episode: "Where did G really sit musing on that fateful evening? The 'ruins of the Capitol' he had only seen in his imagination, for, in 1764, the Capitol was already what it now is. To what extent is the famous sentence fact, to what extent imagination." [29]

The evidence seems to tip the scales in favor of more imagination than fact. Not only is there no contemporary record of this experience in the journal, but Gibbon's few letters from Rome fail to mention the momentous event. There are five letters written from Rome, all to his father (nos. 61, 62, 63, 64, 66). Only one of these, dated October 9, even mentions Gibbon's reactions to Rome, and then says only that "I have already found such a fund of entertainment for a mind somewhat prepared for it by an ac-

---

[29] *Memoirs*, p. 305. In an earlier article Bonnard also questions the vision: "cette phrase est un vrai poéme. Par le choix admirable des mots qui la composent, l'harmonie de leurs sons, le rythme de sa marche, elle agit sur l'esprit du lecteur à la manière d'une incantation. Elle est d'un art si sûr, si maître de ses effets qu'on se demande si Gibbon ici n'a pas sacrifié peut-être la vérité des faits à la recherche de la beauté." See "Le deuxième séjour de Gibbon à Lausanne," p. 401.

quaintance with the Romans, that I am really almost in a dream." [30] And if there is no contemporary evidence to support the vision, there is no corroboration in anything Gibbon wrote after he returned to England. There is not another mention of the project of a Roman history until September 10, 1773. By this time Gibbon was already writing the *Decline and Fall*, and it was now not merely a history of the city, but of the empire. There is no mention of the vision itself until 1787, in the last sentence of the *Decline and Fall*: "It was among the ruins of the Capitol that I first conceived the idea of a work which has amused and exercised near twenty years of my life, and which, however inadequate to my own wishes, I finally deliver to the curiosity and candour of the public." [31]

This elegant sentiment should perhaps be taken as the first sketch of the vision of 1764. This adieu to his readers points directly to the autobiographical versions of 1790. At the conclusion of a long and successful work Gibbon was already in that frame of mind manifest in the *Memoirs*. "The historian of the Roman empire" had become a distinct *persona* to be contemplated with objectivity. This attitude emerges in the course of the *Decline and Fall*, and by 1787 Gibbon is anxious to fix in his own mind the moment of inspiration, the moment when "the historian of the Roman empire" became distinguished from Edward Gibbon, Esq.

When the emotional content of the vision is separated from its biographical details, the issue becomes clearer. Gibbon is trying to do two things in this account of his vision: the first is to explain his emotional relationship to Rome; the second is to explain the circumstances that decided him on a history of Rome's decline and fall. These are quite different things. It is not altogether clear that Gibbon discovered, for the first time, the central problem of European history as he sat on the Capitol in 1764. There is good evidence that he had already hit upon the importance of Rome's decline as the beginning of European civilization. His "Outlines of the History of the World," written between 1758 and 1763,

[30] To Edward Gibbon, Sr., *Letters*, I, 183-185.
[31] LXXI, 325.

according to Lord Sheffield, is practically a scenario for the *Decline and Fall.*[32]

The realization that Europe emerged out of the ruins of Rome is not original with Gibbon. The humanist historians of the Renaissance had recognized the connection, and Montesquieu's *Considérations sur les causes de la grandeur des Romains et de leur décadence* (1734) was familiar to Gibbon. The relationship of the declining Roman empire to the Dark and Middle Ages of Europe was a serious concern of the Enlightenment.[33] That Gibbon thought about it is not surprising: that he wrote the history of this relationship is one of the supreme achievements of the Enlightenment. But it is doubtful that he first saw the problem as he sat on the Capitol. Gibbon's vision then is not so much the vision of a subject for his great historical work, but rather a vision of his feelings about Roman and European civilization.

Gibbon's philosophy of history insisted that the feelings of the historian about his topic are at least as important as the topic itself. This was clear when he decided to write a history of Swiss liberty. It was the combination of a "philosophic" theme and the historian's personal involvement in that theme that decided him. The same is true of his Roman history. What he is describing in the *Memoirs* is the discovery of an emotional identification with Roman civilization. As a picture of his feelings, the vision is accurate. Without these feelings, these enthusiasms, Gibbon could not have become "the historian of the Roman empire." But he was not converted in a moment, and he was not converted by a vision. It is not so

[32] The "Outlines of the History of the World" is printed in *MW*, III, 1-55. Sheffield says it is "written in Mr. Gibbon's early handwriting between 1758 and 1763." It does not deal directly with Roman history, but rather sketches world history from the ninth to the fifteenth centuries. But from this essay it is clear that Gibbon, before the trip to Rome, was thinking seriously about the genesis of European civilization. "Outlines" says much about the connection between Rome's fall and the rise of Christian Europe.

[33] H. R. Trevor-Roper suggests that the vision may be an invention of the artist. His cogent argument is that Gibbon's own persistent interest in antiquity led him to Rome, and that in the *Decline and Fall* the aspirations and historical development of the Enlightenment find their fullest expression and realization. See "Edward Gibbon after 200 Years," *The Listener*, LXXII, no. 1856 (October 22, 1964), 617-619; and *The Listener*, LXXII, no. 1857 (October 29, 1964), 657-659.

important that the vision is not strictly true. What is important is that Gibbon wanted it to be true.

Gibbon's own propensity for antiquity, his years of diligent labor on the literary sources, his phenomenal appetite for commentaries, his familiarity with French culture and the Scottish Enlightenment, and the general movement of ideas in the eighteenth century all pointed toward Rome as his life's work. But if all the necessary ingredients for the making of "the historian of the Roman empire" were present by around 1765, they were not yet crystallized. Something was needed to mobilize Gibbon's considerable genius and give it direction. That something was the collapse of his father's finances, and the death of his father at the height of this crisis. The seriousness of Gibbon's financial situation is first mentioned in a letter dated December 20, 1768. From this date until at least 1772 Gibbon was absorbed in securing for himself and his stepmother some kind of security for the future. His letters in these years are filled with money matters and personal frustrations. The death of his father, in 1770, only added to his troubles. During these years Gibbon did almost no scholarly work. Then, after 1772, there came a wonderful burst of energy which continued until his death. These years of personal crisis and frustration were a purifying experience. Gibbon emerged from them stronger than he had ever been, and with a sense of his own powers and mission. All of his talents, all the distractions and waverings of his middle years, were concentrated on a single project: the *Decline and Fall of the Roman Empire*. Gibbon became "the historian of the Roman empire."

"The tears of a son are seldom lasting" wrote Gibbon of his reaction to his father's death: "I submitted to the order of Nature; and my grief was soothed by the conscious satisfaction, that I had discharged all the duties of filial piety: Few, perhaps, are the children who, after the expiration of some months or years, would sincerely rejoyce in the resurrection of their parents; and it is a melancholy truth, that my father's death, not unhappy for himself, was the only event that could save me from an hopeless life of obscurity and indigence." [34] This passage from the *Memoirs*, or at least the first half of it, has often been cited as evidence of Gibbon's cold, dispassionate temperament. The point of the passage, however, lies not in Gibbon's epigrammatic statement of his feelings on his father's death, but in his interpretation of what that event meant. His testimony is without ambiguity: his father's death "was the only event that could save me from an hopeless life of obscurity and indigence." This event not only made possible the *Decline and Fall*, but it is—far more than his vision in Rome—the moment from which productive work on that masterpiece can be dated.

His father's death was the most critical and liberating event in the years separating the *Essai* from the *Decline and Fall*. There is not only Gibbon's own testimony, quoted above, but also much other evidence. Immediately after he settled in London (1773) he began writing his *History*. There is, after 1770, an enormous increase in his correspondence. These letters are relaxed, elegant, playful, racy, learned, and wonderfully varied in tone, in range, and in literary art. In a word, the mature and familiar Gibbon, Gibbon the "historian of the Roman empire," is met only after his father's death:

> Independence is a magic thing even when it is saddled with embarrassments. After the first hurry of the new situation—conferences at Child's coffee-house, Doctors' Commons, letters of administration, negotiating for "a daughter of the Poet Mallet to divert poor Mrs. Gibbon during the gloom of winter"—a new Gibbon emerges and grows apace, no longer introspective but confident of future achievement, good-humoured and decisive in the midst of difficulties, unconstrained in his relations with people.[35]

The story of Gibbon's relationship with his father, and the financial embarrassments and crises that punctuated that relationship, is long and sometimes tedious. But the emergence of "the historian of the Roman empire" after 1770 cannot be understood without a sketch of this difficult and complex relationship.

[34] *Memoirs*, p. 150.   [35] Low, p. 208.

Father and son never really understood each other. The Tory squire was puzzled by his studious and retiring son, who was more anxious to make the Grand Tour than sit in Parliament. Gibbon could not but feel constrained and perhaps disapproved of. Before his father's death every major decision in Gibbon's life was made either directly by his father, or indirectly through suggestions which he could not resist. In almost every case Mr. Gibbon's plans and schemes for his son were both capricious and ill-advised. He sent Gibbon to Oxford unprepared for that drastic change. When the boy converted to Catholicism he tried to shake him out of his new religion by exposing him to the atheism of Mallet —"by whose philosophy I was rather scandalized than reclaimed." When this failed he sent the boy in disgrace to Lausanne. There Gibbon remained for almost five years, deprived of all the comforts of home and understanding, and forced to live the painful life of an exile. After numerous petty annoyances, created by his father's capriciousness and penuriousness, Gibbon was called home on the eve of his majority to break the entail on the family estates. "The priests and the altar had been prepared" and "My submission at the time was blind and almost involuntary; but it has been justified by duty and interest to my cooler thoughts; and I could only regret, that the receipt of some appropriated fund was not given into my own hands." [36] Well might Gibbon, in retrospect, lament his blind submission. He had at the time no idea of his father's ineptitude in business.

Not only was Gibbon called home from exile to approve a large mortgage which would sink the family even further into debt, but he returned to find a new Mrs. Gibbon. His father had not troubled to tell his son that he had remarried. Gibbon discovered this fact only from a country neighbor. He, quite naturally, interpreted the event as yet another act of his father's displeasure, and he met his new stepmother "with the most unfavourable prejudice": "I considered his second marriage as an act of displeasure, and the rival who had usurped my mother's bed appeared in the light of a personal and domestic enemy." [37] Soon after his

[36] *Memoirs*, p. 90.   [37] *Memoirs*, p. 91.

return his proposed marriage to Suzanne Curchod was forbidden by his father, and Gibbon meekly submitted. His service in the militia, which took him away from his beloved books, was dictated by his father's desire that the Gibbons cut a good figure in the county and serve together. Major Gibbon, who had no more talent for military matters than for business, dropped onto his son's shoulders all the business of the regiment. Gibbon later took some pride in his successful managing of the regiment, but at the time he complained constantly—but only in his private journal—of his additional tasks, which rightly belonged to the major.

The *Essai sur l'étude de la littérature*, his first book, was published at his father's request, and the shy and reserved author was made to deliver presentation copies to the Duke of York. His father thought this might win him favor in high places. Mr. Gibbon consistently pressed the reluctant Gibbon to stand for Parliament, and Gibbon finally yielded to the pressure, although his bid was unsuccessful. Even Gibbon's first introductions to London society, in 1758-60, were arranged by his father. Gibbon was confined to a circle of old friends and family dinners, both of which he found dull. His father had been buried in the country for twelve years and no longer had any useful, or according to Gibbon, interesting contacts. The Grand Tour, Gibbon's long-cherished dream, was made frustrating by his father's irresponsibility and finally terminated prematurely at his father's insistence. Gibbon's life was not his own, and his emotional development was stunted until he was a man in his thirties. Only with his father's death was he liberated, and almost immediately he marshaled his energies for his life's work.

The first crisis between father and son came with Gibbon's conversion to Catholicism: "The intelligence which I imparted to my father in an elaborate controversial Epistle struck him with astonishment and grief: he was neither a bigot nor a philosopher; but his affection deplored the loss of an only son, and his good-sense could not understand or excuse my strange departure from the Religion of my country." [38] His father responded by sending Gibbon to Lausanne to "effect the cure of my spiritual malady."

[38] *Memoirs,* p. 68.

Gibbon was entrusted to the care of Daniel Pavillard, a Calvinist minister of some enlightenment. Pavillard's house was mean and dirty. Gibbon was ignorant of French and "every object every custom was offensive." After almost forty years he could still recall "the appearance of the table which during eight successive days was regularly covered with the same linnen." [39] From the freedom of Oxford he was reduced "to the dependence of a school-boy." His allowance was meager and thus were his activities carefully controlled.

Two years after his banishment he wrote to his Aunt Porten an agitated letter asking her to intercede on his behalf with his father. Gibbon wanted to make the Grand Tour and then return to England to continue his studies at Cambridge, or perhaps at a university in Holland. Aunt Porten showed the letter—written in halting English—to Gibbon's father. On Christmas eve, 1755, Mr. Gibbon wrote his son a stern letter: "I have never grudged you any reasonable expences, notwithstanding the many unjust and undutiful things you have said of me to the contrary." The letter goes on to tell Gibbon that "the news that you heard of my being married again is very true," and "if you behave as you ought to do, it shall not make any difference to you." This remarkable letter continues: "I am very sorry to hear of the many complaints you make to your Aunt, of the place where you are, and make none, but you may as well make yourself easy for I am determined you shall stay abroad at least two years longer." And the disgrace of his conversion is the reason Gibbon must remain in exile: "Are you thoroughly sensible of the Errors of the Romish Church which you rashly embraced and destroyed all my plan of Education I had laid for you at Oxford." [40] Gibbon retreated, and decided in the future to deal humbly and diplomatically with his father. All of his letters to his father, until those of 1769, are carefully and deliberately constructed to achieve the maximum effect with the minimum direct confrontation.

The whole of the Lausanne correspondence is pathetic. In a letter of March 1, 1755, Gibbon pleads for a "return of your

[39] *Memoirs,* p. 69.
[40] The whole of this letter is printed in Low, p. 60.

paternal tenderness." [41] In another, January 10, 1756, he assures his father that he will love his stepmother as if she were his natural mother.[42] Even on June 4, 1757, after exactly four years of exile, Gibbon is convinced that he remains in disgrace. Certainly his father had done nothing to convince him otherwise. Gibbon assures his father—and perhaps he is trying to assure himself—of his love and devotion. He reiterates his complaint about the length of his exile, but very timidly: "Four years have already elapsed since your decision fixed me in this country. They seem to me like four centuries." [43] After detailing the advantages of Lausanne—friends, study—he asks to be permitted to return home: "But what are these friends at the price of a father to whom I owe everything, an Aunt whom I have loved from my earliest years, and indeed whom I love as much as myself." [44] Gibbon was a born ironist. At least, he continues, if he cannot be invited home, let the circumstances of exile be softened by a little more money and some relaxation of the rules. Apparently this letter went unanswered, for on October 26, 1757, Gibbon writes reiterating his love and asking his father why he has not written in months.[45]

Gibbon's return to England brought some relief. His father "received me as a man and a friend" and they "ever afterwards continued on the same terms of easy and equal politeness." [46] But this is not strictly true: the evidence of the letters belies the recollections of the *Memoirs*. In England Gibbon divided his time between Beriton and London. At Beriton he was bored only when he was forced to leave his books; in London he was dutiful to his father's wishes, and also bored. "I endeavour to see no company in town but such as you yourself would approve of" he wrote to his father on December 30, 1758.[47] But this company was distressingly dull: "I found myself a stranger in the midst of a vast and unknown city, and at my entrance into life, I was reduced to some dull family parties, and some scattered connections which were not such as I should have chosen for myself." [48] At Beriton there were also difficulties. Gibbon could never feel comfortable

[41] *Letters*, I, 5-6.   [42] *Letters*, I, 11-13.   [43] *Letters*, I, 56.
[44] *Letters*, I, 57.   [45] *Letters*, I, 73-74.   [46] *Memoirs*, p. 91.
[47] *Letters*, I, 117.   [48] *Memoirs*, p. 93.

as a country squire: "My father could never inspire me with his love and knowledge of farming: When he galloped away on a fleet hunter to follow the Duke of Richmond's fox hounds, I saw him depart without a wish to join in the sport; and in the command of an ample manour, I valued the supply of the kitchen much more than the exercise of the field." [49]

Gibbon continued the study habits laid down at Lausanne, and his father continued to try to transform his son into a Tory squire. He pressed Gibbon to stand for Parliament, and was ready to put up the 1,500 pounds necessary to secure a seat. Gibbon hoped to divert this money to his Grand Tour. In the summer of 1760, while living at Beriton, he wrote his father a curious letter. Gibbon was living in the same house with his father, yet rather than face him with his proposal, he wrote a long, closely argued letter: "An address in writing, from a person who has the pleasure of being with you every day may appear singular. However I have pre- ferred this method, as upon paper I can speak without a blush and be heard without interruption." [50] After an elaborate marshaling of arguments, Gibbon comes to the point: "I should affront your penetration, did I not suppose you now see the drift of this letter. It is to appropriate to another use, the sum you destined to bring me into Parliament; to employ it not in making me great, but in rendering me happy." [51] The response to this singular letter is not known, for the calling up of the militia suspended all plans. But if the question of the Grand Tour did not come up while father and son served together, the question of Parliament did. Gibbon stood unsuccessfully for a seat from the borough of Petersfield. It was only with the disbanding of the militia that Gibbon was able to convince his father that perhaps the Grand Tour was a fitting enterprise for a gentleman. Within a month of the disband- ment Gibbon left for the Continent.

Gibbon's letters to his father from Paris, his first stop, are chatty and affable. For the first time they have the ease and familiarity of his letters to others. But in Lausanne, where he next went, dif- ficulties began. The family finances were again in serious trouble,

[49] *Memoirs*, p. 95.
[50] *Letters*, I, 123.
[51] *Letters*, I, 125.

and Mr. Gibbon wrote his son proposing yet another mortgage. "I hardly thought it possible any letter of yours could have given me so much uneasiness," Gibbon wrote.[52] This opening phrase is to become a familiar feature of his letters to his father. In a carefully reasoned reply Gibbon suggested two plans for raising money, neither of which would involve another mortgage. His father, always sensitive about his lack of business sense, took Gibbon's suggestions as a personal affront, and wrote a sharp reply. Gibbon describes this letter in his journal as being a refusal of one of his proposals and a willful misunderstanding of the other.[53]

The letter also complained about Gibbon's expenses, and Gibbon wrote trying to convince his father that his station in life demanded no less: "In this age, it would be almost impossible for me to do it [the tour of Italy] under 7 or 8 hundred; every thing is much altered since you were abroad and I believe if you consult those who have travelled lately, they would name scarcely less than a thousand." [54] In his journal he entered this: "Ma situation est facheuse, mais des que je m'y trouve l'extreme prudence seroit une imprudence reelle." [55] His father continued to make difficulties about his son's expenses, and on February 1, 1764, Gibbon wrote: "Upon reading over what I have wrote, I am afraid Dear Sir you will suspect me of murmuring and being out of humor. Such sentiments are far from me. I am convinced there is nothing occasions your complaints but your not being able to support it, and in that case tho' I cannot lessen my expence I can put an entire stop to it. May I beg Dear Sir your speedy directions for my conduct. If I am to pass the mountains (which I wish and hope still) I must not wait for the month of April as it [is] the very worst in the year." [56]

He was even bolder in his journal, where he says he sent his father an ultimatum.[57] But any direct confrontation with his father was never a good idea; and any criticism of Mr. Gibbon was always a mistake. Mr. Gibbon became petulant and Gibbon's difficulties

---

[52] *Letters*, I, 156 (dated September 10, 1763).
[53] *Jour. B.*, p. 92 (February 1, 1764).
[54] *Letters*, I, 163 (dated October 15, 1763).
[55] *Jour. B.*, p. 92 (October 15, 1764).
[56] *Letters*, I, 167-168.   [57] *Jour. B.*, p. 205 (February 1, 1764).

continued and increased. On April 28, 1764, Gibbon explains to his father why he should continue his tour: "Thus Dear Sir, you will in the two years and half I may be abroad, have sacrificed about a thousand pounds extraordinary to the most agreeable part of my life; a sacrifice I shall endeavour to repay by the behavior of my whole future life." [58]

For the moment the rift was patched up, and Gibbon continued his trip. But in Rome, on November 10, 1764, began a series of events that culminated in an act of remarkable irresponsibility by his father. Once again Mr. Gibbon proposed to his son a new mortgage. Once again Gibbon wrote that he "could scarcely have thought that any one [letter] from you could give me so much uneasiness as this has done." [59] After detailing the growing list of his father's debts from previous mismanagement Gibbon continues: "What may be one day my fate without half your knowledge of business [he was a natural ironist], and deprived of all those resources which you must have found in living so many years in the Country, and in managing and improving your estate. With less economy and perhaps more wants, I may very easily find my way to a Gaol." [60] Gibbon proposed an expedient that would not further lead his father into debt, and suggested that Mr. Gibbon give up the pretensions of a man of enormous wealth. His father had suggested, as a motive for taking a new mortgage, that the money thus raised would be sufficient to improve his holdings, and thus leave something for the Elliots—Gibbon's closest relations on his father's side—at his death: "My views will never extend beyond the happiness of your life, that of Mrs. Gibbon's and of my own. Let us mutually consult what may the most contribute towards that object without calculating what estate may at last remain *for the Elliots.*" [61]

If this constant problem of trying to modify his father's unrealistic schemes for raising money was an annoyance—albeit a seri-

---

[58] *Letters*, I, 172.   [59] *Letters*, I, 185.
[60] The estate consistently lost money under his father's management. *Letters*, I, 186.
[61] This is Gibbon's first written declaration that he had no intention of marrying. *Letters*, I, 187 (Gibbon's italics).

ous one—it was nothing compared to what happened next. In December, 1764, Gibbon's father withdrew his son's credit and left him stranded in Rome without money and without the possibility of cashing a draft. Gibbon had no inkling that something so drastic might happen. "My character is ruined in every great town in Italy," Gibbon moaned.[62] The letter goes on to remind Mr. Gibbon that they had mutually agreed to a sum of 700 pounds for the Italian tour, and that unless the credit were restored Gibbon would be hopelessly stranded. Still agitated, he wrote, later the same day, another letter to his father. He was now aware that the letter suspending credit was a circular letter. It would be sent to all the Italian banks. Not only could Gibbon have no credit in Rome, but he could not cash a draft anywhere in Italy. In addition, the ominous letter had taken some days, perhaps weeks, to reach Rome: "How can it have happened Dear Sir that a letter can have had the time to go from London to Florence, from Florence to Lausanne and from Lausanne to Rome without my having had the smallest intimation of it from you."[63]

The circumstances behind Mr. Gibbon's behavior are not known. Perhaps he withdrew Gibbon's credit as a punishment for his son's criticism of his financial schemes. At any rate, he made the last months of Gibbon's tour a hellish experience. Not only did he force his son to live in a strange country without enough money, but also he exposed him to an even keener humiliation. Gibbon was especially sensitive about his position as a gentleman. He was often more concerned that he be treated as a gentleman than as a man of letters. The collapse of his credit ruined his name in Italy, and this was more painful than the immediate discomfort caused by lack of money. Indeed, so profound was his pride of station that he hid his financial embarrassment from his traveling companion, William Guise. Not only would he not borrow money from Guise, but he also behaved as if nothing had happened. When the travelers reached Venice, in April, 1765, Gibbon believed his credit had been restored. He went, with Guise, to draw funds. The banker in

[62] *Letters,* I, 188 (dated December 5, 1764).
[63] *Letters,* I, 189 (dated December 5, 1764).

Venice proved difficult and Gibbon arrogantly told him that he wanted neither his money nor his company. But the damage had already been done. The Venetian banker had raked up the story of Gibbon's unreliable credit, and in Guise's presence. Gibbon had just spent several months of very real distress in his company without saying a word about his troubles. He was mortified.[64]

The whole Italian trip had been distressing, and as a final blow, Gibbon was forced to cut short his tour. His father insisted he return home. Gibbon's last letter from the Continent (from Lyons) is marked by a tone of resentment: "Perhaps one day you may spare me Dear Sir some months to compleat what I have left unfinished at present." [65]

Gibbon's second return to England, and his resumption of his ordinary life of dividing his time between Beriton and London, brought him neither peace nor leisure. What had been satisfactory during his first stay in England, when he was in his early twenties, was now vexatious. Gibbon was almost thirty, and itching for independence. Financial problems and his own guilty sense of duty toward his father kept him in bondage. His increasing restlessness is best expressed in his writings during these years. The fragment of Swiss history, the *Mémoires littéraires*, and the *Critical Observations* have in common a lack of overall design and evident purpose. They are occasional works, and show none of the architectural genius which designed and built the *Decline and Fall*. They are also partial and fragmentary works, narrowly focused on problems which constrict the author's style and imagination. Gibbon was, during these years, distracted, frustrated, and confused. He was unable to find a station in life that would permit him to pursue a literary career. He drifted, he wavered in the face of many distractions. And in the midst of these personal difficulties came the final catastrophe: the simultaneous collapse of his father's health and his father's finances.

The financial affairs of Mr. Gibbon, which were to plague his son for the remainder of his own life, are complex. There is no need to present all of the evidence. A useful summary has been

[64] See Low, p. 189.
[65] *Letters*, I, 196 (dated May 29, 1765).

prepared by J. E. Norton, the editor of Gibbon's *Letters*.[66] The relevant documents are in Gibbon's papers, the papers of his step-mother (now in the Yale University Library),[67] and the Public Record Office. In brief, Gibbon's father had mortgaged his estates heavily, and he was seriously in debt to a number of men from whom he had borrowed additional money. In addition he had no steady income and had seriously mismanaged his properties. Some old gambling debts had long before exhausted his savings, and he had always lived beyond his means. To further complicate this situation, his haphazard methods resulted in almost all the important papers relating to his finances being lost or mislaid. His sensitivity about his financial abilities made it almost impossible to bring him to turn his affairs over to qualified advisers. Only when his health began to deteriorate could he be persuaded to seek expert help, and even then he willfully interfered with those who were trying to save him from complete ruin. So desperate were the family finances that Gibbon did not achieve financial security until 1790, when the death of his Aunt Hester gave him a modest inheritance. But from 1768 until 1772 Gibbon was involved in complicated legal proceedings, which amounted to having to sell one half of his father's lands to pay the mortgages on the other half.

These were years of acute distress and enormous emotional pressure. Gibbon was suddenly thrown into a series of business arrangements which were absolutely necessary, yet for which he had neither the experience nor the inclination. His father proved the greatest problem. Mr. Gibbon brooded, dragged his heels, accused his son of lack of interest, and aggravated all those near him. His declining health intensified these problems, and his death in 1770, without a will, was his final act of irresponsibility. Gibbon spent the majority of his time in London, living in temporary quarters and devoting almost every day to conferences on his father's af-

[66] See *Letters*, I, appendix III, 402-407.
[67] The collection consists of letters, drafts of letters, and one or two other documents relating to the family finances, to and from Dorothea Gibbon. No new facts about Gibbon's life are to be found here, but these papers confirm the bleak picture of Gibbon senior's financial ineptitude and the difficulties thus created for his heirs.

fairs. His nights were given over to explaining, defending, pleading, threatening and placating his father. His letters for these years are a painful record of these transactions, and a remarkable testimony to his diligence, patience, and humanity. Gibbon was an exceptional man, and he brought to the melancholy task of saving his father from ruin all of his talents and energies.

When the finances collapsed, in late 1768—and this final collapse had long been delayed by his father's schemes and secrecy—Gibbon was given complete responsibility. He moved to London and began his work. At the outset he had no idea of the depth of the family's distress. Only slowly, as the relevant documents trickled to London from Beriton, and as the lawyers explained things to him, did he grasp the seriousness of the situation. Gibbon was soon convinced that only the most radical arrangements could save his father and, ultimately, himself. But before anything could be done, deeds and bills, mortgage papers and marriage settlements, were needed, and Mr. Gibbon had lost many of these: "The deed itself formerly in your possession is what he wants, for says he any purchaser would naturally be allarmed at its not being to be found, and would immediately suspect that some incumbrance (perhaps for your life only) had been contracted on that security." [68] Without the papers nothing could be done. Without his father's co-operation nothing could be done: "Depend on it, Dear Sir, we do not wish to flatter you with vain hopes (indeed to what end could they serve?), and let this consideration dispell the Fantom which torments you and makes me so unhappy." [69]

Each letter closes with an assurance that Gibbon is doing everything he can to help, and that complete ruin can be averted if his father cooperates and resigns himself to drastic remedies. For the first time, in this correspondence, a streak of independence emerges. The polite and diplomatic style of the earlier letters to his father is gone. In its place is a direct and manly confrontation of the problems and of his father. Gibbon is growing up, and his growth can be traced in these letters. He repeats, time and again, like a

[68] *Letters*, I, 230 (dated January 1, 1769).
[69] *Letters*, I, 233 (dated January 14, 1769).

recurring lament, that he should have prevented his father from
making so many irresponsible decisions: "As for myself, I shall
only say that I cannot be happy, without your being so I am willing
to make every reasonable sacrifice to your tranquillity. The only
restraints I shall wish to impose on you are such as will be con-
ducive to our common good. Perhaps it had been better for us all,
had I insisted on them some years sooner." [70]

Gibbon is surer of himself and of what must be done than he
has ever been. And when his father accuses him of ruining the family, and offers yet another wild scheme, Gibbon remains firm in his
resolve: "Let me beg of you Dear Sir, not to suffer any indolence
or false delicacy to prevent your going to the bottom of your affairs. The time of temporary Expedients is now passed." [71] When
his nerves were frayed and his patience exhausted by his father's
accusations and his refusal to face the crisis, Gibbon would write
to his stepmother, asking her to mediate and to convince Mr. Gibbon of the seriousness of his affairs.

It was an extremely delicate situation. Mr. Gibbon's pride was
profoundly wounded by his financial collapse and he was constantly depressed by his failing health. Despite his accusations, despite his sulking, despite his complaints, he knew that he must sub-
mit to the advice of his son, a son he had always dominated. And
Mr. Gibbon took out his frustrations on his son: "I scarce thought
that our present melancholy situation could receive any addition
of uneasiness, but the displeasure your last letter expressed, convinced me that the mere blows of fortune are trifling when compared with the unexpected reproaches of those we love." [72] A
month later an even more depressing letter from his father arrived:

> It is impossible for me to express how much your last letter sur-
> prized and grieved me; as well from the particular contents of it,
> as from the general strain of resentment & dis-satisfaction which
> runs thro' the whole. To be accused of neglect, of indifference, of
> unjust insinuations are reproaches, which I can only bear because

[70] *Letters*, I, 233 (dated January 14, 1769).
[71] *Letters*, I, 234 (dated January 21, 1769).
[72] *Letters*, I, 239-240 (dated February 23, 1769).

I am conscious of not having deserved them. I wish to look for-
wards, & if at any time I look back it is only where such a retrospect however unpleasant becomes necessary.[73]

In the midst of the crisis Gibbon's father died without a will.
Gibbon had left London to be with his father during his last weeks.
In his *Memoirs* he has condensed the frustrations of two years into
a single sentence: "My quiet was gradually disturbed by our domestic anxiety: and I should be ashamed of my unfeeling philosophy, had I found much time or taste for study in the last fatal
summer (1770) of my father's decay and dissolution." [74] Gibbon's
letter to his Aunt Hester (his father's sister), written in December,
1770, some weeks after his father's death, describes the progress of
Mr. Gibbon's illness, his death, and the reactions of himself and
his stepmother:

> Long before the melancholy event my father was sensible of his
> approaching end, and prepared himself for it with the truest resig-
> nation; besides his private prayers he was attended by the Clergy-
> man of the Parish from [whom] he received the Communion who
> testified the highest satisfaction in his edifying behaviour. But my
> father's best preparation was the comfort of a well spent life. He
> was followed to the grave by the tears of a whole Country which
> for many years had experienced his goodness and charity.[75]

Gibbon's problems did not end with his father's death:

> As soon as I had paid the last solemn duties to my father, and ob-
> tained from time and reason a tolerable composure of mind, I be-
> gan to form the plan of an independent life most adapted to my
> circumstances and inclination. Yet so intricate was the net: my
> efforts were so awkward and feeble, that near two years (Novem-
> ber 1770-October 1772) were suffered to elapse before I could
> disentangle myself from the management of the farm, and transfer
> my residence from Buriton to a house in London.[76]

[73] *Letters*, I, 244 (dated March 22, 1769).   [74] *Memoirs*, pp. 148-149.
[75] *Letters*, I, 273. "Country" was regularly used in the eighteenth century for
"county."
[76] *Memoirs*, p. 151. See also p. 154 for another description of these years.

Gibbon was fortunate in having in this crisis the help of his dearest friend, John Holroyd, Lord Sheffield. He gratefully dumped onto Sheffield's shoulders all his financial cares. Indeed, Sheffield was to remain his financial mentor for the rest of his life, and took upon himself the handling of Gibbon's English interests when he moved to Lausanne. It is interesting to notice that Sheffield had all of those qualities which Gibbon himself lacked, but more particularly, all of those qualities which his father lacked. Gibbon's friendship with Sheffield was deep and testifies to Gibbon's immense capacity for friendship. Sheffield was his dearest friend. When Gibbon read that Sheffield's wife had died, he literally killed himself traveling from Lausanne to London—and Gibbon could at this time scarcely move because of gross corpulence and the gout—so that he might be with his dear friend in his grief.

Gibbon emerged from these years of crisis a more emotionally stable man. Just as his physical disorders had most wonderfully vanished on his fifteenth birthday, so did his frustrations and distractions most wonderfully vanish with his father's death. The years separating his return to England (1765) and his father's death and the financial difficulties following it (1770-72) were crucial in the making of "the historian of the Roman empire." Gibbon's genius now had direction, he had personal liberty, and his ambition was focused on his *History*. His shyness, his hesitancy, his lack of self-confidence were all gone. The crisis had been a purifying experience. The pride he had discovered in the militia when he realized that despite his foreign education and retiring manners he could run a battalion, and run it better than most men—especially his father—was repeated in 1768-72. He had been thrown into a situation over which he had no control, and he had handled it with distinction and humanity. It is pride in his ability more than the release provided by his father's death that is important in Gibbon's development.

There were to be no more false starts. Gibbon had now attained "the first of earthly blessings, Independence." The prospects and the activities of his life expanded immediately. An enormous amount of energy was released. A new Gibbon appeared in London: member of the most fashionable clubs, Member of Parliament, friend of the mighty and the talented, master of "the solid comforts of life, a convenient well-furnished house, a domestic table, half a dozen chosen servants, my own carriage, and all those decent luxuries whose value is the more sensibly felt the longer they are enjoyed." [77] He continued his practice of early rising, and gave the entire morning and part of the afternoon to his work. In February, 1773, he moved into 7 Bentinck Street: "No sooner was I settled in my house and library than I undertook the composition of the first Volume of my history." [78] The crisis of 1768-72 had made Gibbon "the historian of the Roman empire."

[77] *Memoirs*, p. 154.   [78] *Memoirs*, p. 155.

CHAPTER II

GIBBON THE SCHOLAR

". . . in the ardour of my enquiries I embraced a large circle of historical and critical erudition."

GIBBON WAS PROUD of his learning. His conversation became, as he advanced through the Roman empire, a magnificent monologue of erudition and anecdote. In his *History* he cast his immense learning into the text, and threw into the notes that excess of erudition which would have hopelessly clogged the narrative. The notes, which occupy about a fourth of the *Decline and Fall*, became for Gibbon almost as important as his narrative. At the bottom of the page, in what one biographer has called his "table talk," [1] Gibbon carries on, with himself and his readers, a dialogue on the materials for Roman history. He also indulges his considerable vanity about his vast learning. In literary and scholarly virtuosity, in pungency, in mordant criticism, the notes for the *Decline and Fall* are unique in English literature. Gibbon knew more about Roman history than any of his contemporaries and most of his predecessors, and he ostentatiously displayed this fact at the bottom of every page. He made very clear, to his readers and himself, the scholarship which supported his Roman empire.

That Gibbon's learning was extraordinary was recognized in his own day. William Robertson, himself a respectable scholar, took the trouble to check many of Gibbon's citations: "I have

---

[1] Low, p. 328.

traced Mr. Gibbon in many of his quotations (for experience has taught me to suspect the accuracy of my brother penmen), and I find that he refers to no passage but what he has seen with his own eyes."[2] Robertson's praise was matched by Richard Porson's,[3] and there were not in the eighteenth century two men better qualified to judge such matters. J. B. Bury, Gibbon's most respected modern editor, has stamped Gibbon's accuracy with the imprimatur of a later and better informed generation of scholarship.[4] There is no need to defend Gibbon the scholar. He prepared his own defense in the *Decline and Fall*: in the notes the serried ranks of folios and authorities march along with "the historian of the Roman empire." The foundation of the *Decline and Fall* is as impressive as the superstructure. It is, however, useful to describe the state of classical scholarship in Gibbon's day, to notice his attitude toward this scholarship, and to explain the remarkable accuracy of his *History*.

There are nearly 3,000 references to secondary authorities in the *Decline and Fall*:[5] if Gibbon's references to works such as Muratori's *Rerum Italicarum scriptores* are included the number exceeds 4,000. These figures are meaningless in themselves, but when compared to the total number of references in the *Decline and Fall* a distinct picture of Gibbon's reliance on secondary authorities is obtained. There are approximately 8,000[6] notes in Gibbon's *History*. Thus more than 50 percent of Gibbon's notes make reference to secondary authorities.

Several other relationships should be noticed before abandoning this game of numbers. Gibbon's references—either including or excluding the compilations—are to authorities from the sixteenth to the eighteenth century. Of these almost 60 percent refer to works in French or by French scholars. The next highest representation is from works in Latin (about 23 percent), followed by

[2] Quoted by Young, p. 112.   [3] See Young, p. 126.
[4] See Bury's introduction to his edition of the *Decline and Fall* (7 vols., London, 1909).
[5] These and subsequent figures are from I. W. J. Machin, "Gibbon's Debt to Contemporary Scholarship," *Review of English Studies*, XV (1939), 84-88. Hereafter cited as Machin.
[6] Machin mentions 8,362 references and allusions.

English (about 14 percent), Italian (5 percent), and Spanish (about .5 percent). These references are to 409 authors, and those of French nationality predominate (about 47 percent).[7]

In addition to proving the extent of Gibbon's scholarship the figures provide a reliable map of classical scholarship in the eighteenth century.[8] European scholarship in the seventeenth and eighteenth centuries was practically a French monopoly. The great cooperative enterprises, like the work of the Maurist community, and the work of individual men, like Tillemont, were among the most impressive achievements of classical France. Gibbon was one of the very few men of enlightenment who loved and respected this work. His forced exile in Lausanne made him bilingual and a profound admirer of French scholarship.

Gibbon fell heir to the traditions of French scholarship which stretched back to the Renaissance. He had at his command a remarkable collection of the sources of ancient history. There was no important literary source for Roman history which had not been thoroughly edited in the course of the seventeenth century. Gibbon was an armchair historian. He worked only from printed materials, and only in his own study. For no other period of the past could he have found a set of sources to equal those available for Roman history.

In addition to these traditional materials Gibbon also had available a growing series of books which had been generated by the historical scepticism of the seventeenth century. The sceptical tradition in modern Europe began first in theology and philosophy, with the recovery of the text of Sextus Empiricus in the sixteenth century.[9] It was only a matter of time before the arguments of Sextus were applied to historical studies, and by the seventeenth century men were questioning seriously the nature, indeed the

[7] Machin, pp. 85-86.

[8] The best guide to the problem is A. Momigliano, "Ancient History and the Antiquarian," reprinted in *Contributo alla storia degli studi classici* (Rome, 1955), pp. 67-104. Momigliano, in another article, "Gibbon's Contribution to Historical Method," reprinted in *Contributo alla storia degli studi classici*, pp. 195-211, traces the growing sophistication of classical studies through Gibbon's intellectual development. See especially pp. 195-199.

[9] See Richard H. Popkin, *The History of Scepticism from Erasmus to Descartes* (Assen, 1964), especially pp. 17-43.

possibility, of historical truth. Along with this theoretical questioning went a more direct attack on the methods and assumptions of historians. The traditional approaches to history, that is, through the literary remains of the past, were preserved in the universities.[10] The sceptics, or historical Pyrrhonists as they came to be known, were outside the universities. And the Pyrrhonist attack on historical truth took the form of marshaling the findings of antiquarianism to support sceptical assumptions. The Pyrrhonists were mostly amateurs. They were gentlemen and proud of the title of dilettantes. They preferred travel and coin-collecting to the emendation of texts. Their great contribution to classical studies was the supplementing of literary texts with the study of coins, statues, vases, and inscriptions: what Gibbon called the "subsidiary rays" of history.

These amateurs, with an interest in nonliterary evidence, at first modified, and then changed, the traditional methods of historiography. Their work proved a valuable control for testing the reliability of literary sources. In England their interests are reflected in such organizations as the Society of Dilettanti, and in the pages of the *Gentleman's Magazine* and the reviews. In France the Académie des Inscriptions was their spiritual home. The number of books published or sponsored by the antiquarian societies far exceeded those of the universities, and the intellectual vigor of the new movement put the traditional methods on the defensive. Ideas, in the long run, never suffer from controversy. The immediate impact of historical Pyrrhonism was negative and destructive, but by the time of Gibbon's maturity the Pyrrhonist attack had cleared the ground of much rubbish and had established new and more stringent tests for historical truth.

The Pyrrhonist position was simple: they insisted that the truth about the past could not be definitively established. Literary evidence was suspect on several grounds. Men being what they are, written accounts of events unless there is corroborating evidence from other sources cannot be trusted. The haphazard survival of some documents and the destruction of others made any historical

[10] This discussion is based on Momigliano, "Ancient History and the Antiquarian,"

reconstruction only tentative. The best kind of evidence, free of human vanity and bias, was nonliterary evidence—coins, inscriptions, and archaeological testimony. Such evidence provided the only reliable proof of events, for such evidence was not subject to forgery, to the corruptions of time, or the ineptitude of scribes and transcribers. In addition, nonliterary evidence was reliable because its original purpose was the innocent commemoration of events at the time of those events.

The Pyrrhonists found close at hand a growing body of antiquarian studies on Rome, and these they used to attack the reliability of literary evidence. Louis de Beaufort's *Dissertation sur l'incertitude des cinq premiers siècles de l'histoire Romaine* (1738) is an extended attack on Livy's account of the early republic. Louis-Jean Lévesque de Pouilly, a man of some importance in the Académie des Inscriptions, regularly presented the Pyrrhonist position at Académie meetings.[11] But the most famous and articulate defender of uncertainty in history was Pierre Bayle. All of these men leaned heavily on the work of the antiquarians, and Gibbon read them all.

Antiquarianism is at least as old as formal historical writing.[12] Whether a satisfactory way can be found to distinguish antiquarians from historians is not as important as the fact that the men of the seventeenth and eighteenth centuries saw a clear distinction. Bacon, in the *Advancement of Learning* (1605), distinguished between memorials, antiquities, and perfect histories. He defined antiquities as "history defaced or some remnants of history which has casually escaped the shipwreck of time."[13] Seventeenth-century historiography considered this definition a truism. Throughout the age of the antiquaries—and this is an accurate characterization— "perfect histories" of antiquity were understood to be those of Tacitus and Livy. The truth and completeness of these accounts was unquestioned. No one had the audacity to suggest that a his-

---

[11] His most famous paper, which influenced Beaufort, was "Dissertation de M. Pouilly sur l'incertitude de l'histoire de premiers siècles de Rome," which he read on his entry into the Académie des Inscriptions, in 1723.

[12] Momigliano, "Ancient History and the Antiquarian," pp. 69-79, traces the development of antiquarianism from ancient Greece to the Enlightenment.

[13] *Advancement of Learning* in *Works* (1605), ed. Spedding and Ellis, VI, 188,

tory of antiquity could be written which would replace the classics. Those who wrote ancient history in the seventeenth century usually produced work that was little more than a recapitulation of what the ancient historians had said. Commentaries on ancient historians were encouraged, and considered positively meritorious, so long as they did not question the ultimate authority of the text. It is only when the Pyrrhonists borrowed the work of the antiquarians in order to undermine this reverence for ancient historians that things changed.

The antiquaries collected most of their evidence from outside the traditional literary sources, and they apparently had no desire to use this new evidence to write histories of antiquity. Their discoveries often contradicted the ancients, or called for modifications in an accepted tradition. Almost inadvertently, their work called into question the accuracy of the ancients. With the accumulation of more and more antiquarian evidence, it became apparent that new histories of Greece and Rome were needed: histories which would incorporate this new evidence.

The Pyrrhonists, who were neither antiquaries nor historians, but rather controversialists and philosophers, were not prepared to write new histories of antiquity.[14] But if the Pyrrhonists did little constructive work themselves, they hammered away at the traditional modes of historical composition, and by the eighteenth century had managed to lower the prestige of the old history, raise the prestige of the antiquaries, and make the need for new histories of antiquity both obvious and popular. Men of letters and gentlemen scholars became convinced that the new methods had much to offer to students of antiquity. Even so conservative a tradition-

---

[14] Louis de Beaufort is an exception. In addition to his polemical *Dissertation sur l'incertitude des cinq premiers siècles de l'histoire Romaine*, he wrote a constructive and respectable Roman history: *La république Romaine, ou plan général de l'ancien gouvernement de Rome* (1766). This work and the earlier *Dissertation* influenced Niebuhr. His other historical work, *Histoire de César Germanicus* (1741), was written for Prince Frederick Charles Louis Guillaume, Landgrave of Hesse-Hombourg. Beaufort was his tutor, and the work is rather a pious exhortation to the young prince to be a benevolent ruler than a serious history. Gibbon met Beaufort, in 1758, but says little about the meeting: "In our halt at Maestricht I visited Mr de Beaufort a learned Critic who was known to me by his specious arguments against the five first Centuries of the Roman history." *Memoirs*, p. 87. Beaufort's *Dissertation* is discussed in chapter xxviiff. of Gibbon's *Essai*.

alist as Joseph Addison wrote a popular treatise on numismatics, *Dialogues upon the Usefulness of Ancient Medals*.[15] Gibbon read the work with interest and delight; it introduced him to the serious study of numismatics. Gibbon was not the first to take up the challenge of the Pyrrhonists and the antiquaries, but he was certainly the most successful. In erudition alone the *Decline and Fall* is the masterpiece of the age. It is a completely reliable guide to the state of classical scholarship—both literary and nonliterary—in the eighteenth century.

"It is seldom," wrote Gibbon of the author of an obscure but learned article, "that the antiquarian and the philosopher are so happily blended." [16] It would be difficult to imagine a better description of the author of the *Decline and Fall*. Gibbon's contribution to historical method—leaving aside his obvious personal genius—is his synthesis of the antiquarian and the philosopher: the scholarship of the seventeenth century and the philosophy of the Enlightenment.

Gibbon's unorthodox education led him beyond the confines and concerns of English scholarship. Perhaps none of his contemporaries was so avid a reader of scholarly periodicals and the transactions of learned societies: "I cannot forget the joy with which I exchanged a bank-note of twenty pounds for the twenty volumes of the Memoirs of the Academy of Inscriptions; nor would it have been easy by any other expenditure of the same sum to have procured so large and lasting a fund of rational amusement." [17] Had he finished his education at Oxford he would doubtless have been sunk "in port and prejudice" with the monks of the corporation. But his conversion sent him into exile, and there he discovered the joys of scholarship. So intoxicated was Gibbon with the pleasures of pure scholarship that his early aspirations seem to have reached no higher than becoming a corresponding member of a learned

---

[15] Joseph Addison, *Miscellaneous Works* (1830), III, 59-199.

[16] IX, 236, n. 89. The dissertation referred to discussed the origins and migrations of nations, with particular reference to the early history of the Germanic peoples. It was published in volume xviii (pp. 48-71) of the *Mémoires de l'Académie des Inscriptions*.

[17] *Memoirs*, p. 97.

society. He never achieved the "scrupulous ear of a well-flogged critic" but he possessed the "sense and spirit of the classics." He might occasionally offend university-trained Latinists "by a false quantity" [18] and his mastery of Greek might be incomplete—he occasionally "committed errors of translation" in the *Decline and Fall* [19]—but he had a passion for classical scholarship. He preferred the scholarship of the seventeenth century to that of his own day, and it was his singular achievement to domesticate the erudition of a controversial age and make it serve the ends of philosophy:

> Nothing is more agreeable than a good journal; and the Bibliothèque Raisonnée certainly merits that title. It can, however, be divided into two parts, roughly equal in length but different in character. The first follows the fashion of serious studies of the seventeenth century: a great deal of theology, jurisprudence, and *belles-lettres;* erudition directed towards the original sources and a healthy science of criticism. The spirit of religious controversy dominates this work too much: it also displays too much bitterness and minuteness.[20]

But he found these shortcomings preferable to those of eighteenth-century scholarship: "There is a great indifference to theology, a superficial learning, a bold philosophy, a dogmatic tone, and a style both more figurative and more laconic." [21]

In the *Essai sur l'étude de la littérature* Gibbon set out his thoughts on scholarship and scholars. In the *Essai* he carefully distinguishes between mere antiquarians and real scholars. A good scholar, Gibbon argues, must have more than learning. Henry

---

[18] In addition to Gibbon's own candid evaluation of his mastery of Latin, there is the testimony of an eminent scholar and classicist, D. M. Low. Low studied and translated Gibbon's Latin correspondence with Professor J. J. Breitinger—the five surviving letters are printed in *Letters*, I, nos. 7, 9, 11, 12, 14. Low concludes: "It may be said at once that Gibbon's Latin is fluent but faulty. . . . The chief weakness, Gibbon's latter-day examiner must report, is an uncertain grasp of the syntax of Latin moods." But Low adds: "Had Gibbon continued the pursuit of pure scholarship he would no doubt have become more correct and more fastidious, and the present letters indicate that he might have been an accomplished Latinist with an individual style." See *Letters*, I, appendix I, especially p. 89. Gibbon was not yet twenty when he wrote these letters.

[19] See Bury's introduction to the *Decline and Fall*, ix.

[20] *Jour. B.*, pp. 246-247 (March 21, 1764).   [21] *Jour. B.*, p. 247.

Dodwell (1641-1711), for example, whose "learning was immense" is criticized: "The worst of this author is his method and style; the one perplexed beyond imagination, the other negligent to a degree of Barbarism."[22] Men whose minds are "drowned in pedantic erudition" are the consistent butts of Gibbon's mordant wit, both in the *Essai* and the *Decline and Fall*. "Mere critics" or "mere compilers" are, in the *Essai*, a subspecies of scholar; they "never deserve our admiration" and "rarely gratify our taste."[23] Their manners are "gross, their labors sometimes trifling."[24]

Thoroughness, exactness, and diligence are the characteristics and the virtues of scholarship, but these can easily be pushed beyond moderation. When the "minute diligence of an antiquarian" became excessive, Gibbon considered his work either foolish or fruitless.[25] Antiquarian zeal, like religious zeal, was to be condemned. The urge to emend every text that fell into their hands is the great sin of pedants: "The passage is perfectly clear: yet both Casaubon and Salmasius wish to correct it."[26] And often these men so encumbered a text with worthless commentary that its original clarity is buried: "With regard to the time when these Roman games were celebrated, Scaliger, Salmasius and Cuper, have given themselves a great deal of trouble to perplex a very clear subject."[27] Gibbon had no patience with the finicky tamperings of antiquarians: "the more I read the Antients, the more I am persuaded that the originals are our best commentators. In this article of ancient Gymnastics (for instance), when I have read with care Homer, Pausanias, and some few more ancients, M. Burette has little to teach me, excepting perhaps what he may have picked up from some obscure Lexicographer."[28]

Even more than misdirected curiosity and an acrimonious spirit, Gibbon abhorred the lack of common sense among antiquarians.

---

[22] *Jour. A.*, p. 82 (June 8, 1762).   [23] *Essai*, VI, p. 22.
[24] *Essai*, IV, p. 18.
[25] He wrote, for example (LI, 430, n. 19): "Claudian [the fifth-century poet and panegyrist] is not prepared for the strict examination of our antiquaries." And he complained (XXX, 284, n. 91): "How labourously does the curious spirit of Europe explore the darkest and most distant antiquities."
[26] XII, 322, n. 15.   [27] XII, 346, n. 106.
[28] *Jour. A.*, p. 113 (August 12, 1762).

Claude Salmasius, Milton's unfortunate opponent in a famous pamphlet battle of the seventeenth century, was frequently the victim of Gibbon's venom: [29] "On the texture, colours, names, and use of the silk and linen garments of antiquity, see the profound, diffuse, and obscure researches of the great Salmasius, who was ignorant of the most common trades of Dijon or Leyden." [30] Or: "I leave Scaliger and Salmasius to quarrel about the origin of Cumae, the eldest of the Greek colonies in Italy; already vacant in Juvenal's time, and now in ruins." [31] In addition to irrelevance, ignorance, and naïveté, Gibbon condemned all forms of special pleading. Those antiquarians whose patriotic zeal drew them to study the past were serious corruptors of historical truth. Gibbon referred to them contemptuously as "national" antiquaries. The past was, for these men, a series of examples apparently designed for no other purpose but to flatter the present. To achieve their purpose these "national" antiquaries "variously tortured" the texts and did not blush at inserting conjecture in the place of evidence. Their ignorance of world history was astonishing. British antiquaries, for example, wrote as if the British Isles were the center of the Roman empire, instead of its most obscure and neglected province: "Our antiquarians, even the great Cambden himself, have been betrayed into many gross errors by their imperfect knowledge of the history of the continent." [32] When Gibbon destroyed the plausibility of the Ossian poems in the *Decline and Fall* [33] he did so by arguing that the traditional evidence for the reign of Caracalla, perfectly acceptable on every other point, directly contradicts the evidence presented in the Ossian poems.

Yet even "national" antiquaries had their use. Gibbon knew precisely what he wanted from other scholars. He was perfectly willing to take what was valid and true, and reject what was mere conjecture: "As a great number of medals of Carausius are still preserved, he is become a very favourite subject of antiquarian

[29] Gibbon said in the *Essai*, III, p. 18, that Salmasius "neither deserved the admiration paid him by his contemporaries, nor the contempt which we feel compelled to heap upon him." Whether deserved or not, Gibbon was generous with his contempt.

[30] XL, 244, n. 65.

[31] XLIII, 447-448, n. 75.

[32] XXXI, 371-372, n. 178.

[33] See VI, 141-142, n. 16.

curiosity, and every circumstance of his life and actions have been investigated with sagacious accuracy. Dr. Stukely in particular has devoted a large volume to the British emperor. I have used his materials and rejected most of his fanciful conjectures." [34] The list of antiquarian faults might be extended, but this is perhaps enough to make the point. Gibbon's interests in antiquarian scholarship extended only so far as it could be of direct benefit to the "historian of the Roman empire." He had no desire to be an antiquarian, and he tended to view antiquarians, even the best of them, as below historians. The distinction he makes between antiquarian and historian is not very precise. His view is that only those who construct a narrative of the past are historians; all others are antiquarians or "mere" compilers.

Yet if Gibbon always distinguished between antiquarian scholarship and philosophic history, he took considerable delight in scholarship. A large part of his life was spent, and pleasantly spent, in the company of antiquarian scholarship. Gibbon was not above praising a deserving guide, and his encomiums are as gracious as his contempt is devastating: "but the preceding account is eclipsed by the magnificent description and drawings of MM. Dawkins and Wood, who have transported into England the ruins of Palmyra and Baalbec." [35] "The historian of the Roman empire" was completely dependent on antiquarian scholarship, and he frequently bemoans the lack of "a local antiquarian, and a good topographical map." When dealing with periods of Roman history not adequately investigated by antiquarians, he laments "the insufficiency of my guides."

What little antiquarian scholarship Gibbon himself did was done when he was very young, and before he had clarified, in the *Essai*, his notions of history and the historian. These youthful essays in pure scholarship can be traced in the *Miscellaneous Works*, and some of the titles will give an adequate idea of the direction of Gibbon's early studies. "Remarques critiques sur le nombre des habitants dans la cité des sybarites" [36] contains no original research

[34] XIII, 358, n. 31.   [35] LI, 458, n. 85.
[36] *MW*, III, 178-182.

but attempts to apply the speculations on ancient populations of Hume and Wallace to a specific case. "An Examination of the Catalogue of Silius Italicus" [37] and "An Inquiry Whether a Catalogue of the Armies Sent into the Field Is an Essential Part of an Epic Poem" [38] are brief, occasional essays. "Remarques critiques sur un passage de Plaute," [39] "Remarques sur quelques endroits de Virgile," [40] and "Remarques critiques sur un passage de Virgile" [41] might well have been published in the transactions of an antiquarian society. There were also more ambitious works, which in fact formed the foundations of the massive learning of the *Decline and Fall*. Such were "Principes des poids, des monnoies, et des mesures des anciens, avec des tables construites sur ces principes," [42] "Dissertation sur les anciennes mesures, &c. du bas empire jusqu'à la prise de Constantinople par les Turcs," [43] and his historical geography of ancient Italy.[44] But Gibbon's antiquarian phase did not last long, and in the *Decline and Fall* antiquarian interests are subordinated to those of "the historian of the Roman empire." Gibbon is interested in constructing a narrative of Roman history. This narrative rests on the best scholarship of his day, but there is no doubt that Gibbon looked upon antiquarian scholarship as useful to a philosophic historian, not an end in itself.

Part of Gibbon's definition of a philosophic historian was his ability to live "in distant ages and remote countries." "By reading and reflection," Gibbon believed, the historian "multiplies his own experience." Working alone in his study, in the comfort of a Reynolds portrait and a tasteful collection of Wedgwood plaques, and surrounded by his books,[45] Gibbon lived "in distant ages and remote countries." Through his books Gibbon traveled through the ancient world. Much of his impressive empathy with Rome was

[37] *MW*, IV, 333-335. [38] *MW*, IV, 327-332. [39] *MW*, IV, 435-441.
[40] *MW*, IV, 441-446. [41] *MW*, IV, 446-466. [42] *MW*, V, 66-119.
[43] *MW*, V, 120-169. [44] *MW*, IV, 155-326.
[45] Gibbon owned about 7,000 volumes. He says he never bought a book for ostentation and that every book "was either read or sufficiently examined" before being shelved. The catalog of his library has been ingeniously compiled by the doyen of British bibliographers, Geoffrey Keynes, *The Library of Edward Gibbon* (London, 1940). A shorter and less reliable survey is James W. Thompson, "The Library of Gibbon the Historian," *Library Quarterly*, VII (1937), 343-353.

made possible through the works of travelers. These products of
the lay scholarship of the Enlightenment are among the most attractive books of the age. Gibbon used two distinct categories of
travel literature: the memoirs of individual travelers and the elaborate (and expensive) books of archaeological scholarship then ap-
pearing. He devoured travel literature. His appetite was never
sated, and this passion lasted a lifetime.[46]

Travel, whether his own or that of others, was a serious business.
Gibbon himself had taken months of preparation, including the
composition of a historical geography, before he dared enter Italy.
Because he demanded so much of himself Gibbon had only scorn
for most of the travelers he consulted. They were "blind" because
ill-prepared. Their remarks and observations were uninformed,
and their information uncritical. But there were some philosophic
travelers, and they occupy an honored place in the *Decline and
Fall*. Sir John Chardin, for example, was a trusted guide.[47] His
Voyages en Perse, et autres lieux de l'Orient (1735) is frequently
cited, and always with approval. A handful of other travelers also
escaped Gibbon's acerbic wit: George Sandys, *Travels* (1673);
Thomas Shaw, *Travels or Observations Relating to Several Parts
of Barbary and the Levant* (1757); J. B. Tavernier, *Six voyages
en Turquie, en Perse et aux Indes* (1692); J. de Thévenot, *Voyages
tant en Europe qu'en Asie et en Afrique* (1689); the same author's
Relation de divers voyages curieux qui n'ont point publies (1696),
and *Travels into the Levant* (1687); and J. Pitton de Tournefort,
Relation d'un voyage du Levant (1717).

The second category of travel literature, books of archaeological
scholarship, are similarly represented in the *Decline and Fall*. Gibbon came late enough in the development of archaeological studies
to benefit from several important discoveries. Etruscan antiquities
were beginning to receive serious attention, and the extraordinary
excavations at Herculaneum (1736) and Pompeii (1748) were

---

[46] Some indication of his continuing appetite for travel literature can be found
in his later letters. See especially nos. 488, 620, 722. Letter 722, written to the book-
seller Peter Elmsley, after completion of the *Decline and Fall*, on February 28,
1789, is interesting. Gibbon requests several travel books, telling Elmsley "that in
general I am greedy of Voyages and travels."

[47] Gibbon cites Chardin more than a dozen times.

available to him. So, too, were such splendid books as the *Antiquities of Athens* (1762) by Stuart and Revett, a model of its kind. In the same class were the two works of R. Wood, the *Ruins of Palmyra* (1735) and the *Ruins of Baalbec* (1757), and the re-creation of Diocletian's palace at Spalato, by Adam and Clerisseau (1764). Few were able to afford these handsome folios, and even fewer were privileged to visit the sites discussed. Gibbon's independent income, although modest, was sufficient to allow him both advantages. He had seen Italy, and could enjoy Palmyra, Baalbec, or Spalato in his study.

The use of travel literature in the *Decline and Fall* was always for one of two purposes: either to sketch a "philosophic" contrast between past glories, medieval decay, and present industriousness, or to re-create for his readers the actual physical extent of a city or a location. In the midst of a discussion of the wealth and urbanization of the early empire, Gibbon pauses to consider a minor episode during Tiberius' reign. In the early first century eleven Asiatic cities had disputed the honor of dedicating a temple to the emperor. The literary evidence for this incident comes from Tacitus. Gibbon appends two extensive notes to his discussion in order to show the reader the condition of these cities in the eighteenth century:

> I have taken some pains in consulting and comparing modern travellers, with regard to the fate of these eleven cities of Asia; seven or eight are totally destroyed, Hypaepe, Tralles, Laodicea, Ilium, Halicarnassus, Miletus, Ephesus, and we may add Sardis. Of the remaining three, Pergamus is a straggling village of two or three thousand inhabitants; Magnesia, under the name of Guzel-hissar, a town of some consequence; and Smyrna, a great city, peopled by an hundred thousand souls. But even at Smyrna, while the Franks have maintained commerce, the Turks have ruined the arts.[48]

Of the eleven applicants the Roman senate rejected four as unequal to the honor. One of these was Laodicia, "whose splendour is still displayed in its ruins"; and Gibbon then refers his readers to "a very exact and pleasing description of the ruins of Laodicea,

[48] II, 49, n. 84.

in Chandler's Travels through Asia Minor." [49] This habit of contrasting antiquity with the present is a regular feature of the *Decline and Fall*. The philosophic historian had a responsibility to view the works of man in every possible light. It was an instructive intellectual exercise to compare Roman grandeur, feudal tyranny, and eighteenth-century industriousness, and Gibbon seldom let slip such an opportunity. In these contrasts the philosopher would see not only the vanity of human wishes and the mutations of time, but also the historical process at work. From such a contrast the philosophic historian would be now a Roman, now a feudal lord, and finally a gentleman of the Enlightenment.The program for philosophic history outlined in the *Essai* thus finds expression in the *Decline and Fall*.

The other use of travel literature is less philosophic. From childhood Gibbon had been fascinated by the puzzling out of itineraries in antiquity. In the *Decline and Fall* this hobby is put to good use. He takes great pains to establish the distance between points, and is concerned about fixing the exact number of days necessary to accomplish a journey.[50] Speaking of Heraclitus' expedition against the Persians (A.D. 623), which passed through the Black Sea, Gibbon notes: "From Constantinople to Trebizond, with a fair wind, four or five days; from thence to Erzerona, five; to Erivan twelve; to Tauris, ten; in all thirty-two. Such is the Itinerary of Tavernier, who was perfectly conversant with the roads of Asia. Tournefort, who travelled with a Pasha, spent ten or twelve days between Trebizond and Erzeron; and Chardin, gives the more correct distance of fifty-three parasangs, each of 5000 paces (what paces?) between Erivan and Tauris." [51] Gibbon's reliance upon and use of travel literature is most striking when he was forced to work solely from secondary accounts. The two most famous examples in the *Decline and Fall* are his descriptions of Constantinople and the Muslim empire. Gibbon had seen neither, yet he painted a detailed and memorable picture of each from the travel literature. His re-

[49] II, 49, n. 85.
[50] See, for example, *MW*, IV, 335-354, "A Minute Examination of Horace's Journey to Brundisium, and of Cicero's Journey into Cilicia."
[51] XLVI, 87, n. 102.

creation of ancient Constantinople (chapter XVII) is a tour de force, not superseded until the present century.[52]

His first problem was to determine the extent of the ancient city. Against those who wish to extend the limits of the city "over the adjacent villages of the European, and even of the Asiatic coast," Gibbon masses the testimony of modern travelers. His preference is consistently for those who had taken the trouble to explore the city itself and pace off the distances. The "accurate Thévenot" had walked around two sides of the triangle—"from the kiosk of the Seraglio to the seven towers"—in one hour and three-quarters. This is "decisive testimony" and Gibbon assigns to the city a circumference of "ten or twelve miles."[53] For his description of the Bosporus, Gibbon compared all the accounts, both ancient and modern: "The Bosphorus has been minutely described by Dionysius of Byzantium, who lived in the time of Domitian, and by Gilles or Gyllius, a French traveller of the xvith century. Tournefort seems to have used his own eyes and the learning of Gyllius."[54] Gibbon appends this learned note to his majestic description of the Bosporus: "Thévenot contracts the measure to 125 small Greek miles. Belon gives a good description of the Propontis, but contents himself with the vague description of one day and one night's sail. When Sandys talks of 150 furlongs in length as well as breadth, we can only suppose some mistake of the press in the text of that judicious traveller."[55]

Throughout the *Decline and Fall* Gibbon follows this pattern: in the text he paints a picture of the place, and in the notes marshals all the evidence furnished by modern travelers. So addicted did Gibbon become to this habit of furnishing authorities for every geographic description, that he even footnotes things he had himself seen. In speaking of a camp of the Goths, which Procopius described as "seven miles from Rome under the crossing of two principal aqueducts," Gibbon says: "Procopius has forgot to name these aqueducts; nor can such a double intersection, at such a distance from Rome, be ascertained from the writings of Frontinus, Fabretti, and Eschinard . . . or from the local maps of Lamette

[52] See Bury's reservations, in his notes to chapter XVII.
[53] XVII, 159, n. 35.   [54] XVII, 151, n. 3.   [55] XVII, 153, n. 15.

and Cingolani." [56] Only with the support of this battery of authorities, does Gibbon add his own eyewitness testimony: "Seven or eight miles from the city (50 stadia) on the road to Albano, between the Latin and Appian ways, I discern the remains of an aquaduct (probably the Septimian), a series (630 paces) of arches twenty-five feet high." [57] A similar example is Gibbon's description of Trajan's column. Not only had Gibbon seen the column, but he spent some time studying it.[58] But in his *History* the description of Trajan's column is impersonal, drawn entirely from the sources.[59] Gibbon's diffidence in these matters is pedantic, but rests on an assumption about the historian's responsibility to himself, his readers, and his materials. One of his major objections to the works of the *philosophe* historians of his own day was their cavalier attitude toward scholarship. Voltaire's remark that historical details are "the vermin who destroy important works" [60] was anathema to Gibbon. Voltaire is frequently the target of Gibbon's malice in the *Decline and Fall*, and he never dismissed a *philosophe* historian without a sharp criticism: for example Père Daniel, "whose ideas were superficial and modern," or Villaret, "who quotes nobody, according to the last fashion of the French writers." Gibbon bent over backward to avoid this style of historical writing, and it led him into the pedantry noticed above. "The historian of the Roman empire" never missed an opportunity to demonstrate to his readers his own scholarly diligence, and to show them the massive foundations on which his narrative rested.

Gibbon speaks often of "philosophic" travelers, and the designation is one of praise. The adjective "philosophic" is often loosely applied by Gibbon, but in this case, from his *Memoirs* and journals a definition can be extracted. "The use of foreign travel," he writes, "has been often debated as a general question; but the conclusion must be finally applied to the character and circumstances of each individual." The use of travel in "the education of boys" is dismissed as an expedient to get them "over some juvenile years with

---

[56] XLI, 342, n. 100.   [57] XLI, 342, n. 100.   [58] See *Letters*, I, 184.
[59] II, 47.
[60] Voltaire's complete statement, from his letter to the Abbé Dubos, which is prefixed to *Le siècle de Louis XIV*, is: "Malheur aux détailes: la postérité les néglige tonus: c'est une vermine qui tue les grands ouvrages."

the least mischief to themselves or others." Travel must be reserved for maturity, for it demands "the previous and indispensable requisites of age, judgement, a competent knowledge of men and books, and a freedom from domestic prejudices." In addition to a strong constitution, the traveler should have "a copious stock of classical and historical learning" and "blend the practical knowledge of husbandry and manufactures." "The benefits of foreign travel," he adds, "will correspond with the degree of these qualifications." A man thus prepared will be a philosophic traveler. He will live in foreign lands with ease, his impressions and judgments will be informed by learning, and he will be able to put his immediate impressions into historical perspective. Gibbon, obviously, considered himself a "philosophic" traveler, and assured his readers that "those to whom I am known will not accuse me of framing my own panegyric." [61]

In a sense the *Decline and Fall* is a piece of travel literature, for Gibbon conducts his readers through the Roman empire as an urbane, witty, and philosophic Cicerone. The philosophic traveler should "compare the monuments of Roman conquest, of feudal or Austrian tyranny [he is speaking of northern Italy], of monkish superstition, and of industrious freedom." [62] Such a comparison will induce the philosophic traveler to "applaud the merit and happiness of his own times." [63] Gibbon's own travel literature— his journals—are filled with just such reflections, and he carried over to the *Decline and Fall* his own experiences. He also judged the travel literature of others according to this personal standard. Only those who meet Gibbon's criterion of philosophic traveler find a place in the *Decline and Fall*.

Complementary to travel literature was the work of geographers, another of the nonliterary disciplines of ancient history. Gibbon himself was an excellent geographer; certainly more adept and precise than his contemporaries Montesquieu and Voltaire.[64] His

---

[61] All these passages are from *Memoirs*, pp. 135-136.
[62] XXXVIII, 112, n. 25.   [63] XXXVIII, 112, n. 25.
[64] Montesquieu qualified as a philosophic traveler, and his knowledge of geography was impressive. But he lacked the tenacity and pride in minute detail that characterized Gibbon as geographer. Montesquieu traveled to study customs and not geography. See Robert Shackleton, *Montesquieu, a Critical Biography* (Ox-

youthful habit of never reading without a reliable historical atlas at hand continued throughout his life. There is never, in the *Decline and Fall*, any doubt about the precise location of places or events. There is throughout Gibbon's *History* a remarkable quality of geographic solidity, and Gibbon never leaves his readers in doubt about their exact location in the empire. He takes a perverse delight in heaping scorn on men who misplace a city or a bridge, or have a river flow in the wrong direction. The French scholar, Cousin, had not mastered the currents and winds of the Bosporus: "In bold defiance, or rather in gross ignorance, of language and geography the President Cousin detains them [five ships] at Chios with a south, and wafts them to Constantinople with a north wind." [65] Or: "The truth of geography and the original text of Villehardoun place Rodosto three days' journey (trois journées) from Hadrianople; but Vigenère, in his version, has most absurdly substituted *trois heures;* and this error, which is not corrected by Ducange, has entrapped several moderns, whose names I shall spare." [66]

Gibbon early discovered—while composing his historical geography—that the ancients were not to be trusted in geography. Rather than waste his time, as had so many other scholars, in trying to reconcile their inaccurate measurements, Gibbon turned to modern geographers for clarification.[67] "Their exactness is so far inferior to that of modern critics (a Nardini for example) that the moderns are constantly put in the position of supplying the defects of the ancients." [68] Gibbon had no false piety about antiquity: he recognized that he knew more about geography than did the ancients, and he never apologized for discounting the testimony of a classic author. His favorite geographer was Jean-Baptiste Bourgui-

---

ford, 1961), p. 95, where a part of Montesquieu's journey to Rome is recorded. He spent the majority of his time in society, not with an antiquary studying the ruins. Voltaire traveled only for political expediency. A single example of Gibbon's scorn is sufficient (I, 26, n. 96): "M. de Voltaire, unsupported by either fact or probability, has generously bestowed the Canary Islands on the Roman empire."
[65] LXVII, 189, n. 54.   [66] LXI, 443, n. 33.
[67] In the *Essai*, XXXVII, p. 47, Gibbon points out that the ancient poets were bad geographers. In the following chapter he accused them of faulty chronology. He later extended the charge to include most of the ancient writers.
[68] *Jour. B.*, p. 47.

gnon d'Anville (1697-1782), a Parisian who seldom ventured out of the archives.[69] Gibbon's admiration for d'Anville was unbounded. He was "the first of geographers," "that excellent writer," "that ingenious geographer." D'Anville is cited no less than 128 times, and always with approval. Only once did Gibbon catch his French guide in an error. He took the occasion to reprimand him playfully: "For my own justification, I am obliged to mention the *only* error which I have discovered in the maps or writings of that admirable geographer." [70]

The geographers are often used in conjunction with the travelers: the former to set the stage, the latter to describe the action: "M. d'Anville has ascertained the true position and distance of Babylon, Seleucia, Ctesiphon, Bagdad, &c. The Roman traveller, Pietro della Valle seems to be the most intelligent spectator of that province." [71] Or: "The local description of Alexandria is perfectly ascertained by the master hand of the first of geographers, but we may borrow the eyes of the modern travellers, more especially of Thévenot, and Niebuhr. Of the two modern rivals, Savaray and Volney, the one may amuse, the other will instruct." [72]

Gibbon's reliance on d'Anville is a clear instance of his use of the new antiquarian scholarship. Yet even d'Anville retained a reverence for the ancient texts that often led him into foolish errors: "even that ingenious geographer is too fond of supposing new and perhaps imaginary *measures,* for the purpose of rendering ancient writers as accurate as himself." [73] His judgments are always sharp and to the point, and these judgments rest firmly on his ex-

---

[69] D'Anville's *Considérations générales sur l'etude et les connoissances que demande la composition des ouvrages de géographie* . . . (Paris, 1777) is a personal statement of what the craft of geography entails. His eulogy was written by Dacier, "Éloge de M. d'Anvile," *Mémoires de l'Académie des Inscriptions,* vol. xiv; and Condorcet, "Éloge de M. d'Anvile," *Histoire de l'Académie Royal des Sciences* (1782).

[70] XXII, 436, n. 35.   [71] XXIV, 529, n. 68.

[72] LI, 479, n. 130. Gibbon's faith in d'Anville's accuracy was so strong that he preferred his testimony to that of travelers who had visited the actual site. For example, in a digression on the precise location of Memphis (LI, 476, n. 124), Gibbon says the travelers place the city at Gizeh, but: "we may not disregard the authority of the arguments . . . of d'Anville, who . . . [has] removed Memphis toward the village of Mohannah, some miles farther to the south."

[73] XXIV, 520, n. 16.

tensive knowledge of all the best works of antiquarian scholar-ship.[74]

The science of numismatics was in its infancy in the eighteenth century. The father of modern numismatics, Ezechiel Spanheim (1629-1710), published his great work, *De usu numismaticus,* in 1671. The work lifted the study of coins out of the realm of mere curiosity by insisting on the application of rigorous principles of classification. The enthusiasm of collectors and dilettantes was channeled in a more orderly course by Spanheim's work. A rash of books, both on the historical importance of coins and the joys of numismatics, began to appear. Charles Patin, a doctor by profes-sion and a militant numismatist by choice, wrote one of the most interesting of these popular handbooks, *Histoire des médailles, ou introduction à la connaissance de cette science* (1665).[75]

This engaging work is a good guide to the state of numismatics when Gibbon wrote. Patin considered coins "les preuves de l'his-toire" and argued enthusiastically: "And one can even say that without numismatic evidence history, thus stripped of reliability [*preuves*], would be seen by many either through the prejudiced eyes of the ancient historians, who wrote only of events in their own day, or would be seen as a simple inventory of the memoirs of contemporaries of the events. Such a view of the past would reduce history either to falsehood or prejudice." [76] Gibbon's view of the importance of coins was less exalted than this, but he clearly recog-nized its importance. At the outset of the Grand Tour he had paid a "superficial" visit to the Académie des Medailles in Paris. The visit opened a "new field of inquiry" [77] and Gibbon immediately began a systematic study of numismatics. He started by "glancing [his] eye over Addison's agreeable dialogues" and then moved on to more scholarly works: "I more seriously read the great work of

---

[74] Gibbon owned fourteen of d'Anville's works, and they were among the most heavily used books in his library.

[75] In addition to this popular work Patin wrote several learned treatises: *Impera-torum romanorum numismata a Julio Caesare et Heraclium, ex aera mediae et minimae formae descriptae et enarratae* (Amsterdam, 1696); *Epistola de antiquo numismate Augusti et Platonis* (Basil, 1675). He also compiled catalogs of his own and other coin collections.

[76] Patin, *Histoire des medailes,* p. 8.

[77] *Memoirs,* p. 131. The actual visit is recorded in *Misc. Gibb.,* pp. 98-99.

Ezechiel Spanheim, de Praestantia de Usû Numismatum, and applied with him the medals of the Kings and Emperors, the families and colonies to the illustration of ancient history." [78] In Italy he visited all the collections open to the public, but these were sightseeing tours, not serious scholarly exercises.

It is unfortunate that the most important numismatic work of the age, Joseph-Hilar Echkel's work on imperial coinage, which appeared in 1792-98, was not available to Gibbon. After Spanheim, Echkel was the most important name in the new science. Familiar only with the work of Spanheim, and the books of several lesser men, Gibbon tended to be conservative in his use of numismatic evidence. Had the science been more sophisticated in the eighteenth century Gibbon might have been bolder; but numismatic evidence occupies a secondary place in the *Decline and Fall*. Gibbon preferred to create the past from literary evidence. There are about thirty specific instances where Gibbon uses numismatic evidence,[79] and he was sufficiently interested to write two occasional essays on the subject.[80]

Gibbon carefully differentiated himself from the enthusiastic claims of the Pyrrhonists, who argued that coins were the only reliable evidence for the past. Numismatics were, for Gibbon, but a useful supplement to the literary evidence. He speaks of "the treacherous language of . . . medals" [81] and used such evidence only when it could be checked against other sources. His view of numismatics is identical to that recently expressed by a respected historian of the Roman empire.[82] Gibbon thought coins the best possible evidence for events which they directly celebrate, but he refused to go much further than this. He uses coins to support the testimony of Julian the Apostate regarding Constantine's ridiculous

---

[78] *Memoirs*, p. 132.

[79] Those instances where Gibbon makes specific reference to numismatic works, or uses the evidence of coins in his discussion, are included.

[80] See *MW*, V, 66-120, "Principes des poids, des monnoies, et des mesures des anciens, avec des tables construits sur ces principes" (1759); and *MW*, V, 33-39, "A Dissertation on the Allegorical Beings Found on the Reverses of Medals" (1764).

[81] X, 256, n. 87.

[82] A. H. M. Jones, "Numismatics and History," *Essays in Roman Coinage Presented to Harold Mattingly*, ed. R. A. C. Carson and C. H. V. Sutherland (Oxford, 1956).

costumes [83] and to prove that the voters under the republic passed across a narrow bridge, one at a time, to give their votes.[84] He uses coins to prove that the emperor Maximin's wife died before her husband [85] and to prove the magnificence of Aurelian's triumph in A.D. 274.[86] He ventured a translation of "the treacherous language of . . . medals" by suggesting that "the restraints of civil institutions" under Aurelian was suggested by the words *Deus* and *Dominus* on his coins.[87] And he cites a coin of king Theodoric as a representation of "the oldest and most authentic model of Gothic architecture." [88]

He was delighted when he was able to find numismatic evidence which supported his hostile attitudes toward the early church, and he gleefully cited this evidence for his readers: "The Christian humility of the popes was not offended by the name of *Dominus*, or Lord; and their face and inscription are still apparent on the most ancient coins." [89] He uses the evidence of coins to refute Tertullian [90] and to date Constantine's conversion later than the battle of the Milvian Bridge.[91] Gibbon was aware of numismatics, and he made good use of this discipline when he could. But in this specialized study he was wholly at the mercy of his guides, and as a general rule Gibbon was "not fond of repeating words like a parrot." The limited use of numismatic evidence in the *Decline and Fall* is due to Gibbon's own lack of expertise, the infant state of that science in his day, and the fact that his narrative interests naturally led him to concentrate his attention on literary evidence.

Gibbon's hesitancy in using methods and materials with which he was not intimately familiar is clear throughout the *Decline and Fall*. The sophisticated techniques developed by Jean Mabillon, perhaps the greatest of the Maurist scholars, were known to Gibbon, but only casually. Mabillon's *De re diplomatica* (1681), which virtually created the science of diplomatics, had been read by Gib-

---

[83] XVIII, 217, n. 6.   [84] LXIV, 477, n. 28.   [85] VII, 173, n. 12.
[86] XI, 311, n. 87.   [87] XI, 315, n. 101.
[88] XXXIX, 205. Gibbon also uses numismatic evidence to prove the extensive travels of Hadrian (I, 8, n. 27), the fact that Antonius Pius passed over his two sons to adopt Marcus as his successor (III, 76, n. 50), and the fact that Caracalla had his brother Geta consecrated after he had murdered him (VI, 133, n. 26).
[89] XLIX, 282, n. 46.   [90] XVI, 116.   [91] XX, 308-309, n. 11.

bon, yet there is no evidence in his *History* that he ever applied these principles to a single medieval document. The same is true of the work of Mabillon's successor, Bernard Montfaucon. His *Paléographie grecque* did for Greek documents what Mabillon had done for those in Latin, and is worthy of standing beside the latter's medieval paleography. Here is Gibbon's description of these important studies:

> My visits, however superficial to the cabinet of medals and the public libraries opened a new field of enquiry, and the view of so many Manuscripts of different ages and characters induced me to consult the two great Benedictine Works, the *Diplomatica* of Mabillon, and the *Palaeographica* of Montfaucon. I studied the theory, without attaining the practise of the art; nor should I complain of the intricacy of Greek abbreviations and Gothic alphabets since every day, in a familiar language, I am at a loss to decypher the Hieroglyphics of a female note.[92]

These are the attitudes of a gentleman scholar, who had only a dilettante's interest in pure scholarship.

Gibbon refused to enter the labyrinth of specialized medieval studies, but he gratefully used the literary evidence edited and collected by the Maurists. His respect for Benedictine scholarship was immense. In the *Memoirs* he contemptuously compared the "port and prejudice" of Oxford "to the Benedictine Abbeys of Catholic countries": "The shelves of their library groan under the weight of the Benedictine folios, of the editions of the fathers, and the Collections of the middle ages, which have issued from the single Abby of St Germain des Préz at Paris." And "If I enquire into the manufactures of the monks at Magdalen, if I extend the enquiry to the other Colleges of Oxford and Cambridge, a silent blush, or a scornful frown, will be the only reply."[93] Gibbon owned and used many of these monuments of Benedictine scholarship, and he praised them at every opportunity. Such splendid editions permitted him to deal conveniently with materials both unfamiliar and uncongenial to "the historian of the Roman empire": "as I am *almost* a stranger to the voluminous sermons of

[92] *Memoirs*, p. 131.   [93] *Memoirs*, p. 52.

Chrysostom, I have given my confidence to the two most judicious and moderate of the ecclesiastical critics. . . ." [94]

The monumental work of the Bollandist scholars is similarly praised. Their great *Acta sanctorum*, begun in 1607, is still incomplete. For Gibbon the *Acta* were an indispensable repository of information about the lives of the saints: "This immense calendar of the saints, in one hundred and twenty-six years (1644-1770), and in fifty volumes in folio, has advanced no farther than the 7th day of October. The suppression of the Jesuits has most probably checked an undertaking which, through the medium of fable and superstition, communicates much historical and philosophical instruction." [95]

The work of the legal historians, the collectors of inscriptions, the compilers and editors, and the hagiographers all figure prominently in the *Decline and Fall*. The forty-fourth chapter of Gibbon's *History* is justly famous as a brilliant explication of the complexities of Roman law.[96] It is perhaps the most impressive synthetic chapter in the *Decline and Fall*, and without the patient labors of generations of legal historians and obscure scholars, would have been unthinkable. Gibbon entered "with just diffidence" on the subject of civil law, and relied completely on the scholarship "which has exhausted so many learned lives and clothed the walls of such spacious libraries": "At the head of these guides I shall respectfully place the learned and perspicuous Heineccius, a German professor, who died at Halle in the year 1741. His ample works have been collected in eight volumes. . . . The treatises which I have separately used are, 1. Historia Juris Romani et Germanici . . . 2. Syntagma Antiquitatum Romanam Jurisprodentian Illustratium . . . 3. Elementa J. C. Secundum Ordinem Pandectarum." [97] Gibbon owned the books mentioned here, and his journal records

[94] XXXII, 396, n. 42.

[95] XXXIII, 438, n. 48. Despite interruptions—during the eighteenth century when the Jesuits were suppressed, and during World War I when the Belgium house was dispersed—this remarkable order has continued its work to the present day.

[96] Bury thought it one of Gibbon's best chapters. Harold Laski thought the chapter the finest exposition of Roman law he had ever read. In the eighteenth century it was translated into German and served as an introduction to the study of Roman law in the universities.

[97] XLIV, 471, n. 4.

that he read Heinecke as a young man: *"L'Histoire du Droit Romain,* by Heineccius, is especially interesting for a man who concerns himself with jurisprudence only in so far as it relates to literature." [98] This was long before Gibbon became the "historian of the Roman empire," but when he reached the chapter on Roman law he returned naturally to the books that had stimulated him as a young scholar. Gibbon's treatment of Roman law, although brilliant, is limited by the state of scholarship in the eighteenth century. The bulk of his famous chapter concerns the Justinian code, and is no longer an adequate treatment. Mommsen's *Romisches Staatsrecht,* based on the corpus of Latin inscriptions, was not then available. The discovery of the important manuscript of Gaius has also altered the current view of the subject. Gibbon broke no new ground, but he synthesized for his age all that was then known about the subject.

His use of epigraphical evidence presents a similar picture. Gibbon was restricted to the available scholarship. The corpus of Latin inscriptions was not yet published. What he had was the *Inscriptiones antiquae totius orbis Romani,* collected by J. Gruter, and a few lesser collections. Gibbon relied heavily on this work, but it represents a mere beginning in an important branch of ancient history. It is praiseworthy that he recognized the importance of inscriptional evidence and incorporated it in his *History,* but he was never happy with either the quality or the quantity of the evidence. But if the available evidence was inadequate, Gibbon's instincts were correct. He applied epigraphical evidence as it is today applied: to prove the occurrence of an event (the defeat of the Germans by Aurelian) [99] or to throw a ray of light into the more obscure corners of ancient civilization: "See in Gruter, and the other collectors, a great number of inscriptions addressed by slaves to their wives, fellow-servants, masters, &c. They are all most probably of the Imperial age." [100] It would be unfair to expect from Gibbon the sophisticated applications of epigraphical evidence which are now familiar, not to mention the prosopographical studies of recent years.

---

[98] *Jour. B.,* p. 9 (August 25, 1763).   [99] XI, 298, n. 43.
[100] II, 40, n. 51.

When working in the more traditional modes of ancient history, that is, using the literary evidence, Gibbon was more at home. His touch was surer, his speculations bolder, and his command of materials nothing short of remarkable.[101] The names of the great scholars of Roman history—Tillemont, Pagi, Muratori, Baronius, DuCange—are familiar to any reader of the *Decline and Fall*. The twenty-two volumes of Tillemont ("my incomparable guide") and the thirty-seven of Muratori ("my ordinary and excellent guide") divide between them almost a third of the citations from secondary authorities in the *Decline and Fall*. For the history of Italy Gibbon found Muratori indispensable: "Through the darkness of the middle ages I explored my way in the Annals and Antiquities of Italy of the learned Muratori; and diligently compared them with the parallel or transverse lines of Sigonius and Maffei, Baronius and Pagi, till I almost grasped the ruins of Rome in the fourteenth Century. . . ."[102] For France Gibbon used the *Recueil des historiens des Gaules et de la France* in eleven volumes, a worthy continuation of the heroic labors of the seventeenth-century historians: "By the labour of Dom Bouquet and the other Benedictines, all the original testimonies, as far as A.D. 1060, are disposed in chronological order and illustrated with learned notes."[103] For England he was less fortunate: "Such a national work [the *Recueil des historiens*], which will be continued to the year 1500, might provoke our emulation."[104] Gibbon was so convinced of the need and value of such a collection, that after the completion of the *Decline and Fall* he seriously considered editing the British historians of the Middle Ages. It was the last project he proposed and, alas, was never done.[105]

---

[101] Gibbon's memory was not the amazing repository possessed by Macaulay, but he seldom needed to verify a quotation. This may account for some of the occasional slips in Latin syntax noticed by his more scrupulous critics.

[102] *Memoirs*, p. 147.   [103] XXXVIII, 106, n. 1.   [104] XXXVIII, 106, n. 1.

[105] *Letters*, III, 34-43 (dated July 25, 1793), to the English antiquarian, John Pinkerton (1758-1826). Gibbon proposed an edition of the English historians to 1500 (*Scriptores rerum anglicarium*), which Pinkerton was to edit. Gibbon offered "to be always ready to assist at your secret committees, to offer my advice with regard to the choice and arrangement of your materials, and to join with you in forming a general outline of the plan." Illness and death prevented him from carrying out the project. Pinkerton's extract of the original plan, accompanied by his letter to Lord Sheffield, is printed in *MW*, III, 578-590.

Gibbon thought it rare for the philosopher and the antiquarian to be so happily blended. It is rarer still for the artist and the scholar to be united, as they are in Gibbon. Gibbon was not a great scholar in the sense of a Tillemont, a Montfaucon, a Mabillon, a Muratori. He made no original contributions to scholarship or to method. His supreme genius was as a narrative artist who imposed, for the first time since antiquity, a superb, constructive, and personal vision on the history of Rome. But if Gibbon cannot claim an important place in the history of scholarship, he most certainly has a place as the greatest synthesizer of his age. It is in Gibbon's pages that the state of classical scholarship before the French Revolution can be seen. It is in Gibbon's pages that the achievements of Christian humanism since the Renaissance can be surveyed. It is in Gibbon's pages that the triumph of French scholarship and the hegemony passing on to Germany can be discerned.

Gibbon is the *locus classicus* for any student of classical scholarship on the eve of the Germanic inundation. If Gibbon was not the greatest scholar of his age, he was certainly the most learned amateur of that, or any other, age. The scholarly foundations of the *Decline and Fall* were laid down early by Gibbon. Long before he became "the historian of the Roman empire" he was acquiring erudition about Rome. There is almost something ludicrous about this small boy, with an oversized head, studiously puzzling out recondite folios while still a child. This passion for scholarship continued for a lifetime, but always remained subordinate to the needs of "the historian of the Roman empire."

Gibbon the scholar is not easy to characterize. He had the instincts, the patience, and the talents necessary for scholarship, and he had a genuine admiration for scholarship. Yet he seemed happiest snapping at the heels of scholars and pedants alike. He was contemptuous of mere antiquarians, but showed little interest in the technical aspects of great scholarship. He lavished praise on the Bollandists and the Maurists without really appreciating their achievement. His history of medieval Europe, which is the least satisfactory part of the *Decline and Fall*, might have been much improved had he followed the Maurists and Bollandists more closely. The inadequacies of Gibbon's treatment of Byzantine and medieval civilization are not the fault of his guides. He often gave the impression—which has been reenforced by his commentators— that had he better materials for medieval history the *Decline and Fall* would not be weak in these areas. It was not, however, the quality or the quantity of medieval studies that hampered Gibbon. It was his lack of sympathy.

Even in the area of classical scholarship Gibbon was arrogant. He refused to learn German and maintained throughout life the contemptuous disdain toward Germany of a Roman senator. The few pieces of German scholarship which were translated into French—Winckelmann, Niebuhr, Schmidt—made no impact on Gibbon or his *History*. And his myopia prevented him from reading the most intelligent and substantial contemporary reviews of his *History*.[106] He wrote as if France were still the most important country in Europe. For all his pride in England he was insensitive to what was happening around him. Gibbon was, in many ways, a figure of the seventeenth century. His friend Adam Smith published the *Wealth of Nations* in the same year as the first volume of the *Decline and Fall*. But Gibbon was as myopic about the new capitalistic England as he was about Germany.

His mind had been formed by the late French Renaissance, or rather the great achievements of classical France. And he remained, despite profound historical changes, devoted to his tradition. His dismissal of the *philosophes*, or German scholarship, or the new values of a changing English society are all of a piece. The great classicist was indifferent to all things, whether in the past or the present, which were not classical. His values were those of the humanist tradition, especially the expression of that tradition in classical France. This is clearly reflected in his scholarship. His favorite authors as well as his favorite scholars—with the exception of Montesquieu—were of the seventeenth century. This was

---

[106] A favorable review in the *Göttingische gelehrte Anzeigen*, band 3, (December 25, 1788), notices Gibbon's debt to Heineccius, and points out his general ignorance of other German scholarship (p. 2052). The same point is made by Professor Hugo, the translator and editor of chapter XLIV, in his preface to *Gibbon's historische Uebersicht des Römischen Rechts* (1789). For a list of some of the contemporary reviews of the *Decline and Fall*, see J. E. Norton, *A Bibliography of the Works of Edward Gibbon* (London, 1940), pp. 72-75.

not because there was no scholarship worthy of the name in the eighteenth century, far from it, but rather because he preferred the mentality of a previous age.

Gibbon had the unique good fortune, and the unique genius, to express for his age its attitudes, feelings, and debts to classical antiquity. The *Decline and Fall* is not only a masterpiece of classical art, it is a celebration of European humanism. He rescued from neglect and scorn—the neglect and scorn of the new men, the bourgeois intellectuals—the scholarly traditions of Christian humanism. The real heroes of the *Decline and Fall* are not the great historical actors of Roman history, but the historians and scholars who have, through the ages, studied and created Rome. Tillemont, Muratori, Montfaucon, Mabillon, Erasmus, Godefroy, and dozens more, are enthusiastically commemorated in the *Decline and Fall*. These great scholars are practically the only contemporary figures to appear in Gibbon's *History*. They occupy a conspicuous place in the *Decline and Fall,* and rightly so, for Gibbon saw himself as a direct heir of this splendid tradition. In his own historical development he came to see the historian himself as more important than the history being recounted. He came to see Roman history not as an objective reality external to himself, but rather as a created thing. And those who had created Rome before Gibbon are his true heroes. The *Decline and Fall* is almost a history of the historians of Rome. Gibbon's Roman empire is a unique creation, but it rests on the previous creations of scholars. All the threads of humanistic scholarship meet in the *Decline and Fall*. And the "historian of the Roman empire" sums up this tradition and gives it superb artistic expression.

CHAPTER III

GIBBON AND THE ENLIGHTENMENT

"Attached to no party, interested only for the truth and candour of history, and directed by the most temperate and skilful guides, I enter with just diffidence on the subject. . . ."

O N MARCH 1, 1781, Gibbon published the second and third volumes of the *Decline and Fall*. He added a postscript to his original preface: "The entire History, which is now published, of the Decline and Fall of the Roman Empire in the West abundantly discharges my engagements with the Public. Perhaps their favourable opinion may encourage me to prosecute a work, which, however laborious it may seem, is the most agreeable occupation of my leisure hours." [1] The public reception of the work was not only favorable, but enthusiastic, and Gibbon, who needed little encouragement, continued this "most agreeable occupation" and carried the story down to 1453 and the fall of Constantinople. But in 1781 he had realized his first plan, and he attached to his final chapter [2]

---

[1] *DF*, I, vii (preface).
[2] This is chapter XXXVIII and deals with the loss of all the Western provinces to the barbarians: "Reign and Conversion of Clovis—His Victories over the Alemanni, Burgundians, and Visigoths—Establishment of the French Monarchy in Gaul—Laws of the Barbarians—State of the Romans—The Visigoths in Spain—Conquest of Britain by the Saxons."

an essay surveying his work and speculating on his subject. Here one might legitimately look for a statement of Gibbon's philosophy.

This essay, *General Observations on the Fall of the Roman Empire in the West*, has two distinct parts. The first is a sketch of the causes of Roman greatness and decay: "The rise of a city, which swelled into an empire, may deserve, as a singular prodigy, the reflection of a philosophic mind. But the decline of Rome was the natural and inevitable effect of immoderate greatness." [3] The second part is an attempt to apply "this awful revolution . . . to the instruction of the present age." The two parts are unequal in intellectual content: the first is brilliant and melancholy, clearly in the style of Montesquieu; the second is didactic and superficial, clearly in the style of Voltaire. Both parts reveal Gibbon's relationship to the intellectual currents of his day. In the *General Observations* it is made clear that the self-conscious "philosopher" is far less effective and far less comfortable with himself than is the "historian of the Roman empire." Gibbon was in fact no philosopher: "Gibbon was much more of an artist than perhaps he suspected, and less of a philosophic thinker on history than he would have been willing to allow." [4] His philosophy is to be found embedded in his narrative. His deliberate philosophic stances are almost always shallow and disappointing.

Gibbon was the most successful and most brilliant disciple of Montesquieu. In his native France the didactic school of Voltaire soon overwhelmed Montesquieu's work, but in England Gibbon rejected Voltaire and preserved for English historiography the more fruitful methods and concerns of Montesquieu. [5] The *General Observations* begin with a consideration of Polybius' sixth book which Gibbon uses as an introduction to the *esprit général* of Roman civilization. It is not the capriciousness of Fortune, that inconstant goddess, that explains Rome's greatness. This explanation, the result of the "envious flattery" of the Greeks who "had been reduced into a province," explains nothing. The genius of the

[3] XXXVIII, 161.
[4] J. Cotter Morison, *Gibbon* (London, 1880), p. 107.
[5] See H. R. Trevor-Roper, "The Historical Philosophy of the Enlightenment," *Studies on Voltaire and the Eighteenth Century*, XXVII (1963), 1667-87.

Romans lay in their customs, their laws, their institutions, and their ambitions. In a word, Rome's *esprit général*, first identified by Montesquieu, made her great: "The fidelity of the citizens to each other, and to the state, was confirmed by the habits of education and the prejudices of religion. Honour, as well as virtue, was the principle of the republic; the ambitious citizens laboured to deserve the solemn glories of a triumph; and the ardour of the Roman youth was kindled into active emulation, as often as they beheld the domestic images of their ancestors." [6] The ruin of the empire came, inevitably, with the corruption of the *esprit général*:

> The victorious legions, who, in distant wars, acquired the vices of strangers and mercenaries, first oppressed the freedom of the republic, and afterwords violated the majesty of the purple. The emperors, anxious for their personal safety and the public peace, were reduced to the base expedient of corrupting the discipline which rendered them alike formidable to their sovereign and to the enemy; the vigour of the military government was relaxed, and finally dissolved, by the partial institutions of Constantine; and the Roman world was overwhelmed by a deluge of Barbarians. [7]

This is pure Montesquieu, and Gibbon adds to the causes of the corruption of the *esprit général* the insidious penetration of Christianity. The clergy "successfully preached the doctrine of patience and pusillanimity." The active virtues of society were discouraged, "and the last remains of the military spirit were buried in the cloister." The state, as the church gained in power, was distracted by religious factions "whose conflicts were sometimes bloody, and always implacable." The emperors were "diverted from camps to synods" and the empire became the victim of "a new species of tyranny." Christianity destroyed the manly virtues of Rome: it also "broke the violence of the fall, and mollified the ferocious temper of the conquerors." [8] The barbarians who overwhelmed Rome were mostly Christians, and Constantine's victorious religion saved Rome from even more frightful devastations.

There is nothing very original here. Indeed all of these ideas are explicit in Montesquieu's *Considérations sur les causes de la gran-*

[6] XXXVIII, 160.   [7] XXXVIII, 161-162.   [8] XXXVIII, 162-163.

deur des Romains et de leur décadence. Some of the contemporary French critics of the *Decline and Fall* wrote it off as nothing more than a verbose exegesis of Montesquieu. Gibbon's originality lies not in his recapitulation of the familiar ideas of his age, nor does one find here his authentic philosophy. His originality and his philosophy are to be found in the arrangement of the *Decline and Fall,* and in his assumptions about history and the historian, civilization and society, character and motivation, and in his art. But before taking up these topics, the argument of the second half of the *General Observations* must be sketched.

When Gibbon lays aside the concerns of Montesquieu, with which he is in agreement, and assumes those of Voltaire, his argument becomes flabby and unconvincing. From the second half of the *General Observations* it appears that Gibbon thinks the lessons to be learned from Rome's fall are simply that it cannot happen again. Gibbon moves from history to "philosophy" in this section, and he dutifully repeats the arguments about progress and the ongoing civilization of Europe.

Europe no longer confronts hoards of barbarian nations, driven from Asia and destroying everything in their path. True, a few pockets of barbarians remain in Europe, but "the remnant of Calmucks or Uzbecks, whose forces may be almost numbered, cannot seriously excite the apprehensions of the great republic of Europe." Still, he cautions, "unknown dangers, may *possibly* arise from some obscure people, scarcely visible in the map of the world." Gibbon had in mind some semicivilized people who might be mobilized to conquest by a great leader who could breathe into "those savage bodies the soul of enthusiasm." In 1781 the only possible threat to European civilization was barbarian invasion.

Not only were there no sizable barbarian populations threatening Europe, but the very progress of civilization would make it impossible for a barbarian nation to overrun Europe. The technology in warfare of the Romans and the barbarians was not different in quality, only in quantity. By the time the barbarians entered the empire they had mastered most of the weapons of the Romans, and their superior vigor and numbers were sufficient to defeat the moribund empire. In eighteenth-century Europe no barbarian hoards

could stand against the military technology of the day. Should barbarians invade, they must first become civilized in order to conquer: "Cannon and fortifications now form an impregnable barrier
against the Tartar horse; and Europe is secure from any future
irruption of Barbarians; since, before they can conquer, they must
cease to be barbarous. Their gradual advances in the science of war
would always be accompanied, as we may learn from the example
of Russia, with a proportionable improvement in the arts of peace
and civil policy; and they themselves must deserve a place among
the polished nations whom they subdue."[9] Even if they manage to
invade Europe successfully "ten thousand vessels would transport
beyond their pursuit the remains of civilized society; and Europe
would revive and flourish in the American world, which is already
filled with her colonies and institutions."[10]

All of this reads like a *philosophe* pamphlet. But it should be
pointed out that Gibbon repeats these arguments with little enthusiasm. There was much that was French in Gibbon's intellectual
makeup, but he had none of the French *philosophe*'s sense of anger,
of frustration, perhaps even of alienation. Gibbon felt at one with
his society and his civilization; he certainly had no desire to change
it. The second half of his *General Observations* lacks the sincerity
and conviction of the first half. Gibbon's philosophy was not taken
from the *philosophes*. It came from another tradition. He was essentially a humanist and had no difficulty in finding in the Renaissance and in the seventeenth century—not to mention the ancient
world—men and ideas with which he was more comfortable than
with the *philosophes*. He thought Voltaire superficial. D'Holbach's
atheism offended him. The Abbé Raynal was shallow and aggressive. He had no interest in Rousseau and his ideas, and he thought
d'Alembert and the *Encyclopédie* doctrinaire and intellectually
hollow. Gibbon was, like all men, a child of his age, but his heart
and his mind were formed by another tradition.

If Gibbon did not mean by "philosophy" what the encyclo-
pedists meant, he certainly did not mean the construction of a
system of epistemology, politics, logic, and ethics. What Ernst

[9] XXXVIII, 167.   [10] XXXVIII, 166.

Cassirer calls the *esprit de système* had no appeal, and not one of the great system-makers of the seventeenth century is discussed in any of Gibbon's works. Descartes is considered only a mathematician, and Leibniz is mentioned only as the historian of the House of Brunswick. Hobbes is ignored, as is Spinoza. Pascal is discussed only as a literary artist, and the Cambridge Platonists made no impact on Gibbon. The philosophers of the seventeenth century are ignored, and so, too, are their predecessors. Aristotle is treated respectfully as a literary critic and theorist, but his metaphysical works are not noticed. Plato is mentioned as a companion of Gibbon's leisure hours after the completion of the *Decline and Fall*, but Gibbon is clearly uninterested in his ideas: "After a full repast on Homer and Aristophanes, I involved myself in the philosophic maze of the writings of Plato, of which the dramatic is perhaps more interesting than the argumentative part." [11] The medieval philosophers, as one might expect, are all scorned:

> The numerous vermin of mendicant friars, Franciscans, Dominicans, Augustins, Carmelites, who swarmed in this century [the 13th century], with habits and institutions variously ridiculous, disgraced religion, learning, and common sense. They seized on scholastic philosophy as a science peculiarly suited to their minds; and excepting only Friar Bacon, they all preferred words to things. The subtle, the profound, the irrefragable, the angelic, and the seraphic Doctor acquired those pompous titles by filling ponderous volumes with a small number of technical terms, and a much smaller number of ideas. [12]

Of modern philosophers Bayle is favorably mentioned. He was, indeed, Gibbon's favorite philosopher, yet he is the great critic of philosophic systems and of metaphysics. Locke is also praised, as the exploder of innate ideas. But Hume is respected primarily as a historian, not a metaphysician. Here and there in Gibbon's work are scattered the names of logicians, but not a single metaphysician finds a conspicuous place in Gibbon's work or his mind.

Gibbon had no interest in the traditional concerns of philoso-

[11] *Memoirs*, p. 183. [12] *MW*, III, 29.

phers, and he had a profound distrust for metaphysics. He accepted the sensational philosophy of Locke, and the sceptical tradition running from Bayle to Hume. But Gibbon, like many of his English contemporaries, was more interested in a philosophy which celebrated common sense and concentrated on things rather than words. Despite his French education Gibbon was decidedly English. The Continental tradition, with its rationalism and idealism, was ignored. Gibbon's library, a faithful reflection of his interests and his mind, contained almost no philosophical works except those of antiquity. He owned no Descartes, no Spinoza, no Kant, and it is doubtful that he read these men. Of Hume's philosophical works, Gibbon owned only the *Dialogues Concerning Natural Religion*, which was published long after Gibbon had formed his philosophical notions. Of Berkeley's works Gibbon owned only *Alciphron*. Metaphysics and systematic philosophy held no interest for "the historian of the Roman empire."

What then was "philosophy" for Gibbon? It is clear that he understood something different from the modern definition. It is equally clear that "philosophy" had at least as much emotional content for Gibbon as intellectual. That is, the word and the concept described a state of mind, a way of life, and a set of individual and social values. Gibbon used "philosophy" in much the same way "science" is used today. He was not troubled by the imprecision of the concept. "Philosophy" was a general word adequately describing all those things Gibbon most admired, and since neither he nor his contemporaries found any difficulty in understanding what the word or the concept meant, there was no need to be more precise.

Some of the applications of the word in the *Decline and Fall* make clear this easy application of "philosophy." In one place he says that the philosopher should deplore "the loss of the Byzantine libraries" more than the sack of Santa Sophia during the iconoclastic riots.[13] In another place he laments that the theological literature of the Arian and Monophysite controversies had not suffered a similar fate. Had these tedious and intemperate works been lost,

[13] LXVIII, 206-207.

"a philosopher may allow, with a smile, that it was ultimately devoted to the benefit of mankind." [14] But Gibbon was aware that this witty advocacy of book-burning was not worthy of a philosopher. He argues in another place that "it is unworthy of a philosopher to wish that any opinions and arguments the most repugnant to his own should be concealed from the knowledge of mankind," [15] and he excoriated those who had suppressed or destroyed evidence. This particular use of the concept of "philosophy" is identical to that of the *philosophes*. Philosophy is used to distinguish the cultural and intellectual achievements of man from mere politics. The word is used as Voltaire used it, to celebrate enlightenment and the progress of the human mind.

There are profound differences between the *philosophes* and Gibbon, yet there remains in his mature views much *philosophe* rhetoric. His anticlericalism, for example, is more French than English. Gibbon had, personally, no experience of clerical oppression. The English clergy was enlightened and could hardly be characterized as *l'infâme*. Gibbon's anticlericalism is historical, and to excoriate the hierarchy he borrowed the very effective rhetoric of the *philosophes:* "to a philosophic eye, the vices of the clergy are far less dangerous than their virtues." [16] Similarly, Gibbon sometimes used the *philosophe* argument that progress in the sciences is the best weapon of civilization against "the prejudices of popular superstition."

Gibbon's philosophy was not that of the French intellectuals. A better analogy would be with Renaissance humanism. Philosophy is Gibbon's general term for all of the values of his humanistic faith, and he is perhaps closest to Milton's concept of rational freedom. "Freedom of the mind" is for Gibbon "the source of every generous rational sentiment." And "freedom of the mind" is the greatest gift of philosophy. Philosophy insulates a man from "the herd of bigots," from "the grovelling or visionary schemes of superstition," and "the pride of the human heart." "The dark and implacable genius of superstition" is an ever present threat to civilization. Only the philosopher can see the threat and preserve for future gener-

[14] LI, 483-484.   [15] XXXVIII, 473, n. 39.   [16] LXIX, 318-319.

ations the precious and fragile heritage of civilization. The advances
of reason, science, and the arts of peace had been "slow and la-
borous" and Gibbon thought "a philosopher, according to his temper, will laugh or weep at the folly of mankind." [17] Gibbon was an
intellectual snob, and he understood philosophers to be those men
like himself who had a high degree of literary culture. Philosophy
was a way of life, but a way of life reserved only for an elite. In
a bourgeois age filled with democratic rumblings, Gibbon was an
aristocratic reactionary. He harked back to the past for his values,
and he enshrined in the *Decline and Fall* the humanism and clas-
sicism which he so loved, and which were to be attacked within his
lifetime. His profound hatred of the French Revolution was the
hatred of a man who had the misfortune to live through the death
throes of his civilization.

Gibbon's philosophy is the humanism of a previous age adapted
to the scientific and bourgeois Enlightenment. The synthesis was
never complete, and perhaps only Gibbon's superb art held together
the disparate elements. At one and the same time he believed in an
intellectual elite, material progress, government by the minority,
the importance of the classics, a human nature that was flawed by
self-love, creature comforts, Catholic oppression, civic spirit and
martial vigor, civilization through conquest, rigid social distinctions,
the refinement of taste, the importance of money, the irrationality
of the majority of men, and the traditions of aristocratic Europe.
All of these ideas or emotional responses he expressed under the
heading of "philosophy." In art as in politics Gibbon was a conservative, even a reactionary. He was, in Bagehot's colorful phrase,
"the kind of man crowds hang."

Like so many humanists Gibbon responded with more excitment
to the creations of man than to the creations of nature. All of his
landscapes are peopled, and there is hardly a passage in the *Decline
and Fall* where the beauties of nature are celebrated. His imagination was fired by the splendor and mystery of Oriental or Near
Eastern history, but he was indifferent to the "sublime" landscapes
of Europe which were just beginning to excite a younger genera-

[17] LXV, 86.

tion. When living in the country, at Beriton, Gibbon spent most of his time in the library. When he did venture outside his "philosophic walks were soon terminated by a shady bench where I was long detained by the sedentary amusement of reading or meditation." [18] When he crossed the Alps into Italy Gibbon described not the natural, even stunning, beauty of the place: instead he described the skill and endurance of the men who carried his litter over the mountains. When he retired to Lausanne and lived with Georges Deyverdun, Gibbon was still indifferent to natural beauty. The remarkable prospect of his house meant little to him except a pleasant place in which to work.

The works of man, however, awoke in Gibbon genuine enthusiasm. He was especially keen about architecture, and was often inspired to moral ecstacy by the contemplation of architectural ruins. Such is the famous description of the moment of inspiration for the *Decline and Fall*, not to mention the conclusion of his *History* and the numerous passages on the ruins of the Roman empire. But even more important than architecture for Gibbon were books. More than any other object, a book was the work of man, and Gibbon's respect and reverence were unbounded: "what is a council, or an university, to the presses of Froben and the studies of Erasmus?" [19] His *Memoirs* are primarily a record of books read. The *Decline and Fall* is a bibliographical survey of European civilization from the second to the fifteenth century. All the great writers are commemorated, all the famous books are noticed, and on each occasion Gibbon carefully tells his readers what his own reactions are to these creations of man. The intimate relationship felt by the Romantics between man and nature is felt by the humanist Gibbon between man and man's creations. It is the works of men that will endure, and Gibbon's contention that "the Romance of Tom Jones, that exquisite picture of human manners will outlive the palace of the Escurial and the Imperial Eagle of the house of Austria" is an eloquent and unequivocal confession of faith.

Gibbon's humanism, his profound respect for literature and

[18] *Memoirs*, p. 95.   [19] LXVI, 105, n. 41.

especially the classics, and his equally profound faith in man's ability to make sense of his experiences and to order, through thought, his life, forms the basis of his philosophy of history. He valued intelligence and insisted that the urge toward order, rationality, and creativity was a part of human nature. Despite his Pascalian despair about the power of the passions and the potential wickedness of *amour-propre*, Gibbon believed that the gifted few might rise above their own human sordidness and the circumstances of their times. He believed not in the progress of the race or the human mind, but rather in the rational and creative powers of a few individuals in every age. Amidst the barren stretches of Roman history, or the history of the Middle Ages, he found, and celebrated, these remarkable men. Alexander Severus, St. Athanasius, St. Bernard, Erasmus: these are the heroes of his *History*, for these men managed to escape the gloom and evil of their times. They managed to make sense of their own lives and to pursue, with pathological tenacity, their own values. They managed to think clearly and somehow to leave a record of their struggles against their times. Gibbon's heroes are not the men who yield to the historical pressures of their age, or whose decisions complement the movement of events. His heroes are always men spiritually outside their age. It is the enemies of Alexander Severus, of Athanasius, of Bernard, of Erasmus, who represent for Gibbon their respective ages. But these great men are different. The force of their characters, their talent, sets them apart.

This is not to argue that Gibbon saw the lives of great men as the essence of history, or even as *exempla* to be imitated. He never advocated that a man model his life on some historical predecessor. Gibbon had no use for those historians or theorists, like Bolingbroke, who treated the past as a collection of *exempla*, or wrote history as character sketches. Gibbon's view is more subtle. The movement of history, the passage of time, is an overwhelming process. Most men are fatalistically trapped by history and live lives determined by events which they cannot even understand, let alone control. This is the meaning of his remark that history is but a catalog of the crimes and follies of mankind. This aspect of Gibbon's historical thought is melancholy, and he is saved from utter despair only by his taste for irony. There is nothing to be learned from a study of history precisely because the only lesson is despair. Yet Gibbon avoids the fatalistic implications of his theory by focusing on individuals. Ultimately, he believes, men—however few—can impose an order on their lives, and can escape history. The Roman empire was destroyed by overmighty greatness, by time, by the fury of the barbarians and the zeal of the Christians, but Roman civilization—her books, her art, her ideals—have survived. And they have survived because individual men preserved them. The philosopher, for Gibbon, is a man able to see the inevitable movement of time, the inevitable force of historical circumstances, and yet impose on these things the imprint of his rationalism and creativity. Gibbon took delight in the morbid and sardonic periods of Tacitus. The very fact that there existed a man named Tacitus, who recorded the wickedness of his times, is for Gibbon sufficient reason for optimism.

Gibbon's humanistic faith is perhaps best seen if his development as a historian from the *Essai* to the *Decline and Fall* is surveyed. It is a long way from the rather enthusiastic pronouncements of the youthful *Essai* to the somber concluding chapters of the *Decline and Fall*, but there is in this development a logical consistency. The historian that Gibbon imagined, or rather created, in the *Essai* is not realized until the middle of the *Decline and Fall*. Gibbon was, in 1759, incapable of becoming the historian he created. It would take more than twenty years for the author of the *Essai* to become "the historian of the Roman empire."

The *Essai* has, like everything Gibbon wrote, been forced to live under the shadow of the *Decline and Fall*: nothing but another stupendous masterpiece could survive without sunshine. The *Essai* is not a masterpiece, but it is much more than a puerile work. With all its faults, and they are many, the *Essai* can stand as one of the more interesting essays on literature of the eighteenth century. It is interesting not merely because it was the first book of a great man, but also because the *Essai* presents—in a disorganized form— Gibbon's highly original speculations on the nature of history and the role of the historian.

The *Essai* is the product of Gibbon's exile in Lausanne. It is a summing-up of his foreign education and the only theoretical work he wrote. It marked for Gibbon, as it does for his readers, an event of some importance.[20] The *Essai* had little success, and it has remained, unfortunately, neglected. Several Continental journals gave the work a serious review, yet these favorable notices were read by few.[21] The complimentary copies, carefully distributed among those who might help the young author and aspiring diplomat, brought little reward. Gibbon did not become an immediate sensation. His literary reputation would come only with his great *History*.

His own appraisal of the *Essai*, written twenty-eight years later, is both just and accurate. Gibbon thought the *Essai* a spirited defense of *les érudits*—as classical scholars were then contemptuously called—and an impressive first book by a man still in his early twenties. His stock of erudition might be meager compared to the enormous learning of the mature historian, but at least the "Essay does credit to a young writer of two and twenty years of age, who had read with taste, who thinks with freedom, and who writes in a foreign language with spirit and elegance." [22] He thought his thesis of "the patriotic and political design of the Georgics" to be happily conceived, and he was "not displeased with the enquiry into the origin and nature of the Gods of Polytheism." The defects of the work are those of youth and inexperience: loose organization and imprecise definitions; an aggressive urge to impress his readers with his erudition; and a style still derivative—"alas how fatal has been the imitation of Montesquieu!" [23] Despite these reservations—which are reiterated by the contemporary reviews—Gibbon was happy to observe that he found in the *Essai* "some dawnings of a philosophic spirit" which enlightened "the general remarks on the study of history and of man." [24]

The "general remarks on the study of history and of man" are

[20] See *Memoirs*, pp. 99-103, for Gibbon's account of how he came to publish the *Essai*.

[21] For an account of the reception of Gibbon's first work see Georges A. Bonnard, "Gibbon's *Essai sur l'étude de la littérature* as Judged by Contemporary Reviewers and by Gibbon Himself," *English Studies* (Amsterdam), XXXII (1951), 145-153.

[22] *Memoirs*, p. 104.   [23] *Memoirs*, p. 103.   [24] *Memoirs*, p. 104.

certainly the most interesting feature of the *Essai*. The years of exile had been intellectually stimulating for Gibbon. His love of reading and thinking, blighted at Oxford, revived at Lausanne. There he embarked on a program of systematic reading. There he confronted the Enlightenment on its own grounds, and there he formulated, in a somewhat unsophisticated way, his ideas "on the study of history and of man."

The theme of the *Essai*, announced in the title, is how to study literature. But it soon becomes obvious that Gibbon understands literature in its broadest sense: "The title itself, the sense of the word *Litterature* is loosely and variously applied." Gibbon is concerned, almost exclusively, with the Latin classics of the late republic and the early empire. He is not interested in literature per se, but rather in the classics as historical documents revealing the thought, the life, and the society of Roman civilization: "Que ce contraste est parlant pour un homme instruit dans l'antiquité! Qu'il est fade aux yeux de celui qui n'apporte à la lecture de Virgile, d'autre préparation qu'un goût naturel, et quelque connoissance de la langue Latine!" [25] The study of ancient literature, for Gibbon, is essentially a study of ancient history through literature. The *Essai* also has a polemic purpose. Gibbon believed that "all the faculties of the mind may be exercised and displayed by [the] study of ancient literature." [26] He was shocked by d'Alembert's argument, in the *Discours preliminaire* to the *Encyclopédie*, that the study of ancient literature exercised only the memory, the least important part of man's mind.

When Gibbon wrote the *Essai* in 1759 this scorn of the *philosophes* for scholarship was a commonplace. Historical studies, in France at any rate, were not in high favor. *Philosophe* arrogance on the one hand, and the attack of the Pyrrhonists on the other, had temporarily dethroned history. Only the academies and the learned societies remained productive, and they were clearly not in the mainstream of Enlightenment thought. The Pyrrhonists, represented by Bayle and Beaufort, questioned the historian's

---

[25] *Essai*, XVII, 31. I have given these quotations in the original French to provide the reader with some samples of Gibbon's remarkable command of the language.
[26] *Memoirs*, p. 99.

ability to know the past. They pointed out the disparity between the testimony of literary and nonliterary evidence. They hammered away at the unreliability of even eyewitness accounts. They insisted that special pleading and deliberate falsification tainted what literary evidence had survived. Historical truth was probably impossible, and certainly unlikely.

At the time of the *Essai* no one had successfully answered the Pyrrhonists. Their major opponents were the historians who saw a providential scheme in history. Despite the acknowledged genius of Bossuet, the providential view had been almost completely exploded by mid-century. In England the picture was more hopeful. David Hume's first volumes appeared in 1754, and William Robertson's *History of Scotland* in 1759. But Gibbon had read neither of these when he wrote the *Essai*. He was, however, familiar with Bolingbroke's *Letters on the Study and Use of History* (1752). This famous little book was England's major contribution to the philosophy of history at the time. Bolingbroke's famous maxim, that history is philosophy teaching by example, represents a view of history distinct from those of the Continent. Bolingbroke had little interest in the past for its own sake. Rather he saw history as containing numerous *exempla* which might instruct the contemporary statesman. He also saw in the past a discernible movement toward the present, and viewed his own age as the progressive and inevitable outcome of the past. His interests were confined exclusively to politics, and he considered the historian to be little more than a specialist who extracted the useful *exempla* from the past, for the benefit of politicians. Gibbon had never found Bolingbroke stimulating. He characterized the *Patriot King* as a work filled with vitality and highmindedness, but concluded that the author "est petit philosophe." [27] His judgment on Bolingbroke's notions about history is similar.

Finally, there were the *philosophes*. Voltaire published his *Siècle de Louis XIV* in 1751, and with it established a new model of the new history. For Voltaire, as for the *philosophes* generally, the study of history should be confined to those epochs when the hu-

[27] *Jour. B.*, p. 224 (February 25, 1764).

man spirit made palpable progress. Along with this myopia went the assumption that the past was not so much interesting in and for itself, as it was interesting as a series of laboratory experiments in the movement of the human spirit toward enlightenment. History was also, for the *philosophes*, a didactic exercise: the sticks of the past were used to beat the present.

Gibbon rejected all these views. With Montesquieu as his inspiration and his mentor, he offered another alternative. The *Essai* argues for a new synthesis of enlightenment and erudition, such as is found in Montesquieu. Most important, the *Essai* argues against all systems, all schemes, and all constricting patterns. The Pyrrhonists are, in their way, as rigid and schematic as the providentialists. The former prove too little, the latter too much, about man and his history. The *philosophes* disregard scholarship, while those who search the past only to discover useful *exempla* are too narrow.

The *Essai* is full of the rhetoric and the sentiments of the *philosophes*: "L'histoire des empires est celle de la misère des hommes. L'histoire des sciences est celle de leur grandeur et de leur bonheur. Si mille considérations doivent rendre ce dernier genre d'étude précieux aux yeux du philosophe, cette réflexion doit le rendre bien cher à tout amateur de l'humanité." [28] But amidst these conventional pieties can be discerned the workings of an original mind. Gibbon had no formal education to speak of. His illnesses as a child and his disgrace at Oxford forced him to educate himself. He never achieved the "well-flogged ear" of the professional scholar, and he often stumbled painfully over difficult ground, guided only by his own stamina and determination. But these were very minor shortcomings compared to the genuine benefits of his private education. Gibbon's reading was omnivorous, and he was bold and original. The core of his learning was the Latin classics, and few have read the classics with such passion. He wrote in his *Memoirs* that the *Essai* grew out of "the desire of justifying and praising the object of a favourite pursuit." He was understating the case. Study was his life, and he had, during the Lausanne years, thought deeply

[28] *Essai*, I, 15.

about the problems of history. The *Essai* is the fruit of this thought.

For Gibbon history is a study of cause and effect: "L'histoire est pour un esprit philosophique, ce qu'étoit le jeu pour le Marquis de Dangeau. Il voyoit un système, des rapports, une suite, là, où les autres ne discernoient que les caprices de la fortune. Cette science est pour lui celle des causes et des effets." [29] The Marquis de Dangeau discovered the science of cause and effect not by bringing to the gaming table preconceived systems, but by extracting from his experience those facts which gave him a coherent view of gambling. The science of cause and effect is a general science. The Marquis could not say what this or that roll of the dice would bring, but he knew what he could expect. Gibbon argues for an exact parallel with history: it is a science of cause and effect and the philosophic historian is able to discover these laws by studying the record of the past.

This emphasis on cause and effect—which becomes decreasingly important as the *Decline and Fall* progresses—is doubtless one of the many lessons Gibbon learned from Montesquieu. Whatever the source, Gibbon believes that there are some general rules of procedure for the historian. The first is not to attribute the wrong cause to the wrong effect:

> A ceux qui ont plus de jugement que d'érudition, il paroîtra peu nécessaire d'avertir qu'on doit toujours proportionner les causes aux effets, ne pas bâtir sur l'action d'un homme le caractère d'un siècle, ne pas chercher dans un effort unique, forcé et ruineux, la mesure des forces et des richesses d'un état, et se souvenir que ce n'est qu'en rassemblant qu'on peut juger, qu'un fait éclatant éblouit comme un éclair, mais qu'il instruit peu, si l'on ne le compare avec d'autres de la même espèce. [30]

The Pyrrhonists—and indeed all those who come to history with preconceived schemes—have no difficulty in finding supporting evidence: "L'incertitude est pour nous un état forcé. L'esprit borné ne sauroit se fixer dans cet équilibre dont se piquoit l'école de Pyrrhon. Le genié brillant se laisse éblouir par ses propres conjectures:

---

[29] *Essai*, XLVIII, 63.   [30] *Essai*, XLIX, 63-64.

il sacrifie la liberté aux hypothèses. De cette disposition naissent les systèmes." [31] These historians are, in fact, picking up the stick by the wrong end: "Déférez plutôt aux faits qui viennent d'eux-mêmes vous former un systême, qu'à ceux que vous découvrez après avoir conçu ce systême." [32] The Pyrrhonists "ont banni l'art du monde moral, pour y substituer le hasard." They are, consequently, too simplistic: "La fureur d'un écervelé établit un empire: la foiblesse d'une femme le détruit." [33] The love of his own systems, Gibbon concludes, is the "dernière passion du sage." In place of systems Gibbon wants philosophic criticism.

"Si les philosophes ne sont pas toujours historiens," Gibbon argues, "il seroit du moins à souhaiter que les historiens fussent philosophes." [34] The first step for a philosophic historian is to have a science of facts, a method of study, and a direction. The philosophic historian must be "Prompt et fécond en ressources, mais sans fausse subtilité, il ose sacrifier l'hypothèse la plus brillante, la plus spécieuse, et ne fait point parler à ses maîtres le langage de ses conjectures." [35] And to sift all the facts, sorting out the important from the unimportant, demands not only a love of detail and precision— something scorned by the *philosophes*—but also reliable collections of the sources of history—something not thought very important by the *philosophes*. "Je m'oppose, sans crainte du nom flétrissant d'érudit, à la sentence par laquelle ce juge éclairé, mais sévère, ordonne qu'à la fin d'un siècle on rassemble tous les faits, qu'on en choisisse quelques-uns et quo'on livre le reste aux flammes." [36] From these facts "Un Montesquieu démêlera dans les plus chétifs, des rapports inconnus au vulgaire." [37]

Montesquieu occurs time and again in the *Essai* as the model of a philosophic historian. Indeed he remained, throughout Gibbon's life, a favorite author. For Gibbon only Montesquieu, among his contemporaries, had understood the complexities of history. Only Montesquieu had known how to transform the enormous bulk of historical evidence into a science of cause and effect: "Parmi la multitude des faits, il y en a, et c'est le grand nombre, que ne

[31] *Essai*, LIV, 68. [32] *Essai*, L, 64. [33] *Essai*, LIV, 68-69.
[34] *Essai*, LII, 66. [35] *Essai*, XXV, 39. [36] *Essai*, LIII, 67-68.
[37] *Essai*, LIII, 68.

prouvent rien au delà de leur propre existence. Il y en a encore qui peuvent bien être cités dans une conclusion partielle, d'où le philosophe peut juger des motifs d'une action, et d'un trait dans un caractère: ils éclaircissent un chainon." [38]

It is the philosophic spirit, working on the record of the past, that creates history. But Gibbon's understanding of the philosophic spirit is quite different from that of most of his contemporaries. This spirit is, for Gibbon, a quality of mind and temperament which allows the historian to escape from his own time and place, and to live in the past. By this Gibbon does not understand anything like Michelet's "spirit of France," not to mention Michelet's belief that he could identify himself with inanimate objects, like Gothic cathedrals. Gibbon's philosophic spirit is more refined.

There is no program of study that can teach this "esprit philosophique"; it is a "don du ciel." [39] But this talent can be cultivated and developed. The best practice for refining such a talent is the study of ancient literature. Thus does a man learn "cette habitude de devenir, tour à tour, Grec, Romain, disciple de Zénon ou d'Epicure." [40] The philosophic historian must "become"—and the choice of word is deliberate—a Greek or a Roman, a disciple of Zeno or of Epicurus. In so doing the historian sees with the eyes of the ancients. The historian also becomes a part of history. Gibbon's ideal historian, even in the early *Essai*, is no dispassionate observer. He is the controlling, creating intelligence, sifting the past through his own mind and presenting it as his own. The historian creates history, and he creates it by being now a Greek, now a Roman. It is this very process that allows the philosophic historian to see more than other men. It is this very process that gives him wisdom and tolerance:

Quel spectacle pour un esprit vraiment philosophique de voir les opinions les plus absurdes reçues chez les nations les plus éclairées, des barbares parvenus à la connoissance des plus sublimes vérités, des conséquences vraies, mais peu justes, tirées des principes les plus erronés, des principes admirables qui approchoient toujours de la vérité sans jamais y conduire, le langage formé sur les idées, et

[38] *Essai*, XLIX, 63.   [39] *Essai*, XLVII, 59.   [40] *Essai*, XLVII, 59.

les idées justifiées par le langage, les sources de la morale partout les mêmes, les opinions de la contentieuse métaphysique partout variées, d'ordinaire extravagantes, nettes seulement pendant qu'elles furent superficielles, subtiles, obscures, incertaines, toutes les fois qu'elles prétendirent à la profondeur! [41]

These ideas are not fully developed in the *Essai*. They reach perfection only in the later volumes of the *Decline and Fall*. But already by 1759 Gibbon had thought out a view of history and the historian distinctly different from those of his contemporaries. The first component in the making of "the historian of the Roman empire" was already present. What Gibbon needed now was a subject and the opportunity to put into practice his speculations.

Gibbon did not, in the *Essai*, tackle the problem of the importance of a theme or a thesis in writing history. His primary concern was the relationship between the historian and his data. In the *Essai* he implies that a science of facts, a pursuit of cause and effect relationships, and a philosophic spirit, that is, a rational imagination giving the historian both empathy and detachment, is all that is necessary for the writing of philosophic history. Nowhere in the *Essai* is there a discussion of narrative technique, nowhere in the *Essai* is there a discussion of what gives meaning and order to facts, nowhere in the *Essai* is there a discussion of the role of character in history, or the balance between men and the impersonal forces identified by Montesquieu. Before he achieved his final synthesis, in the last volumes of the *Decline and Fall*, Gibbon would wrestle with these problems. His concept of a philosophic history was but half-formed in the *Essai*, and before becoming "the historian of the Roman empire" Gibbon will become other historians. That is, he will experiment. He will try, and reject, several varieties of historical writing before hitting upon his mature approach.

The arguments in the *Essai* are bold and precocious, but the intellectual self-confidence displayed there did not lead immediately to fruitful practice. The emotional and psychological difficulties standing between Gibbon and the writing of the *Decline and Fall* have already been discussed. How Gibbon modified the theories

[41] *Essai*, XLVII, 60.

of the *Essai* as he developed as a historian will be examined. The *Essai* announced, and celebrated, the dawnings of a philosophic spirit, but not the emergence of a philosophic historian.

Pierre Bayle had argued that a true history would be equally unacceptable to all parties. Characteristically, Bayle devoted his energies to sceptical criticism: he never wrote a work of history. Gibbon, too, was dissatisfied with the histories he had read, but he did not experience Bayle's dilemma because he did not insist that history be as objectively true as, say, mathematics (although Bayle's scepticism extended even here). Gibbon always considered historical truth to be tentative and subjective. The philosophic historian was not the historian who presented objective truths. Only the facts of history met such a criterion of truth, and facts were not history, nor were the collectors of facts—the antiquarians—historians. To give order, meaning, and significance to facts was the historian's task, and these are intensely personal operations. Gibbon did not, like Bayle, despair for historical writing. He admired several historians, and hoped to emulate them if not equal their achievement. Among his contemporaries he admired Hume and Robertson. He similarly admired Montesquieu, Giannone, Sarpi, Tillemont, de Thou, and Muratori. But most of all he admired Tacitus. Yet never did he argue that any of these great historians had written objective, true history. Their conclusions, their interpretations, even their facts, were merely tentative and perhaps to be replaced or superseded. Even about the *Decline and Fall* Gibbon had no illusions. He knew that he had written a great book, and he knew he had taken his place among the great historians. But he would not have been disturbed by the fact that more is known now about the Roman empire. Indeed, this was for him the very nature of history.

Gibbon could no more accept the sceptical attack on history than he could accept providential schemes. His notions of historical truth, not clearly formulated in the *Essai* or until the 1780's, were not schematic or deductive. He insisted, more than any of his contemporaries, on the role of the historian in creating history. He early rejected the historical orthodoxies of his age, and after the *Essai* set out to find a topic for his first historical work. These years of looking for a subject are instructive, for Gibbon is seen trying to find a mold into which he might cast the theories of the *Essai*. The problems of theme, of narrative voice, of order, all of which were neglected in the *Essai*, are tackled in the historical projects between the *Essai* and the *Decline and Fall*.

Historical writing, like all crafts, is best learned, indeed only learned, through practice. The program of the *Essai*, derived from books and not practice, was quickly modified when Gibbon tried writing history.

The young historian in quest of a topic considered first the possibility of writing a biography. The first project mentioned in his journal for these years (1761-63) is a history of Charles VIII's invasion of Italy: "Having thought of several subjects for an Historical composition, I chose the expedition of Charles VIII of France into Italy. I read two memoires of M. de Foncemagne. . . . I likewise finished to-day a Dissertation in which I examined the right Charles had to the Crown of Naples and the pretensions of the houses of Anjou and Arragon." [42] This dissertation [43] is the only thing Gibbon wrote about Charles, or about any other project, until August 4, 1761, when Charles VIII is dismissed "as too remote from us, & rather an introduction to great events than great in itself." [44] Several projects quickly followed Charles VIII, and were as quickly abandoned: "I successively chose and layed aside, the Croisade of Richard I, the Barons wars against John, & Henry III, the history of the Black prince, the Lives and comparaisons of Titus and Henry V, The Life of Sir Philip Sidney, and that of the Marquis of Montrose." [45] His reasons for dropping these topics are

[42] *Jour. A.*, p. 24 (April 14, 1761).

[43] The dissertation is published as "Critical Researches Concerning the Title of Charles the Eighth to the Crown of Naples," in *MW*, III, 206-222.

[44] *Jour. A.*, p. 30 (August 4, 1761). I quote from Gibbon's original journal entry. The same passages, freely altered, appear in *Memoirs*, pp. 119-123. In writing this part of his life Gibbon transcribed "some passages, under their respectible dates from a Journal which I kept at that time." In fact, Gibbon transformed rather than transcribed, and this is yet another indication of the nature of the *Memoirs* and the motives of the author.

[45] *Jour. A.*, p. 30. During these years Gibbon often confused French and English syntax and spelling. His letters for these years show the same confusion, and his autobiographical statement that he was more at home in French than in English is not hyperbole.

not given, but Gibbon "at last fixed upon Sir Walter Raleigh" for his hero. His use of the word "hero" is deliberate. At this stage of his development Gibbon was looking not so much for a biographical subject as for a hero. A hero who might hold the reader's attention and whose dominating personality would give unity and coherence to the past. For the moment he thought Raleigh was just such a hero. He found in Raleigh's life "a subject important, interesting and various, with such a quantity of materials as I desired, and which had not yet been properly made use of." [46]

From these journal entries some idea is obtained of Gibbon's conception of history and the historian as he moved slowly toward the practice of his craft. All of these subjects are biographical, and with good reason. Biography would furnish the historian with an organizing principle: he had merely to narrate events through the eyes of his hero and order and direction would automatically follow. Biography also offered Gibbon a chance to be now a Stoic, now an Epicurean. His belief that the philosophic historian must enter into his subject, even become his subject, seemed perfectly adapted to biography. All of the "heroes" Gibbon entertained as possible subjects for a biography were men he admired, men he hoped to emulate. His interest in biography—and he had a genius for characterization—finds a distinctive place in the *Decline and Fall.* But at this stage of his development none of the biographical projects was attempted.

These few journal entries reveal Gibbon searching early modern history for a subject: the remainder of the journal records a persistent, detailed, and systematic concentration on ancient history. These occasional worries about Raleigh, and others, do not even interrupt the smooth flow of Gibbon's classical studies. Only in January, 1762, does Gibbon return to Raleigh. He mentions some reading of the sources for Raleigh's life, and also a biographical study, and declares: "My subject opens upon me, and in general gains by being considered more nearly." [47] But the next entry in the journal concerns Hurd's study of Horace. Raleigh does not reappear until July 26, 1762. The intervening months are filled, almost exclusively, with a study of Homer and the *Iliad.*

[46] *Jour. A.,* p. 30.   [47] *Jour. A.,* p. 45 (January, 1762).

When Gibbon does return to consider Raleigh he decides to abandon him. There exists already a dull but thorough life of Raleigh, and "I could hardly add anything to them except some few particularities . . . so that my utmost ambition (exclusive of the uncertain merit of style and Reflections) must be giving a good abridgement of Oldys." [48] The other reasons Gibbon gives for abandoning the project are perhaps more to the point. Tudor and Stuart history, then as now, was a well-plowed field. Should Gibbon decide to write a life of Raleigh he would find himself in competition with "the laborious diligence of *Birch*, the minute curiosity and acuteness of *Walpole*, the ingenious criticism of *Hurd*, the strong sense and bold imagination of *Mallet* and *Robertson*, and the original philosophic genius of *Hume*." [49] Gibbon was not yet ready to try himself against such men, especially "the original philosophic genius of *Hume*" whose "calm philosophy" and "careless inimitable beauties" often forced Gibbon "to close the volume, with a mixed sensation of delight and despair." [50] If these were not sufficient drawbacks, there was the added difficulty that the historian of Tudor and Stuart England "is supposed to hang out a badge of party, and is devoted to destruction by the opposite faction." A history of Raleigh and his age might be an ideal topic for a historian persuaded of Bolingbroke's view that the historian was to look in the past for political *exempla* which might be useful in the present. Gibbon was not such a historian.

Gibbon abandoned biography and looked for a great theme running through several centuries. The first of these projects was *The History of the Liberty of the Swiss*. The subject had everything: "From such a subject, so full of real virtue, public spirit, military glory, and great lessons of government, the meanest writer must catch fire." [51] And if the meanest writer must catch fire Gibbon—who certainly did not consider himself the meanest writer— had an additional advantage. He himself would be a part of this history: "What might not I hope for, who to some talents perhaps add an affection for the nation which would make me labour the composition *con amore*." [52] Here is Gibbon's first formulation of

---

[48] *Jour. A.*, p. 102 (July 26, 1762).   [49] *Jour. A.*, p. 103 (July 26, 1762).
[50] *Memoirs*, p. 99.   [51] *Jour. A.*, p. 103 (July 26, 1762).   [52] *Jour. A.*, p. 103.

the importance of the historian's relationship to his subject. It is not merely the theme that is important, it is Gibbon's reactions to that theme, for the past will be filtered through his mind and seen through his eyes. Already in 1762 he is suggesting that other *persona*, "the historian of Swiss liberty."

At the same time that he contemplated a history of Swiss liberty, Gibbon also considered another subject: *The History of the Republic of Florence, Under the House of Medicis.* This was "the direct contraste of the former." Switzerland was a poor, virtuous state which emerged into glory and liberty: Florence was a rich and corrupt republic which "sinks into the arms of a master." The Florentine history is the more attractive of the two. Not only are the materials readily accessible—not "fast locked up in the obscurity of a barbarous old German language"—but there are "two fine *morceaux* for a Philosophical historian, and which are essential parts of it, the Restoration of Learning in Europe by Lorenzo de Medicis and the character and fate of Savanarola." [53] The Florentine history has both a "philosophic" theme and characters around whom the historian can group events. In these two contemplated subjects the authentic voice of "the historian of the Roman empire" is heard. An introduction into the intensely personal concept of the past that distinguishes the *Decline and Fall* is obtained. But again no progress is made. The journals continue to record only an intense interest in ancient history, and the Grand Tour intervenes. Even in Gibbon's journal for his Italian trip there is no mention of working at, or even thinking about, the Florentine history. His months in Lausanne, before leaving for Italy, are taken up with his historical geography of ancient Italy. There is no mention of the Swiss history.

In the *Memoirs* Gibbon says that he began work on the Swiss history in the first summer after his return to England. This would be in 1765, for he returned home in June of that year. It was Deyverdun's extended visit to Beriton that decided Gibbon on the Swiss rather than the Florentine history: "the two historical designs which had balanced by choice were submitted to his taste; and in that parallel between the revolutions of Florence and Switzerland

[53] *Jour. A.*, p. 104 (July 26, 1762).

our common partiality for a country, which was *his* by birth and *mine* by adoption, inclined the scale in favour of the latter." [54] Gibbon's choice thus falls on the topic to which he is most intimately related, although certainly Deyverdun's visit made the Swiss history possible: Deyverdun knew German. The first mention of the Swiss history in his letters is a long letter to his Swiss friend, Victor de Saussure, dated September 23, 1766. Not only was Gibbon ignorant of German, and thus totally dependent on the translations and abstracts made for him by Deyverdun, but also he did not have an adequate library for the project. He wrote Saussure asking him to check something in the Neufchâtel library, to wit, *Les entreprises du Duc Charles de Bourgogne . . . contre messeigneurs des ligues*, part of a chronicle written at the end of the fifteenth century.

To Deyverdun fell the heavier task of translating and abstracting the German sources, especially the medieval chronicles. The two men worked together preparing the materials [55] and "such was the distance and delay that two years elapsed in these preparatory steps; and it was late in the third summer (1767) before I entered with these slender materials on the more agreeable task of composition." [56] The rest of the story is well known. The first book of the Swiss history, written in French, was read in the winter of 1768 "in a litterary society of foreigners in London." Gibbon "listened without observation to the free strictures and unfavourable sentence" of his judges. And "their condemnation was ratified by my cooler thoughts; I delivered my imperfect sheets to the flames." [57]

This is not quite accurate. Gibbon did not burn the Swiss history, and it can be read in his *Miscellaneous Works*. Nor does he mention sending the manuscript to David Hume, with a covering letter (dated October 4, 1767) [58] offering to burn the manuscript

---

[54] *Memoirs*, pp. 140-141.

[55] See *Memoirs*, p. 141, for a detailed description of Deyverdun's part in the project.

[56] *Memoirs*, p. 141.   [57] *Memoirs*, pp. 141-142.

[58] The letter to Hume is interesting as evidence of Gibbon's confusion between French and English. It is punctuated with French and much of the syntax is French. Even as late as 1767 Gibbon was not yet a master of his own language.

if Hume so advised. The London reading was probably only a public test of Hume's reservations—although Hume's reaction was kind and favorable. At any rate, Gibbon suppressed the work, and seriously considered Hume's advice to write in his native tongue.[59]

The fragment of the Swiss history, printed by Sheffield, fills ninety-one printed pages.[60] It is difficult to tell from an incomplete work the intentions of an author. Yet even with only this partial evidence it is clear that the Swiss history was a false step for Gibbon. There is nothing distinguished about the work, nothing announcing the greatest historian of his age. Here and there one finds some glimmerings of a philosophic spirit, but the whole is dull and without Gibbon's characteristic genius, either for narrative, characterization, or analysis. Only a careful reader can extract from the mass a few Gibbonian gems, like this note:

> Within this small walled area are to be found the monuments of every century. The ruins of Vindonisse, an old Roman town destroyed in the fourth century by the Alemani, against whom it had been erected as a rampart, can still be discerned. The town was the home of the twenty-first legion, and of the first bishops of Constance. Close to these ruins lies the tower of the Habsburgs, offering an image of feudal tyranny; and the cradle of twenty emperors. The more extensive ruins of the Abbey of Konigsfeld reveals the tropies of superstition. Finally, the small village of Bruck, which completes the picture, presents a view of industry and prosperity. The contrast is very favorable to our own century.[61]

Here is one of Gibbon's favorite devices: the melancholy and invidious comparison of Roman civilization, barbarian inundation, medieval superstition, feudal tyranny, and industrious city life. It lacks the pungency of such passages in the *Decline and Fall*, but it is Gibbon's authentic voice.

Another of Gibbon's mature characteristics, the bold debunking

---

[59] Hume's letter (dated London, October 24, 1767) is printed by Sheffield in his edition of the *Autobiography, MW*, I, 204-205, note. Gibbon's reply is in *Letters*, I, 222-223 (dated Beriton, October 25, 1767).

[60] *MW*, III, 239-330.

[61] *MW*, III, 243-244.

of a favorite legend, is found in his treatment of the William Tell story:

> The happiness of Tell, his flight and his vengeance, are much celebrated. But our century, which questions the credulity of our ancestors, seems to discount a fable which has not even the merit of originality; and we discern in William Tell only a heavy imitation of one of the Danish heroes, perhaps as fabulous as Tell himself. Whatever might be the truth, the deeds of this famous citizen scarcely influenced the Swiss revolution. All the conspirators awaited in silence the beginning of a year which was to be the signal of their enterprise, and the epoch of Swiss liberty.[62]

But these *morceaux* do not make up for the tediousness of the work. Far from inflaming him, the Swiss history seems to have bored Gibbon. He originally decided to write a history of Swiss liberty because he himself so closely identified with the subject, and in his role as creator would bring to his materials his own enthusiasm for the events. In fact his imagination never took fire. Gibbon might owe his education and his culture to Switzerland, but he felt nothing positive about the men and the intrigues which had, in those Gothic centuries, created Swiss liberty. For all of his ambition, Gibbon was unable to breathe life into the chronicles of medieval Switzerland. The Swiss history plods on, page after page, with Gibbon closely following the chronicles. He is accurate and diligent, but he is also dull.

Another problem was Gibbon's decision to write in French. His youthful ambition to achieve a place in French literature still persisted. He argued, both in the *Memoirs* and in a letter to Hume, that French, in which he spontaneously thought and wrote, was more familiar to him at the time than English. This is doubtless true. Yet his decision to write in French was an error, and Gibbon learned from this error a most useful lesson. His command of French was remarkable. The French reviewers of the *Essai* all commented on the excellence of his French style. But what had served so well for the argumentative *Essai* failed in the narrative

[62] *MW*, III, 265-266.

history. Gibbon could not find in French a tone proper for historical narrative. He conceived of historical narrative as grandiose and
rhythmic, and one has but to imagine the difficulties of translating
the *Decline and Fall* into classical French to realize Gibbon's problem in the Swiss history. This problem, too, affected the Swiss history, and in the *Memoirs* Gibbon commented on it: "Perhaps I may
suspect that the language itself is ill adapted to sustain the vigour
and dignity of an important narrative. But if France, so rich in
litterary merit, had produced a great original historian, his Genius
would have formed and fixed the idiom to the proper tone, the
peculiar mode of historical eloquence." [63] But Voltaire, the outstanding French historian of the age, was not Gibbon's ideal of a
historian. France would have to wait for those great liberal historians of the nineteenth century, especially Michelet, for a true
historical style. Gibbon's style, in the Swiss history, was "above
prose and below poetry" and it "degenerated into a verbose and
turgid declamation." [64]

The Swiss history was important in Gibbon's development, but
it did little to improve his technique. Its impact was largely negative. Gibbon learned from the Swiss history what he could not
and should not do. The single positive result was his realization that
a historical subject must be thematic and that the historian himself
must be intimately related to his subject. The other lessons learned
are mistakes to be avoided. The historian must find a subject in
which he can master all the sources, and he must write in his native
language. He must not concentrate on the Middle Ages, nor should
he embark on a project that demanded years of original research
in the archives. The Swiss history was a failure, but an important
failure in the making of "the historian of the Roman empire."

Gibbon first looked to biography as providing that principle of
organization which he hoped would give coherence to the past.
He had rejected all the deductive schemes of his day, and he believed a biographical approach to the past would fill the gap. In
the first place he had a profound humanistic conviction that man
is the object of history, and what could be more obvious than writing the history of one man. All of the technical problems Gibbon

[63] *Memoirs*, p. 142.   [64] *Memoirs*, p. 142.

had noticed in the work of others—Voltaire's habit of separating out the various aspects of history into separate chapters, Montesquieu's disregard for the role of individuals in history—might be solved by a biographical approach. He had also the example of a favorite author, Plutarch, and even toyed with the idea of writing parallel lives. The biographical approach was also popular in Augustan England. "Lives" were almost daily tumbling off the presses and were eagerly devoured by the public. Gibbon might hope for literary success and fame—always present to his mind whenever he contemplated a literary project.

Biography had numerous advantages, but it also had disadvantages. Most serious for an aspiring philosophic historian was the danger of friendship: "The historian of a great man is almost always his friend. The sculptor prostrates himself before his work. This species of *amour-propre* is as familiar as it is singular." Biography would lead the historian from objectivity, and at this stage of his development Gibbon was not ready to give up the idea of objectivity and disinterested pursuit of the truth. He could not yet see the historian as the creator of the past and a work of history as a self-contained object of artistic unity. The mature Gibbon was not troubled by friendship for his characters: he in fact celebrated his friendships with certain Romans. But in the 1760's he was far from this position. So he abandoned biography and looked for a subject that would provide a principle of organization that was more impersonal.

He thought he had found such a subject in the Florentine and the Swiss histories. Both had a thematic unity which would give coherence to events, both had episodes and implied theses which would appeal to a philosophic historian, and both seemingly avoided the objection that might be raised against biography. It is unfortunate that Gibbon decided on the Swiss history rather than the Florentine. It is the latter than would have proved more congenial. Indeed, in the *Decline and Fall* he returns to this Florentine project, and the chapters on the revival of learning in the West are the brilliant realization of this youthful project. As usual, in 1765 Gibbon's instincts were correct, but he allowed himself to be persuaded—this time by Deyverdun—to undertake the Swiss history.

The Florentine project was closer to his real interests, he was competent in Italian and devoted to the classics. In addition, the revival of learning was something Gibbon could put into a vast perspective of world history: Swiss liberty was but a minor episode in the evolution of European civilization. For Florentine history he had guides and examples, and this was crucial for a historian of Gibbon's temperament. He was never willing, or perhaps able, to bury himself in the archives and do original spadework on the sources. This is exactly what was required of a historian of Swiss liberty. But for Renaissance Florence, and even medieval Florence, he had the brilliant works of Muratori, not to mention the histories of Machiavelli and the humanists.

Gibbon saw the past best when he saw it through the eyes of other historians. For Swiss history he had no such eyes to use. In addition, he found in the history of Swiss liberty none of those characters—like Savanarola and the great humanists—who might exercise his biographical interests. The heroes of Swiss liberty were often obscure men or fictional characters, like William Tell.

The failure of the Swiss history made it clear to Gibbon that he must choose a subject that had scope, familiarity, a theme, characters, and philosophical importance. It must be a subject with an abundance of sources already collected, and with a minimum of antiquarian work demanded. It must be amenable to narrative treatment and not yet adequately treated. A history of the Roman empire presented Gibbon with all these things, and when he fixed upon Roman history his intellectual development, and his evolution as a historian, became coherent and seemingly inevitable. How could the most accomplished amateur classicist of the eighteenth century have thought of becoming the historian of Swiss liberty, or Renaissance Florence? How could the greatest narrative historian in the English language have desired to be the biographer of Raleigh?

His next historical work was the *Decline and Fall*. Once he fixed upon Rome as his subject many of the earlier problems evaporated. Rome was a grand theme with which Gibbon could identify. He was master of the sources and the subject was both philosophically and temperamentally satisfying to a man who had spent his life among the classics. A history of Rome not only had a thematic unity, but it also was filled with great characters who might exercise the ingenuity and the art of the historian. Even Gibbon's style, an authentic translation into English of Ciceronian eloquence, was perfectly suited to the subject. The major difficulties he experienced were style and proportion, his narrative stance, and the order of his materials: "At the outset all was dark and doubtful: even the title of the work, the true aera of the decline and fall of the Empire, the limits of the Introduction, the division of the chapters, and the order of the narrative; and I was often tempted to cast away the labour of seven years." [65] But these worries are radically different from those encountered in his earlier historical works. Gibbon now saw the historian's craft to lie in his style, his narrative stance. Once he had solved this problem, his history ran smoothly: "The style of an author should be the image of his mind: but the choice and command of language is the fruit of exercise: many experiments were made before I could hit the middle tone between a dull Chronicle and a Rhetorical declamation; three times did I compose the first chapter, and twice the second and third, before I was tolerably satisfied with their effect." [66]

With the *Decline and Fall* Gibbon descends from the theoretical considerations of the *Essai* to the more practical problem of how to write the history of Rome. He fixes his attention on how to tell the story of Rome's fall, and in so doing moves toward his final solution of the historian's problem. Once Gibbon found his narrative voice he never again went astray: "In the remainder of the way I advanced with a more equal and easy pace: but the fifteenth and sixteenth Chapters have been reduced by three successive revisals from a large Volume to their present size; and they might still be compressed without any loss of facts or sentiments." [67]

The problem of historical writing for Gibbon was how best to tell a story. Bayle's scepticism about historical truth, the refined analytical tools of the Maurists, the ponderous and exhaustive collection of sources are all of secondary importance. It is the historian's narrative voice that creates the past, and it is Gibbon's narrative voice which develops in the course of the *Decline and*

[65] *Memoirs*, p. 155.   [66] *Memoirs*, p. 155.   [67] *Memoirs*, p. 156.

Fall. He spent twenty years writing his *History*, and as might be expected there is a discernible development from the early volumes to the later volumes. As Gibbon encountered different problems, he refined his narrative voice to deal with them. The almost fatalistic implications of "decline" and "fall," faithfully followed in the first two volumes, are gradually replaced by a more sceptical attitude toward patterns or movements in the past. The early volumes have a distinct flavor of determinism, and the general considerations of chapter XXXVIII sum up this determinism: Rome fell, inevitably, through immoderate greatness.

In the later volumes Gibbon became dissatisfied with the trope of decline and fall, and indeed, dissatisfied with the implications of fatalism in history. He abandoned his earlier stance, and he did so by altering his narrative voice. This new awareness of multiplicity, complexity, pluralism is expressed by a language filled with the rhetoric of tentative judgment, sceptical asides, and limpid irony. As Gibbon's historical views changed, his art also become more refined. The historian himself recognized the change: "The style of the first Volume is in my opinion somewhat crude and elaborate: in the second and third it is ripened into ease and correctness and numbers: but in the three last, I may have been seduced by the facility of my pen." [68] To the man who believed that style should be the image of the mind, this artistic growth is a direct reflection of Gibbon's changing attitudes toward the past. Gibbon became increasingly sceptical about the possibility of writing a definitive history of Rome. Not only did the enormous complexity of his subject lead to this conclusion, but also the very nature of historical truth pressed constantly upon his mind. In the middle two volumes of his *History* he moves away from the easy fatalism of the first two volumes. Causal patterns, even so general a pattern as Rome collapsing under the weight of immoderate greatness, vanish. In their place are found the personal pronoun.

History is becoming, for Gibbon, the creation of the historian rather than the philosophic identification of cause and effect relationships. He does not abandon cause and effect, rather he softens the impact of the concept through a "rhetoric of relative judg-

[68] *Memoirs*, p. 179.

ment." [69] Definitive statements become rarer and rarer, until the final two volumes where one looks in vain for the aggressive judgments of the earlier volumes. More and more Gibbon retreats into irony to express the tentative and personal nature of historical truth. Those familiar doublets, the hallmarks of his style—"by art or by accident," "in truth, or in opinion," "genuine or fictitious," "chance or merit"—appear with increasing frequency. And these doublets are but another of Gibbon's devices for expressing the multiplicity and complexity of history.[70] The prominence of the personal pronoun "I" is Gibbon's device for expressing the subjective nature of historical truth and the central importance of the historian as creator of the past.

The evolution of Gibbon's style, his narrative voice, is directly related to his evolution as a thinker about history. His growing scepticism about historical truth and his growing irony are two aspects of the same problem. So, too, is Gibbon's increasing interest in historiography. As the *Decline and Fall* moves on through the empire Gibbon becomes more and more interested in what other historians have said about Rome. At times the accounts of historians become more important to him than the events themselves. Gibbon comes to see the past as the creation of the historian, and there can thus be as many pasts as there are historians. Gibbon's Roman empire is one of several Roman empires, and for all his personal vanity it is doubtful that Gibbon would have insisted on the validity of his own creation for all time.

Gibbon comes more and more to see himself as but another in a long series of historians, and his frequent and eloquent commemorations of Tacitus, or Ammianus, or Livy, or Tillemont, are salutes across the centuries to fellow craftsmen similarly engaged in creating the past. Unlike many modern historians Gibbon had no desire for consensus. He was content to express his own views. The notes might bristle with authorities for almost every factual statement, but the text of his *History* is written in the first-person voice. Divergent opinions need not be reconciled. In fact, this would destroy

[69] Leo Braudy, *Narrative Form in History and Fiction: Hume, Fielding, and Gibbon* (Princeton, 1970), p. 247. Hereafter cited as Braudy.
[70] See Braudy, pp. 246-248. Much of this discussion is based on Braudy.

the essence of history for Gibbon. The true hero of Gibbon's final volumes becomes "the historian of the Roman empire," and that *persona* appears regularly as the intelligence ordering events and making sense out of the past. The historian's task is to impose an intellectual and artistic order on the chaos of events.

Gibbon's mature philosophy of history, described here, is also evident in his specific treatment of the past. The historian imposes an order on events and gives them rational coherence. He may even give to events a rational coherence not possible for contemporaries of the events. Men living in the midst of historical developments are incapable of seeing what is happening. Gibbon frequently speaks of the "insensible" development. What he means by this is that the development was "insensible" to contemporaries. Such is the slow progress of Christianity in the empire. Contemporaries treated the new religion as yet another troublesome Eastern religion, unfortunately embraced by the lower classes, but not really threatening to the empire. In fact they were wrong. The vantage point of the historian allows him to see the whole of the development. "The historian of the Roman empire" is better able to understand Christianity, for example, than were contemporaries to the events. A favorite device of Gibbon's is to shift his perspective, first viewing events with the eyes of the historical actors, and then as "the historian of the Roman empire." Gibbon is never disturbed by the possibility that he might be distorting the past. The character of Muhammad is difficult to discern across the centuries, but, Gibbon insists, the complexities of Muhammad's character were no clearer to an Arab living in the seventh century. The historian orders and rationalizes the past, just as every man orders and rationalizes his own life. These human creations are equally valid and necessary, whether done by an Arab in the seventh century or an English gentleman in the eighteenth century.

What is lost to the historian through the destruction of records does not upset Gibbon. Even had he all the records his picture of the past could only be tentative. Even had he been a Roman senator his picture of events could be only tentative. The genius of Tacitus was that he saw his own times so clearly, but, Gibbon argues, even specific statements in Tacitus are open to doubt and revision. It is the act of creation that matters, it is the act of creation that gives meaning to life, and to history: "Gibbon's true optimism in the *Decline and Fall* rests not in any case he makes for 'progress,' but in his belief and demonstration that the human mind is capable of imposing order on the flux and arbitrary movement of time." [71]

Man, for Gibbon, is not trapped, fatalistically, in history. Circumstances limit and define man's actions, but he has the possibility of understanding and ordering his life. This is Gibbon's humanistic faith. When this faith is contrasted to Voltaire's pessimism about man's ability to do anything significant to the world around him, or even control his own happiness, the true nature of Gibbon's optimism is seen. Gibbon reiterated the rhetoric about progress and improvement, but never with enthusiasm. Gibbon's emotional and moral world was not that of the *philosophes*. He was no bourgeois, and he lacked the bourgeois assumptions of his French contemporaries. His sympathies were aristocratic and humanistic. Gibbon had no desire to change the world. He wanted only to understand it. If the world could be ordered and rationalized—as he ordered and rationalized the past—it could be understood.

Gibbon's attitudes toward the past, toward history, and toward himself as "the historian of the Roman empire" can perhaps best be seen if his treatment of Christianity in the *Decline and Fall* is examined.

Gibbon's antagonism to Christianity is well known, and the evidence for this is easily found in the *Decline and Fall*. Yet it is not perfectly clear that this antagonism is consistent, nor is it even clear that antagonism adequately describes Gibbon's view of Christianity. Alongside the familiar evidence—the sneering irony of chapters XV and XVI, the mordant wit directed against the desert saints, the literary shudder at all forms of enthusiasm—there are to be found cases which do not fit the pattern. Gibbon's admiration for St. Augustine, St. Athanasius, St. Bernard, for Tillemont and Pascal, his devotion to ecclesiastical history and his interest in theological controversy, these things are not the characteristics of a hater of Christianity. Only if the several threads in Gibbon's view of Christianity are distinguished, will his arguments make sense.

[71] Braudy, p. 268.

There are four aspects to Gibbon's attitude toward Christianity, and to all religions. He is interested in religion as a phenomenon of civilization. This interest might be characterized as a legacy of Montesquieu. Gibbon studied the religion of the Germans, the pagan Romans, the Persians, the Muhammadans, and the Christians as an integral part of their society and civilization. On this level he made no invidious distinctions between the religions of the world. Rather he viewed them as fundamental to any understanding of history. What value judgments he allows himself when treating religion as an aspect of civilization are dictated by his concept of social utility. Those religious systems which express the ideals of a society and which contribute to the genius of a people are praised. Thus the paganism of the Germanic tribes and of Rome is treated sympathetically. So, too, is Islam and the religion of ancient Persia. In each case Gibbon considered the religion to be a creative force in society. Roman paganism inculcated the principles of filial piety, and devotion to the state, and emphasized the civilizing mission of Rome. Islam, despite its enthusiasm, raised the desert tribes from a state of barbarism to a state of civilization, and all the achievements of the Arabs are the direct result of their religion.

When dealing with religion on this level Gibbon is a relativist, and he asks only if this or that religion was beneficial to its adherents and consequently beneficial to society. He is occasionally unsympathetic, as with Byzantine Christianity, but as a general rule he was willing to recognize the importance and the value of different religions. His condemnation of Christianity is not an irrational hatred arising from his own conversion and reconversion. His condemnation of Christianity is historical and utilitarian: the nature of Christianity was hostile to the genius of Rome. It was an alien principle, insensibly growing within the empire, and finally corrupting the martial and civic spirit of Rome. Even this view is modified as the *Decline and Fall* progresses.

The second of Gibbon's concerns is with religion as a theological scheme, explaining man's relationship to God, his fellow men, and to society. From childhood Gibbon had been fond of religious speculation, and the child was father of the man. The *Decline and Fall* is full of the most minute and elegant theological explication.

The sections on transubstantiation or the trinitarian controversy, or the gnostic heresy, are memorable performances. Gibbon always found delight in unraveling the complexities of controversy and theology, and the intellectual integrity shown in his discussions of Islam or the iconoclastic controversy is singular in the Enlightenment. It is true that he had little respect for metaphysics, whether religious or secular, and in all of his theological discussions Gibbon used irony to detach himself from the issues under consideration. Nevertheless, his accounts are both accurate and judicious. Gibbon is not noticeably hostile to theology per se, or at least no more hostile than he is to the philosophies of Plato or the church fathers. He prefers some ideas to others, but all are given the benefit of full and thoughtful exegesis.

The third of Gibbon's concerns is best characterized as institutional. Here Gibbon's hostility is patent. He is antagonistic to all institutionalized religions, and this is especially apparent in his treatment of Christianity. He is anticlerical, he is snide, he is deliberately ironic, and he is actively antagonistic. The institutionalization of religion is, for Gibbon, a genuine evil. And it is precisely here that Gibbon has established his reputation as an enemy of Christianity. In fact he has injected into English literature the anticlericalism of the Continent, especially of France. Those brilliant and coruscating remarks about priests, the papacy, and monks are almost direct transliterations of what the *philosophes* said. There is much wit but little originality in Gibbon's remarks about the church as an institution.

Finally, there is Gibbon's concern with the personal, or humanistic, aspects of religion. The impact of religion on individuals had long interested Gibbon, and the most successful and famous character sketches in the *Decline and Fall*—Julian the Apostate, St. Athanasius, St. Bernard, Constantine the Great, Muhammad—are of men whose lives were profoundly influenced by religion. Even some of Gibbon's favorite authors—Tillemont, Pascal, Milton—are men whose characters have been molded by religion, and whose intellectual work directly reflects religion. As a subcategory to this personal aspect of religion should be added Gibbon's fascination with religious enthusiasm. All of the men who intrigued him were religious enthusiasts. Far from being blind to the power of religion, Gibbon had a profound respect for it. If the orthodox view of Gibbon as a man incapable of understanding the religious spirit were true, he would be the least likely man to paint those brilliant portraits of Julian, or Athanasius, or Muhammad. He would be the least likely man to be a devoted reader of Pascal and Milton. The truth of the matter is that Gibbon clearly recognized the power, even the creative power, of religion. He might, as indeed he did, think the enthusiasm of Julian or Athanasius misplaced and potentially dangerous, but he certainly did not dismiss them as madmen. They were men of remarkable genius, and Gibbon saw that this genius was in part created by and nurtured by religious enthusiasm. It is the *philosophes* who are quick to condemn the religious fanatic, not Gibbon. "The historian of the Roman empire" might laugh at the excesses of St. Simeon Stylites and the other desert fanatics, but he did not laugh at those fanatics who had brains. When he called Voltaire "a bigot, an intolerable bigot" he was not being hyperbolic. He thought the *philosophe* insensitivity to religious enthusiasm to be unenlightened, and he was careful to distinguish himself from this part of the Enlightenment tradition.

Inspired by Montesquieu and Bayle, Gibbon believed that the history of religions could be written, and indeed such a task was the responsibility of a historian. A study of his attitudes toward paganism will make clear the complexity of Gibbon's thought about religion, and also provide evidence that the generally accepted view of his treatment of religion is perhaps too simplistic.

Gibbon first attempted to write a history of polytheism in the *Essai sur l'étude de la littérature*. In his *Memoirs* he remarked that he was "not displeased with the inquiry into the origin and nature of the gods of polytheism" and added that the subject "might deserve the illustration of a riper judgment." He never returned to the subject, but many of his fundamental ideas about religion are to be found in the *Essai*. The first gods of polytheism were created through fear. This was an idea borrowed from David Hume. It gave Gibbon a psychological understanding of the importance of religion, and he built up his picture of polytheism from this assumption.

The savage mentality, illuminated by Bayle, Fontenelle, and Hume, is the prisoner of fear. Feeble and ignorant, the savage fears not only his surroundings, but himself. His self-contempt leads him to invest the terrors of nature with divinity. He hopes to ease his fears by worshiping them. The oak tree and the electric storm were both beyond his powers of comprehension: both became objects of worship. These first polytheistic gods were created not out of reason—as the Deists argued—but out of fear.

"Feelings quickly became ideas" for the savage. Every object he saw appeared more excellent than himself, and every object was worshiped: "The savage conferred on each of them life and power, and prostrated himself before the beings which he had created." [72] At first only natural objects or phenomena were deified and the moral world was neglected. But the savage soon discovered that his fate and his actions were not adequately explained by the multiplication of natural divinities. He was unable to generalize at this stage of his development, so he created yet another pantheon of deities to account for his moral life. Each passion and each division in society received its god.[73] And these two distinct species of divinities, this "chain of errors," formed "a single theological romance." [74]

With the passage of time the two sets of gods crystallized into a single pantheon, and as the savage became more sophisticated he was able to generalize and arrange the parts into a whole. But to bridge the gap between natural deities and moral deities a principle was necessary, and the savage seized upon the device of allegory. Gibbon had no patience with allegory. He considered the allegorizing temper of mind to be a retreat from rationality, and an insidious habit. Instead of seeing allegory as a higher truth, Gibbon considered it the refuge of a weak mind: "But all the allegories which ever issued from the Platonic school are not worth the short poem of Catullus on the same extraordinary subject." [75] The allegorizing temperament is, for Gibbon, dangerous. In the first place it destroys truth. Gibbon believed that the pagan mythologies were to be understood literally. The "lascivious form of a naked Venus"

[72] *Essai*, LXVII, 79.   [73] *Essai*, LXXIII, p. 84.   [74] *Essai*, LXXII, p. 83.
[75] XXIII, 462, n. 15.

and the castration of Atys were exactly that. They were not moral precepts disguised allegorically: "The lascivious form of a naked Venus was tortured into the discovery of some moral precept or some physical truth: and the castration of Atys explained the revolution of the sun between the tropics or the separation of the human soul from vice and error." [76] In addition to replacing truth with fiction, allegory became, in the hands of the priests, a weapon for deceit and social control: "As the traditions of Pagan mythology were variously related, the sacred interpreters were at liberty to select the most convenient circumstances; and as they translated an arbitrary cypher, they could extract from *any* fable *any* sense which was adapted to their favourite system of religion and philosophy." [77] Bards and monks, Gibbon argued, are the "two orders of men who equally abused the privilege of fiction." [78]

Underlying Gibbon's hostility to allegory is a basic assumption about the nature of truth. Gibbon was primarily a literary man, and he loved fiction as entertainment. But he made a rigid distinction between fact and fiction. One turned to poetry, and mythology, and fable, to enjoy its imagery and to stimulate the imagination. The *Arabian Nights* was a favorite book, and Gibbon loved Homer. Yet for truth one must turn to prosaic history: "The *Cyropaedia* is vague and languid: the *Anabasis* is circumstantial and animated. Such is the eternal difference between fiction and truth." [79] Indeed, Gibbon would probably have subscribed to Fielding's radical statement of the problem:

> I am far from supposing that Homer, Hesiod, and the other ancient poets and mythologists, had any settled design to pervert and confuse the records of antiquity; but it is certain they have effected it; and for my part I must confess I should have honoured and loved Homer more had he written a true history of his own times in humble prose, than all those noble poems that have so justly collected the praise of all ages; for, though I read these with more admiration and astonishment, I still read Herodotus, Thucydides, and Xenophon with more amusement and more satisfaction. [80]

[76] XXIII, 462.   [77] XXIII, 462.   [78] XXV, 45.
[79] XXIV, 551, n. 119.
[80] Quoted by Braudy, from Henry Fielding, *The Journal of a Voyage to Lisbon*, intro. A. R. Humphreys (London, 1964), pp. 185-186.

The truth is not to be found in allegories or mythmaking, and when such things cease to be mere literary entertainment—as they often do in religion—they become positively dangerous. Poets and the church fathers are much "addicted to fictions" and the latter are dangerous because they have political power through the church.

When Gibbon comes to consider Christianity he uses the assumptions and ideas adumbrated in the *Essai*. He believes fear to lie at the base of all religious schemes, he believes priestly deceit to be a real and present danger, and he believes that a religion is to be judged by its usefulness and not the cleverness of its myths. When he compares Christianity to Roman paganism he finds Christianity lacking. The absurdities of paganism are not minimized, but at least paganism was not intolerant. The intolerant zeal of the Christians, which they inherited from the Jews, made Christianity a persecuting religion, and the importance of doctrine and theology vanished when men were destroyed in the name of religion. Paganism might be superstitious, it might be false, it might be riddled with priestly deceit, but it was not intolerant: "The various modes of worship which prevailed in the ancient world were all considered by the people as equally true; by the philosopher as equally false; and by the magistrates as equally useful." [81] Gibbon's hostility to Christianity is not that it is more irrational than other religions, that it is more priest-ridden than other religions, but rather that it is both more intolerant and more antisocial than other religions. When Christianity comes to dominate, indeed replace, the Roman empire, it becomes powerful enough to enforce its fanaticism.

Gibbon is antagonistic to the priests and monks of Christianity in direct proportion to their power. As a man, and an enlightened man, he considered celibacy and monastic seclusion to be destructive of humanity. The monastic life "is painful to the individual and useless to mankind." [82] As a historian he considered Christianity to be inimical to the Roman genius and oppressive. The *esprit général* of Roman civilization, as Gibbon saw it, was military, prosaic,

[81] II, 28. The source of this clever sentence might be St. Augustine. In the *City of God* he records an aphorism of Scaevola, that there are three kinds of gods: those established by philosophers, those established by poets, and those established by magistrates. Both Bayle and Montesquieu made use of this distinction.

[82] XX, 346, n. 124.

legal, administrative, and practical. Order, prosperity, and an easy tolerance were the blessings of the Roman yoke. And if Rome civilized through conquest, nevertheless she civilized the world. Roman paganism complemented these virtues, and the emphasis of the religion was worldly and civic. Every aspect of Roman life was filled with religious significance, enhanced by religious ceremony, or encouraged by religious precept. Roman paganism contributed to and supported the *esprit général* of Roman civilization.

Rome's great armies worshiped in the field: "In every Roman camp there was a small chapel near the headquarters, in which the statues of the tutelar deities were preserved and adored; and we may remark that the eagles, and other military ensigns, were in the first rank of these deities; an excellent institution, which confirmed discipline by the sanction of religion." [83] The whole of Roman life was embedded in and commemorated by religious ceremony: "The innumerable deities and rites of polytheism were closely interwoven with every circumstance of business or pleasure, of public or of private life; and it seemed impossible to escape the observance of them, without, at the same time, renouncing the commerce of mankind and all the offices and amusements of society." [84] And these ceremonies were happy occasions, unsullied by the constant reminder of sin and retribution: "The important transactions of peace and war were prepared or concluded by solemn sacrifices, in which the magistrate, the senator, and the soldier were obliged to preside or to participate. The public spectacles were an essential part of the cheerful devotion of the Pagans, and the gods were supposed to accept, as the most grateful offering, the games that the princes and people celebrated in honour of their peculiar festivals." [85] Christianity destroyed all this. It was a bleak and intolerant religion, and instead of celebrating the martial spirit and civic pride of the Romans, it condemned these very things as worldly pomp, likely to prevent salvation. At the very time when Rome was struggling to survive the barbarian invasions, the martial and civic spirit of the empire was being directly attacked and destroyed by the progress of Christianity.

[83] VI, 132, n. 24.   [84] XV, 17-18.   [85] XV, 18.

The remarks which have earned Gibbon the reputation of "infidel"—and this was a term applied to him by contemporaries—are not so much his reservations about Christian mythology as they are his witty and angry anticlericalism, and his historical attack on miracles. The miraculous tradition, Gibbon rightly thought, was essential to the triumph of Christianity. Miracles provided palpable proof of God's providence and gave justification to Christian intolerance. It is precisely here that Gibbon directed his attack. He wanted to discredit the miraculous tradition, but not merely theoretically, as David Hume had done. He wanted to show the historical absurdity of the tradition, and this could best be done, Gibbon believed, by writing a history of miracles.

He began with some of the philosophic assumptions familiar to all educated men in the Enlightenment. Gibbon accepted a Newtonian universe, governed by necessary laws and beyond the control of man. These laws, he argued, were not capriciously suspended to accommodate a saint, or to demonstrate God's power to unbelievers: "Accustomed long since to observe and to respect the invariable order of Nature, our reason, or at least our imagination, is not sufficiently prepared to sustain the visible action of the Deity." [86] And if miracles themselves demanded a rejection of a rational universe, the acceptance of miracles was conditioned by custom and habit. The Catholics and the Protestants could not agree on which miracles were genuine; and this is not to mention the attitudes of the Jews, the Muhammadans, or the Chinese: "The conversion of Constantine is the aera most generally fixed by Protestants. The more rational divines are willing to admit the miracles of the fourth, whilst the more credulous are unwilling to reject those of the fifth century." [87] These two difficulties are but further complicated when the specific miracles are examined.

The first and most obvious fact about the miraculous tradition is that the majority of miracles date from the Dark Ages. It is precisely in those periods of superstition that the most miracles were reported; and the frequency of miracles declines with the advance of science and philosophy. So striking is this correspondence

[86] XV, 33.   [87] XV, 33.

between superstition and miracles that Gibbon even suggests that, in an age without science, supposed miracles were perhaps but ordinary occurrences. In an age which did not understand the laws of nature, a miracle could hardly be defined as a deviation from nature: "But we may surely be allowed to observe that a miracle, in that age of superstition and credulity, lost its name and its merit, since it could scarcely be considered as a deviation from the ordinary and established laws of nature." [88] Further proof of this proposition is to be found in the fact that the progress of science has destroyed miracles. What might once have passed for a miracle can now be explained without recourse to the supernatural: "In modern times, a latent, and even involuntary, scepticism adhered to the most pious dispositions. Their admission of supernatural truths is much less an active consent than a cold and passive acquiescence. Accustomed long since to observe and to respect the invariable order of Nature, our reason, or at least our imagination, is not sufficiently prepared to sustain the visible action of the Deity. But in the first ages of Christianity, the situation of mankind was extremely different." [89]

Complementary to this line of argument is the questionable nature of the testimony regarding miracles. Most often miracles of one saint are reported by another saint: "It may seem somewhat remarkable that Bernard of Clairvaux, who records so many miracles of his friend St. Malachi, never takes any notice of his own, which, however, are carefully related by his companions and disciples." [90] And Gibbon could not resist a malicious rhetorical question in a footnote: "In the long series of ecclesiastical history, does there exist a single instance of a saint asserting that he himself possessed the gift of miracles." [91] As a general rule "the conduct which disclaims the ordinary maxims or reason" should be distrusted. It "excites our suspicion and eludes our inquiry." [92] Merely because these are holy things, our good sense and judgment should not be suspended. The evidence supporting a miraculous tradition is open to serious doubts. Not only are the things reported difficult to accept, but the people reporting them are dubious characters.

Some of the witnesses to miracles Gibbon dismisses as deranged

[88] XXVIII, 223.   [89] XV, 33.   [90] XV, 32, n. 83.
[91] XV, 32, n. 83.   [92] XXII, 422.

fanatics. Monks, buried in their cloister, subject to the regimen of fasting, prayer, and mortification, eventually unhinged their minds. Their "sleeping or waking visions" were "the ordinary effects of abstinence and fanaticism." [93] Their dreams and visions, which often are the only evidence for miracles, are "the production of a distempered fancy, the creation of an empty stomach, and an empty brain." [94] Peter the Hermit is a case in point: "whatever he wished, he believed; whatever he believed, he *saw* in dreams and revelation." [95] The men who performed miracles were often mad: the men who reported the miracles no less so. Even, argues Gibbon, if the miracles are accepted, they prove nothing more than the faith of the man: "The monks of Egypt performed many miracles, which prove the truth of their faith . . . but what proves the truth of those miracles?" [96]

At times Gibbon alters his tactics. Instead of hammering away at the irrationality of miracles, he uses the stories as the vehicles for wit. In these instances there is no attempt made at argument: Gibbon is satisfied with sneering and having fun. On the night before he went into battle in A.D. 394, the great emperor Theodosius reportedly experienced a miraculous vision: "Theodoret affirms that St. John and St. Philip appeared to the waking or sleeping emperor, on horseback, &c." [97] "This is," Gibbon says, "the first instance of apostolic chivalry, which afterwards became so popular in Spain and in the Crusades." Boethius, after his execution by Theodoric, passed into popular legend as a martyr and a saint. He was "styled a magician by the ignorance of the times." He was reported to have "carried his head in his hands a considerable way" [98] after it was chopped off. Gibbon apparently told this anecdote in Madame du Deffand's salon, and he adds: "a lady [Mme. du Deffand] of my acquaintance once observed, 'La distance n'y fait rein; il n'y a que le premier pas qui coûte.' " [99] There is here a genuine flavor of the

[93] XXIII, 466.   [94] LXIII, 529.   [95] LVIII, 270.
[96] XXV, 29, n. 78.   [97] XXVII, 193, n. 122.   [98] XXXIX, 216, n. 113.
[99] XXXIX, 216, n. 113. It might be questioned whether or not Gibbon's quotation from Mme. du Deffand is true. The "mot" was famous in eighteenth-century French society, but had been created not in response to Gibbon and Boethius. See Lytton Strachey, "Madame du Deffand," *Books and Characters* (London, 1922), p. 91: "Her famous 'mot de Saint Denis,' so dear to the heart of Voltaire, deserves to be once more recorded. A garrulous and credulous Cardinal was describing

polite and witty conversation of Enlightenment society. Martin of Tours, Gibbon relates, set out to destroy the idols, the temples, and the consecrated trees of his dioceses, "and in the execution of this arduous task, the prudent reader will judge whether Martin was supported by the aid of miraculous powers or of carnal weapons."[100] And Gibbon adds, in his best salon manner: "The saint once mistook (as Don Quixote might have done) an harmless funeral for an idolatrous procession, and imprudently committed a miracle."[101]

Behind this erudite and elegant mockery, Gibbon is deadly serious. It is in the treatment of miracles in the *Decline and Fall* that Gibbon is most deliberately a *philosophe*. Yet his choice of this *persona*—one which he seldom found comfortable—should not mislead his readers. Gibbon treated miracles and the miraculous tradition *en philosophe* because he thought that mocking, cynical, urbane, and witty tone to be the most effective mode for his attack. What is unfortunate is the fact that many readers of Gibbon have taken this particular *persona*, or perhaps mood is a better description, as Gibbon's dominant attitude toward Christianity. This is not so. Gibbon himself recognized that his treatment of miracles was didactic—as few other sections of the *Decline and Fall* are didactic—and he recognized that he ran the risk of being a polemicist rather than a historian: "the duty of an historian does not call upon him to interpose his private judgment in this nice and important controversy; but he ought not to dissemble the difficulty of adopting such a theory as may reconcile the interest of religion with that of reason, of making a proper application of that theory, and of defining with precision the limits of that happy period, exempt from error and from deceit, to which we might be disposed to extend the gift of supernatural powers."[102] He knew that the historian could neither prove nor disprove miracles. He might repeat the conventional views of the Newtonians or the Deists, or the

---

the martyrdom of Saint Denis the Areopagite: when his head was cut off he took it up and carried it in his hands. That, said the Cardinal, was well known; what was not well known was the extraordinary fact that he walked with his head under his arm all the way from Montmartre to the Church of Saint Denis—a distance of six miles. 'Ah, Monseigneur!' said Madame du Deffand, 'dans une telle situation, il n'y a que le premier pas qui coûte.'"

[100] XXVIII, 207.   [101] XXVIII, 207.   [102] XV, 32.

philosophes, but these could do no more than make clear the historian's personal hostility to miracles. As "the historian of the Roman empire" Gibbon could only indict the testimony of his sources, which he did consistently, and attack a pernicious tradition with irony.

Gibbon's treatment of Christianity as an institution is another instance where the impact of the *philosophes* on his thought can be clearly seen. But here his *philosophe* anticlericalism is tempered by his assumption that social utility is the single yardstick by which institutions are judged. His praise of Roman paganism is based on its utility to the Roman state: his condemnation of the church is based on its harm to the state.

Anticlericalism is not a familiar attitude for English intellectuals, even in the eighteenth century. The English Reformation and the great rebellion removed from daily view the monks, the monasteries, and that familiar continental figure, the great ecclesiastical landowner and politician. The eighteenth-century English church might not be overly zealous in fulfilling its religious mission, but it certainly deserved respect for the intellectual quality of its prelates, and could not be convicted of the sins of French Catholicism. Gibbon's anticlericalism is drawn from books and not from personal experience. He had never been the victim of priestly deceit nor had he seen much ecclesiastical interference in politics. He knew these things only from the *philosophes* and from history. Yet if Gibbon himself was not anticlerical in his own life—he regularly attended the family church when he was living at Beriton, and he numbered among his acquaintances some divines—he was certainly anticlerical in the *Decline and Fall*. With good Protestant indignation Gibbon considered monks particularly unpleasant and dangerous men: "Their natural descent from such painful and dangerous virtue to the common vices of humanity will not, perhaps excite much grief or indignation in the mind of a philosopher." [103] In fact, the philosopher was indignant. "The monks in the lazy gloom of the convents" kept alive "the dark and implacable genius of superstition."

Gibbon's antagonism to monks and the monastic life is that old

[103] XXXVII, 76.

humanistic protest against self-mortification and social uselessness. One finds it in Erasmus and in More, in Milton and in Montesquieu. Gibbon adds little if anything to the old clichés about the monastic life, but he does give Europe its first respectable survey of the history of monasticism. Gibbon's concern is to trace the evolution of this institution while condemning monkish superstition, monkish interference in politics, and monkish oppression. "A cruel unfeeling temper has distinguished the monks of every age and country," [104] and when such men, because of historical circumstances, wield political and economic power, the results are frightful. Their very style of life, which Gibbon saw as the rationalization of personal torment, had not made them "susceptible of any lively affection for the rest of mankind."

For Gibbon the monkish life is inhuman, uncivilized, and unnatural. He uses the phrase "a cruel unfeeling temper" to describe the eunuchs of the Byzantine empire, obviously seeing a parallel between the mutilation of men in the East and the emotional and intellectual mutilation of the monks in the West. The very nature of the institution of monasticism is responsible for his inhuman and unnatural treatment of men. Nevertheless, Gibbon sees instances of the monastic life which are praiseworthy. As usual, it is dangerous to hold Gibbon to a single, linear view. The Benedictines of St. Maur are sincerely admired and celebrated in the *Decline and Fall*. So, too, are the Jesuit Bollandists. Gibbon sees that their splendid intellectual achievements are the direct results of monastic discipline and devotion. Tillemont, who never entered a monastery but created in his own home a regimen identical to that of a monastery, similarly receives Gibbon's lavish praise. It is not enthusiasm per se that is evil, nor even the monastic life. These things have a large potential for evil, but Gibbon carefully singles out those instances when enthusiasm and monasticism have been put to good use; and by good use he means socially worthwhile labor, usually intellectual labor. He even makes a special point of singling out the monastic ideal of Zoroaster for praise. That Persian zealot found a way to render the monastic life if not humane at least civilized:

[104] XXXVII, 80.

But there are some remarkable instances in which Zoroaster lays aside the prophet, assumes the legislator, and discovers a liberal concern for private and public happiness, seldom to be found among the grovelling or visionary schemes of superstition. Fasting or celibacy, the common means of purchasing the divine favour, he condemns with abhorrence, as a criminal rejection of the best gifts of providence. The saint, in the Magian religion, is obliged to beget children, to plant useful trees, to destroy noxious animals, to convey water to the dry lands of Persia, and to work out his salvation by pursuing all the labours of agriculture.[105]

Here again, as in his treatment of miracles, Gibbon is far more flexible and sensitive to differences than his *philosophe* contemporaries.

Gibbon's attitudes toward religion, and Christianity in particular, are more complex than is generally assumed. His so-called "hostility" to Christianity is not clearcut, and there is considerable evidence that he was far from hostile to many of the aspects of Christianity. Macaulay's famous remarks that Gibbon treated Christianity as an enemy who had done him a personal injury is clever but unfair. In the early volumes of the *Decline and Fall* Gibbon set up an invidious comparison between Roman paganism—which he perhaps romanticized—and Christianity. He later abandoned this debater's technique, and admitted to Lord Sheffield in a letter that "The primitive Church, which I have treated with some freedom, was itself at that time, an innovation, and *I* was attached to the old Pagan establishment." [106] This attitude, characteristic of the first two volumes, was afterward abandoned. But the impact made on the public by chapters XV and XVI remained to assure for Gibbon a reputation for doctrinaire hostility to Christianity.

Gibbon is hostile to most monks and prelates, he is hostile to the church as an institution, and he has little use for the metaphysics of theological speculation or debate. But he is remarkably sensitive to particular individuals, Athanasius, or Bernard, or Chrysostom. His increasing interest in ecclesiastical history as the *Decline and Fall* progresses is also worth noting. The ironic sneer is still evi-

[105] VIII, 217.
[106] *Letters*, III, 216 (dated February 5, 1791).

dent, but so, too, is an extraordinary diligence and intellectual honesty. Even the Eastern church, which never appealed to Gibbon or fired his imagination, is fairly treated.[107] The papacy is condemned, but individual popes are celebrated. The desert saints are mocked, but other saints are praised. Monasticism is scorned, but individual monks are commemorated.

The explanation for this enlightened view is to be found in Gibbon's changing, or rather maturing, notions of history as he worked on the *Decline and Fall*. He began with the assumption that barbarism and Christianity destroyed the Roman empire. This thesis loses its importance in the later volumes, and with his increasing sophistication about historical causation, Gibbon also abandons his deliberate hostility to Christianity. The true optimism of the *Decline and Fall*, as has been said before, is not the idea of progress, or indeed any of the bourgeois pieties of the Enlightenment. Gibbon's true optimism is a humanistic assumption that man has the capacity to rise above his historical circumstances and leave a record of his triumph—the triumph of the human mind—over the forces of history. Man is not trapped by the past, nor is man trapped by the rhetoric or the institutions of Christianity. Man for Gibbon is not even trapped by the superstition and fanaticism of his age. The great Athanasius was able to rise above both and to leave his mark on history. St. Bernard was able to overcome the dehumanizing effects of his society and to think and write in a manner worthy of the ancients. If Gibbon was hostile to Christianity on the basis of its historical record, he was not hostile to individual Christians, or indeed to religion. As he came to see history as a series of forces comprehensible only to the historian, and a series of forces ultimately hostile to the individual, he also came to respect those individuals who had freed themselves of the patterns of their times.

Only those things touched by man's mind had value for Gibbon, and the unity of history, the meaning of history, was not to be found in impersonal forces. Acts of creation, like the *Decline and*

---

[107] See the judgment of Deno J. Geanakoplos, "Edward Gibbon and Byzantine Ecclesiastical History," *Church History*, XXXV, no. 2 (June, 1966), 170-185. Geanakoplos gives Gibbon high marks as a historian of the Eastern church.

Fall, become for Gibbon the supreme value. He comes to see history not so much as events but rather as events interpreted by the historian. It is the historian who makes history and who gives it meaning. Christianity is a part of that past created by Gibbon. Christianity is the necessary circumstance in which all Europeans found themselves from the late empire to the Renaissance. It is neither good nor bad in itself: it has no moral properties built into it. Christianity has changed with the passage of time, just as all other ideas or institutions have changed. Institutions are but the framework in which men must live.

Gibbon was a very conservative man. He despised the radicals of his day, just as he despised the French Revolution. He was also a gentleman, distrustful of the masses and devoted to style in life as in the *Decline and Fall*. He had, at one and the same time, a profound scepticism about the human condition, and a profound faith in the ability of exceptional individuals to rise above their historical circumstances. Men, for Gibbon, make history, both as historians and as historical actors. There is perhaps little that the individual can do, but that little is a great deal. Institutions, religious systems, laws, and customs come to interest Gibbon less and less. His historical philosophy begins heavily indebted to the impersonal forces identified by Montesquieu. But by the last volumes these things are less important to "the historian of the Roman empire" than individuals. Great individuals come more and more to occupy the pages of the *Decline and Fall*, and Gibbon finally ends his survey of Roman civilization by contemplating himself sitting amidst the ruins of Rome, contemplating Roman civilization. As he moves toward this final view of the past, his early rigid antagonism to Christianity is abandoned. By the final volumes of the *Decline and Fall* Gibbon views Christianity as but another historical necessity, directing the energies of men into specific channels, but not destroying a human nature which can create order out of chaos and which can imprint on the world the humanizing energies of the mind. It is man's mind that becomes the ultimate hero of the *Decline and Fall*.

Philosophy for Gibbon, if a formulation that will take into account his flexible and impressionistic attitudes can be attempted, is a humantistic faith derived from the classics and reinforced by the humanistic tradition. Gibbon believed in man's ability to rationalize and order his life, just as he believed in the historian's ability to make sense out of the past. He had neither interest in nor patience with rigid formulas, and he distrusted all institutions and schemes which dictated behavior. Within this generous and loose framework he was able to hold all of his views. He could praise and admire individuals while condemning the institutions in which they lived. He could praise the enthusiasm of Islam and condemn that of Christianity. He could praise the monasticism of Zoroaster and condemn that of Christianity. He could escape the fatalistic and deterministic implications of his original thesis about Rome by focusing on those great characters who rose above their historical circumstances. And perhaps most important of all, he could die without regret, and with the elegance of manners and personal dignity which characterized his life and his work.

CHAPTER IV

GIBBON'S
JANSENIST MENTORS

"Ce fanatisme des Jansenistes est une de ces maladies Epidemiques de l'Esprit humain qui meritent beaucoup d'attention."

G IBBON'S DEBT to Tillemont is well known. Yet the nature of that debt raises fundamental problems in the historiography of the seventeenth and eighteenth centuries. It is not sufficient merely to cite the encomiums on Tillemont from Gibbon's *Memoirs* followed by some extracts from the *Decline and Fall*. The relationship between the two men is complex and revealing. Why the "historian of the Roman empire" should have relied so heavily on the work of a Jansenist zealot, and why he should have been willing to stake his reputation as a scholar on Tillemont's work, is no idle inquiry.

Part of the answer can be found in a study of Gibbon's work habits, which were not different from those of the other "philosophic" historians of his day. Nowhere are these habits more evident than in an episode of his last years.

In the 1790's after completing the *Decline and Fall*, Gibbon became bored with literary idleness. Historical composition was, he wrote, "le charme de ma vie" and "a perpetual fund of domestic amusement," and he cast about for another subject. He no

longer had the energy to tackle anything as monumental as the
Decline and Fall. Rather he contemplated a series of historical
aperçus, one of which was to be a history of the house of Brunswick.[1] The subject demanded a knowledge of German, a language
Gibbon always considered barbaric and refused to learn. But this
did not deter him from the project. He assumed that his friend,
Ernst Theodor Langer,[2] would translate the necessary German
materials.

Gibbon wrote Langer, offering him the dubious honor of becoming a "guide" for a philosophic historian. Gibbon explained
that he was ignorant of the language, and had never made German
history his "particular study." Thus it was essential that he have
"in the country itself an accurate correspondent, and enlightened
guide . . . whom he [Gibbon] may consult in every difficulty."
Gibbon flattered Langer by assuring him that he was the ideal man
for the task, but he was not sure that his friend would be willing
to supply "books, extracts, translations, and information of every
kind." As he candidly confessed, the status of "guide" promised
neither "fame nor pleasure." [3] Gibbon wanted Langer to function

[1] Among the other projects entertained—none of which reached completion—
were: (1) an autobiography, undertaken at the prompting of Lord Sheffield, and
(2) an edition of the English medieval historians, modeled on Dom Bouquet's
Recueil des historiens des Gaules et de France, whose eleven volumes Gibbon
much admired (see XXXVIII, 106, n. 1, for Gibbon's judgment on this remarkable
work of Benedictine scholarship). He heard that the English antiquarian, John
Pinkerton (1785-1826), was willing to undertake such a labor, and Gibbon wrote
him offering "to be always ready to assist at your secret committees, to offer my
advice with regard to the choice and arrangment of your materials and to join
with you in forming a general outline of the plan." Gibbon's death prevented
him from furnishing the "ornamental frieze" he promised. Pinkerton's plan, accompanied by his letter to Lord Sheffield, is printed in *MW*, III, 587-590. In addition, as Gibbon wrote William Robertson on March 26, 1788 (*Letters*, III, 100),
he entertained "some visionary designs," none of which ever got off the ground.

[2] Langer (1743-1820) was librarian to Charles William Ferdinand, Duke of
Brunswick, and a friend of Lessing and Goethe. He met Gibbon when he stayed
at Lausanne (1784-86 and 1787-88). Langer is the man who sent Gibbon a copy of
John Gibbon's *Introductio ad Latinum blasoniam* (1682). Gibbon, mistakenly,
assumed this John Gibbon was his great-great-uncle, and he spent a couple of
delightful weeks tracing out his ancestry, based on this false assumption. It is the
kind of error he himself would have delighted to excoriate in the *Decline and
Fall*. See Joseph Ward Swain, *Edward Gibbon the Historian* (London, 1966), pp.
3-6, for a discussion of this episode.

[3] The long letter to Langer is printed in *MW*, III, 356-357.

as a graduate assistant: Langer declined. He wrote Gibbon a polite but firm letter explaining that the difficulties of the project demanded that the historian know German well, and be prepared to do much original research in the archives. Gibbon sighed, soon lost interest in the project, and the *Antiquities of the House of Brunswick* remains a fragment.[4] Gibbon was no more willing than Voltaire—whom he had criticized for precisely this attitude [5]— to turn over "musty monkish writers," especially if they were locked up in an unfamiliar language. He was a philosophic historian, not an antiquary. The point of the story is clear. Gibbon believed that he could write a history of any subject so long as he had competent "guides" to follow.

The philosophic historian embraces *all* history. By definition he is not a specialist; and in Gibbon's case specialization was considered the sign of an inferior mind. The philosophic historian is limited only by his ability to absorb and synthesize, *en philosophe,* the work of others. He must be a man "capable of collecting a numerous assemblage of ideas under one abstract idea." [6] Gibbon valued pure research—as long as others did it. Such work provided the necessary foundations for philosophic history. From such research "a Montesquieu [or a Gibbon?] will extract . . . relationships undreamed of by the vulgar." [7] The Langers of this world have Gibbon's best wishes and sincere gratitude for their antiquarian labors; but his is a higher calling.

Tillemont, on one level, was merely a "guide" for the "historian of the Roman empire," and the most trustworthy guide at that. On another level he was an intellectual opponent of genius who must be confronted and overcome.

---

[4] The fragment is printed in *MW*, III, 353-558.

[5] Gibbon's criticisms of Voltaire as a historian are numerous, although he had an enormous regard for him as poet and playwright. In addition to the numerous witty digs at Voltaire in the notes of the *Decline and Fall* (LI, 446, n. 65; LXIV, 9, n. 26; LXVII, 146, n. 15, etc.) he wrote in his journal, on August 28, 1762 (*Jour. A.,* pp. 129-130), the following: "I finished the *Siècle* of *Lewis XIV.* I believe that Voltaire had for this work an advantage he has seldom enjoyed. When he treats of a distant period, he is not a man to turn over musty monkish writers to instruct himself. He follows some compilation, varnishes it over with the magic of his style, and produces a most agreeable, superficial, inaccurate [*sic*] performance."

[6] *Essai,* XLVI, 59.   [7] *Essai,* LIII, 68.

The two men could not have been more different. Gibbon, the intellectual voluptuary, abhorred all that the pious Jansenist was and represented. Yet he was drawn to Tillemont as he was drawn to another Jansenist, Blaise Pascal. Gibbon's religious views, as set forth in the *Memoirs* or in the fifteenth and sixteenth chapters of the *Decline and Fall*, should not be taken with a strict literalness.

Tillemont was a religious zealot, a recluse, a man who scorned literary art and who delighted in the triumph of Christianity over pagan Rome. His life, religious convictions, and scholarship are inseparable.[8] Tillemont lived the life of a recluse, dividing his time between prayer and scholarship. He was remarkable, even in the Jansenist community, for timidity, piety, and devotion to scholarship.

His biographer and friend, Michel Tronchai, records that his subject fixed on history as his life's work while he was at Port-Royal. He read there the *Annales Ecclesiastici* of Cardinal Baronius, who undertook in many folio volumes the destruction of the Protestant *Centuries of Magdeburg*. Gibbon thought the *Annales* "a copious but partial history" and accused Baronius of being "more inclined to seek the cause of great events in heaven than on

[8] There is much biographical information on Tillemont available in printed sources. The starting point in Michel Tronchai's *Vie de Lenain de Tillemont, avec des réflexions sur divers sujets de morale, et quelques lettres de piété* (Cologne, 1711). This reverent biography is the best introduction to the character of the historian, by a man who knew him personally. The *Réflexions* and the *Lettres de piété* were collected by Tronchai from Tillemont's papers, and are very useful. Additional information must be collected from the memoirs of Tillemont's contemporaries and from the sources for the history of Jansenism. Among the former, the *Mémoires de Pierre Thomas, Sieur du Fossé* (4 vols., Rouen, 1876) is especially valuable for Tillemont's middle years, when the two men were living together in Paris. M. Fontaine, *Mémoires pour servir à l'histoire de Port-Royal* (2 vols., Utrecht, 1736) is also valuable. Jérôme Bésoigne, *Histoire de l'abbaye de Port-Royal* (6 vols., Cologne, 1752), is a mine of information, especially volume five, which contains biographical sketches of all the major Jansenists. Of modern works the outstanding book is Bruno Neveu, *Un historien à l'école de Port-Royal: Sébastien LeNain de Tillemont, 1637-1698* (The Hague, 1966), which presents much new information. For Tillemont's religious attitudes see Henri Bremond, *Histoire littéraire du sentiment religieux en France, depuis la fin des guerres de religion jusqu'à nos jours* (4 vols., Paris, 1920). Volume four of this brilliant work ("La conquête mystique") deals with Jansenism. G. Bardy, "Tillemont," Vacant, Mangenot, *Dictionnaire de théologie Catholique*, 15, part 1 (1946), 1029-33, and Martin R. P. McGuire, "Louis-Sebastien LeNain de Tillemont," *Catholic Historical Review*, 52 (July 1966), 186-200, are brief sketches.

earth." Tillemont thought these very characteristics essential to any historical work and the greatest virtue of Baronius' huge compilation. He read the twelve volumes of the *Annales* in a frenzy of religious and scholarly zeal. So inspired was he by ecclesiastical history that he bombarded his tutor, Pierre Nicole, with a "thousand questions." [9] Nicole, who was himself an erudite man, later told Tronchai "qu'il ne voyoit point alors approcher Mr. De Tillemont, sans trembler, dans la crainte de n'avoir pas de quoi de satisfaire sur la champ."[10] Tillemont determined to become a historian. He started collecting materials and making precise and copious notes on all he could find "concerning the history of the Apostles and apostolic men." He planned to arrange these materials "under various heads, following, in general, the methods used by Usserius in his Sacred Annals, which had pleased him a great deal, and on which he based the plan of his own work." [11]

Tillemont found his vocation early, but it would be years of wavering in the face of distractions before he found a station in life suitable to his temperament. He rejected in turn the life of the seminary, the monastery, and the priesthood. His signal fear was over the state of his immortal soul. He agonized over making a decision, unable to find a station that satisfied his numerous scruples. Finally he became a recluse, and remained in solitude and seclusion for the last eighteen years of his life.

His horror of the world was intense. M. Neveu, his most recent biographer, says that he has found only a single reference to contemporary affairs in Tillemont's surviving letters.[12] His friend, Pierre Thomas, Sieur du Fossé, has recorded a revealing episode from Tillemont's life. The two men were living in Paris (August, 1660) when Marie-Thérèse of Austria—who had just married the king of France—made a magnificent entry into the city. Du Fossé went to see the spectacle, but "M. de Tillemont was not at all

---

[9] Tronchai, *Vie de Tillemont*, p. 3. Hereafter cited as Tronchai.

[10] Tronchai, p. 4. M. de Saci told a similar story of his first interview with Pascal.

[11] James Ussher (1581-1656), Archbishop of Armagh and a noted student of patristics. The work referred to is *Annales veteris et novi testamenti* published at London between 1650 and 1654. See his article in *The Dictionary of National Biography*. Tronchai, p. 4.

[12] Quoted by Neveu, p. 122. Neveu has seemingly found and examined every piece of Tillemont's writings that has survived.

tempted to see this magnificent procession." Even had he thought of going, du Fossé adds, "he would not allow himself such pleasure."[13]

Once Tillemont had escaped from the world and buried himself in seclusion, at his family estate near Paris, he followed a regimen hardly distinguishable from that of a monastery. He discouraged visitors (Tronchai estimates that he received no more than three or four a year)[14] and lived in a single bare room which contained a narrow bed, a desk, and a prie-dieu.[15]

Tillemont's histories are a faithful reflection of his life. Piety, scrupulousness, zeal, singlemindedness, and an abhorrence of worldly things characterize his twenty-two folio volumes of ancient history. The style of his life is everywhere evident in his work, not least of all in his prose. Gibbon believed that "style is the image of character" and Tillemont's style is dry, artless, repetitive, and dull. His vocabulary is small, his sentences devoid of variation. He was a contemporary of the most magnificent period of French literature, yet nowhere in Tillemont's pages is there the slightest suggestion that he was aware of the possibilities of the language. He shared with all the Jansenists—with the obvious exception of Pascal and Racine—a horror of style in life as in writing. "The humble Tillemont," writes a perceptive critic, "is the complete antithesis of the man of letters. One never suspects him of rhetorical devices, or even of eloquence." [16]

This inordinate fear of language was but one of many such fears, the sum of which were a considerable part of the personality of the historian. Anything tainted with worldliness acted as an abrasive on his timid and scrupulous character. The high quality of his historical work, for example, was a threat to his Christian humility. Tillemont feared that he loved scholarship too much. In a series of moving and revealing *Réflexions sur divers sujets de*

---

[13] *Mémoires de Pierre Thomas, Sieur du Fossé*, II, 51. Hereafter cited as du Fossé.

[14] Tronchai, p. 111.

[15] Jérôme Bésoigne, one of the first historians of Jansenism, visited Tillemont's house in 1720. The historian's rooms had been preserved just as he left them. See Bésoigne's description in *Histoire de l'abbaye de Port-Royal*, V, 96.

[16] Bremond, *Histoire littéraire du sentiment religieux*, IV, 259.

morale he explored the relationship between the historian and the saint. On a more superficial level he humbled his pride by refusing to read the reviews (all of which were favorable) of his work.[17]

The *Réflexions,* never intended for publication, are Tillemont's confessional. They cannot be dated with precision, nor is it possible even to connect them with specific events in his life. Nevertheless they are a remarkably candid record of a disturbed soul, seeking to reconcile temperament and character with what Lucien Goldmann calls "radical" Jansenism.[18] In the course of the *Réflexions* Tillemont developed a number of rationalizations for his scholarly work. Some of these exercises in self-justification are pathetic in their naïveté, but all reveal a deeply troubled conscience wrestling with a fundamental issue. He tried, for example, to make historical composition a form of religious devotion:

> It cannot be doubted that the rules laid down by St. Bernard concerning the duties of a saint are to be applied to the writing of history. It is essential that whoever undertakes historical composition be worthy of so great and holy a thing. To be so worthy the historian must have not only erudition but zeal for what he is doing. The authority of his person and the gravity of his style and, above all, the holiness of his life—which should be proportionate to the holiness of his subject—are what give weight to what he says.[19]

[17] Among the contemporary notices of Tillemont's *Histoire des empereurs* are: *Journal des Sçavans* (July 10, 1690), pp. 472-480. Volume seven of the *Mémoires ecclésiastiques* is reviewed in *Mémoires pour l'histoire des sciences & des beaux arts* (Trevoux, 1703), volume for July-September, pp. 1521-32. Bonaventure d'Argonne, *Mélanges d'histoire et de littérature* (3 vols., Rotterdam, 1702), is favorable. Abbé Lenguet du Fresony, *Méthode pour étudier l'histoire avec un catalogue des principaux historiens & sur le choix de meilleurs éditions* (6 vols., Amsterdam, 1737), I, 326, says there "is nothing more exact than the first two volumes of Tillemont's ecclesiastical history" and uses Tillemont as the outstanding example of accurate historical composition.

[18] Lucien Goldmann, *Le dieu caché* (Paris, 1959), distinguishes two kinds of Jansenism. "Liberal" Jansenism still saw hope in the world and believed in reform and change. Goldmann identifies this view with Arnauld. "Radical" Jansenism is a complete rejection of the world, accompanied by physical retreat from society and the company of men. St.-Cyran and Pascal are the great exponents of this view. For the argument see *Le dieu caché,* pp. 202-203, 188-191, 128-129, and 166ff.

[19] Tillemont, who was himself a priest, believed that only those in holy orders were qualified to write ecclesiastical history. Also see Neveu, p. 138. Tillemont, *Réflexions,* p. 114.

This comes to little more than a favorite notion of almost all the ecclesiastical historians of the later seventeenth century, especially the Maurist scholars. The best ecclesiastical history of the age—perhaps even of all time—was written by men in holy orders. The Benedictines especially were fond of repeating that the priestly and the scholarly life could not be separated. For Tillemont as for his contemporaries, the pen was consecrated as much as the person.

This particular argument, which Tillemont reiterated a couple of times in the *Réflexions*, he apparently found unconvincing. He tried another tack. History was, for him, the palpable proof of God's providence, and the historian's task was to point out the working of this marvelous providence and thus induce piety in his readers. Errors in matters of fact are human, admissible, indeed anticipated. Errors in matters of morality are mortal: they mean loss of soul. By elaborating on these two themes Tillemont hoped to justify his work—by setting himself up as the inculcator of moral edification. Tillemont wrote his brother, Pierre, a Trappist monk: "What you tell me about the edifying qualities of the Mémoires [his history of the early church] pleases me more than all that any of the others could say. If the Mémoires do not serve to heal souls it would be best they had never appeared in print." [20] He tenaciously pursued the argument in an attempt to reconcile seclusion from the world and scholarship. The simple facts of ancient history were, he believed, charged with religious significance; and they were charged with religious significance because they concerned the triumph of Christianity. Even the profane history of the Roman empire—and Tillemont had to convince himself that he was not jeopardizing his soul by studying the subject with such intensity—had meaning for a Christian. God had chosen to make the empire the stage for the unfolding of His providence. Thus the historical record, stripped of rhetoric and laid bare by a man of holiness, would inculcate piety and edification in the mind of the reader.

So long as Tillemont was able to see himself as a teacher of morality he was able to excuse his excessive, even obsessive, de-

[20] On Tillemont's brother, see Neveu, pp. 35-36. Quoted in Tronchai, p. 53.

votion to scholarship. As one follows Tillemont's attempts to justify his work one sees the careful and clever unfolding of an argument that will account both for his startling capacity for work, his astounding accuracy, and the dry, annalistic nature of his histories. This is not to say that Tillemont cynically sought such an apologia, but he was aware of the difficulties his abilities presented to a "radical" Jansenist. The historian of Christianity, for Tillemont, becomes a man devoted to accuracy in detail and to the plain presentation of his researches. The two become one for Tillemont, and they also become a general act of piety. The historian must be accurate, for the materials under consideration have Christian significance; but the goal of all historical composition is "to inspire humility and devotion." [21] And "humility and devotion" will be generated in the reader by the brute facts of history. Tillemont's histories are, in the Christian sense of the word, inspired. Prayer was his "resource in all things." [22] When he encountered a difficulty in chronology or a corrupt document, he dropped from his desk to his knees to implore God's assistance: "It was thus in all that he wrote. When he encountered some considerable difficulty on an important point, he referred the matter to God for a period of several days, and did not cease praying for assistance until he had received clarification." [23] Tillemont himself considered his work inspired. Whatever value his histories might have he ascribed to God. He wrote to an admirer: "You know that if there is anything of value in my work it does not come from me, but from the Father of all light, from Whom flows all that is good. The errors which I do not doubt can be found in my work, belong solely to me. They result from my essence (fond). I know what I am capable of doing in the way of achieving exactitude; but I make no claims of infallibility." [24]

Although he worked alone, there is a corporate aspect to Tillemont's work.[25] His reliance on the advice of others, especially the

---

[21] Tillemont, *Réflexions*, pp. 114-115. [22] Tronchai, p. 33.
[23] Tronchai, p. 59. [24] Quoted in Tronchai, p. 59.
[25] Until Neveu explored the complicated relationships of the Jansenists after their expulsion from Port-Royal, and especially Tillemont's relationship with the scattered community, this aspect of his work was unknown. See Neveu, especially pp. 192, 197.

scattered Jansenist community, was excessive. Part of the explanation is his timidity, which constantly drove him to seek advice and occasionally a necessary "push" from friends. Part of the explanation is his childlike temperament, which reduced him to a pathetic reliance on his family and friends for almost every decision.[26] If his personality drew him to consult friends and family on every important point, it also gave to his historical work the imprimatur of the Jansenists.

All issues involving doctrine or theological niceties were circulated among the *messieurs* and their suggestions were gratefully taken by the historian. Tillemont's histories thus became the official views of the Jansenists on early Christianity. The community took great pride in their "official" historian and it is certain that this confessional approval helped the scrupulous Tillemont to write his books without being paralyzed by fears over his salvation.

As a historian—with the help of God and the Jansenist community—Tillemont spoke as more than a mere scholar. He was the conduit by which the divine truths of ecclesiastical history were conveyed from the sources to the public; he was the vehicle of edification. The errors in Tillemont's work are remarkably few. He is still consulted with profit on the history of the early church and on patristics. And it is his "Jansenist fanaticism" that made possible, indeed demanded, such accuracy. History was piety teaching by example, and the historian was merely a man who presented the record of the past in pure form. He believed it a crime against man and God to allow the history of the church to remain dubious or corrupt. Holiness cannot be compromised, and piety and truth are one and the same thing. "The truth," he writes "is not contradictory; and piety cannot contradict the truth since piety must be based on truth." [27]

This new alliance between piety and truth, this Jansenist decision to fight religious error and confessional deviation not by polemic but by "brute facts," is manifest in Tillemont's work. The

[26] At one point Neveu, p. 24, speaks of Tillemont's dependence as that of a five-year-old child.

[27] Tillemont, *Mémoires pour servir à l'histoire ecclésiastiques des six premiers siècles, justifiez par les citations des auteurs originaux* (16 vols., Paris 1701-14), I, ix. Hereafter cited as *Mémoires ecclésiastiques*.

entire apparatus of criticism and scholarship was not only meaningless but positively sinful unless it was used as a means of arriving at the eternal truths of Christianity, as understood by the
Jansenists. In his usual fastidious fashion Tillemont set down a
series of rules for historical composition. Strict adherence to these
rules would insure the achievement of his goals. The slightest deviation from these rules would reduce the historian to a mere scrib-
bler, indistinguishable from infidel, pagan, or heretical practi-
tioners. Not only must the historian of holy things be beyond
reproach in his own life: he must have before him a vision of piety.
This will save him from debasing his subject with worldly affec-
tations. First, the historian must cleanse his style of "any informality that may offend, and any politeness that gives the impression
of affectation." "The style of the work should be grave, but not
austere; it should please while making its point. . . . It should never
appear that the author has sought to have his style and his mind
esteemed by his readers, but that he has tried to esteem, to honor,
to love, and to embrace the holy examples that he reports." [28]

This "grave, but not austere" style is to be the vehicle for carrying the considerable weight of historical details. Should any
reader complain of so much detail, let him remember that "there
is nothing useless concerning the saints" for "if we can know in
the most minute detail what the Apostles have said and done, we
will find salutary instruction in all these things." [29] Although he
does not say it explicitly, only the highest standards of criticism
will be used in order to purify the historical record of early
Christianity. The humble Tillemont was troubled that his severe
standards forced him to destroy a favorite legend that did not pass
critical muster. He apologized for his critical audacity: "it will be
necessary occasionally to point out faults even in the greatest
saints." But these faults will be reported "with the greatest possible
modesty" since one must respect "those who will one day be our
judges." [30]

The pious men of Tillemont's day who brought to history precision, clarity, and accuracy, also did much of the spadework for

---

[28] Tillemont, *Réflexions*, p. 115.   [29] *Mémoires ecclésiastiques*, I, iv.
[30] *Mémoires ecclésiastiques*, I, xvii.

the attack on Christianity to be launched by the Enlightenment. Their labors cleared the ground of ecclesiastical history of the rubbish of centuries. The example was not lost on the enlighteners. The step from the rejection of some legends to the rejection of all legends was very short. Tillemont carefully—and perhaps sadly— pruned from the history of the primitive church some of the most colorful, but spurious, legends. With a sigh (Gibbon imagines) he rejected the Acts of Artemius, "a veteran and a martyr who attests as an eye-witness the vision of Constantine." [31] It is not unusual for the sincere efforts of one generation to provide the next with the preconditions for destroying an old ideology. In the case of Tillemont the case is very clear: it is Edward Gibbon who inherits these labors.

The irony, and it is one of the rare ironies in historiography, is made more poignant when one realizes that Tillemont deliberately wrote his histories—indeed consecrated his life—in the hope that some future historian, with unimpeachable religious credentials, would use these accurate materials as the foundation for a great history of the church. Tillemont himself made this clear in those few autobiographical moments he allowed himself. He knew he was diligent, accurate, thorough, and without imagination. He knew he wrote clumsily, was incapable of constructing a narrative history, and was a slave to chronology. He thought of himself as an annalist, since his central organizing principle was strict chronology. His sole ambition was to be accurate and pious: he aimed no higher. Narrative history was beyond his powers: "It seems to the author that a style without elevation and without ornament, such as is found here, belongs more to annals than to history. . . . The author never entertained the thought of writing a history, and he would like it known that he always regarded the writing of a standard history as not only very difficult in itself, but also far beyond his talents and capacities." [32]

[31] XX, 323-324, n. 50.

[32] Tillemont, *Histoire des empereurs, et des autres princes qui ont régné durant les six premiers siècles de l'eglise, de leurs guerres contra les juifs, des écrivains profanes, & des personnes les plus illustres de leur temps. Justifiée par les citations des auteurs originaux* (6 vols., 1st. rev. ed., Venice, 1732-39), I, xi-xii. Hereafter cited as *Histoire des empereurs*.

Tillemont's histories were a labor of love, of piety, and of tormented pride struggling with Jansenist radicalism. But what of his methods? One might expect such an impressive piece of scholarship to be the product of sophisticated techniques. In fact this is not the case. Tillemont occasionally borrowed the tools developed by the Maurists, but he was no innovator and he left his successors no techniques for historical analysis which had not been known since the Renaissance.

Tillemont's achievement is the triumph of individual genius over methodology. For him the document was everything. To understand the document was to understand the past. He considered the proper dating of a document to be the essence of criticism. To know when a document was written would immediately eliminate any false evidence and would give Tillemont all that he needed to know. He divided documents into two categories: true and false. True documents were, as might be expected, those contemporary to the events they describe and from the hand of a reliable witness. He pays very little attention to nonliterary evidence, although he was familiar with numismatics and epigraphy.[33] The most reliable witnesses were those closest to the source of all truth, God. Hence documents from the hand of a saint were inspired: they are unimpeachable sources. From this belief a hierarchy of historical truth emerges. The scriptures are the highest truth, perhaps subject to interpretation, but otherwise beyond reproach. The church fathers—especially Saint Augustine, the "first" Jansenist—and the other saints are a close second. On a more profane level, a work like Eusebius' *History of the Church* he considered more reliable than the pagan histories of Ammianus Marcellinus.

It is the sources of ancient history that concern Tillemont, and he was extraordinarily familiar with them. Although he has no method worthy of the name, he often characterizes a document with great shrewdness. He would have been incapable of giving the reasons for selecting one version over another, but he was seldom wrong in his choice. Yet for all his shrewdness, he was also

---

[33] Tillemont makes reference to Spon, Seguis, Spanheim, and Gruter, to name only the most famous numismatists and epigraphers of his day.

naïve. His reverence for tradition, a characteristic common to many Jansenists,[34] often prevented him from putting the embarrassing question to a document. Tillemont concentrated on the document before him. If he saw no reason to question the author, and if he saw no contradiction implied in accepting the document as true, then he rested his case. He cross-examined only the witnesses to events, never the events themselves. It never occurred to Tillemont, as it occurred to his contemporary Pierre Bayle, to look beyond the testimony of witnesses to the actual events. The growing intensity of historical pyrrhonism, which was exactly contemporary with Tillemont's work, did not touch him.

Once he had decided on the authenticity of a document, he then fixed it in the chronological scheme. He seldom went beyond a superficial impression of the comparative value of his sources. All true documents—except those which were inspired—were given equal weight. This leveling tendency has the effect of reducing historical events to a dull homogeneity. But this is how Tillemont viewed the past. His own formula for determining what is true in history is worth quoting:

> As to the question "what are the rules by which one discovers the true from the false when using documents from an unknown hand" the author replies: Those who have read the history of the martyrdom of St. Polycarpe, or those of Leon in Eusebius, and other accounts which are generally accepted as incontestable, will soon acquire, from such reading, an inclination (*goût*) for determining what has the authentic flavor of antiquity and truth, and what is fable and popular tradition. . . . The knowledge of history, a feel for style, and some discipline—these are the things that allow one to judge what could and what could not have been written at a given time.[35]

Tillemont's methods of criticism share with Jansenism generally a tough literal-mindedness.

[34] Neveu, p. 132, argues (in another context): "Consequently, one of the keys to Tillemont's character, of his attitude toward the problems of the Christian life, and thus—a thing of the utmost importance for understanding his work—toward history, is this touch of traditionalism, archaism, which Father Ceyssens has pointed out in the thought and the sensibility of the Jansenists." Exactly the same reservations apply to his stature as a critic.

[35] *Mémoires ecclésiastiques*, I, xiv-xv.

Despite the sureness of his instincts, Tillemont was ahistorical in his approach to the past. Here again he is very close to the Jansenist community. He saw meaning in history, that is, God's providence; and he imposed upon his materials a pattern, strict chronology. But he had no interest in the past for its own sake. The eternal truths of Christianity, as seen by the Jansenists, were everywhere and at all times the same. Tillemont lived most of his life in the company of the early Christians, yet he saw them either as timeless symbols of the Christian life, or forerunners of Jansenism. He applied the values of Jansenism to antiquity, and judged it accordingly. The primitive church is seen by Tillemont as but an earlier example of the persecuted Jansenists. The Romans become the Jesuits and the virtuous Christians the Jansenists. God mediates the struggle and finally gives the victory to Jansenism.

Tillemont's myopia about Roman civilization arises directly from his religious views. The Romans were pagans, and paganism was anathema. His Christian charity did not extend to paganism. He delighted in the horrible deaths of the fourth-century emperors who had persecuted Christianity: they provided wonderful proof of a vengeful God.[36] He was deeply disturbed that God had permitted the pagan emperors Marcus Aurelius and Trajan to escape an excruciating death: "Suffer me, O Lord, to ask if You always destroyed those who did not understand the work of Your hands . . . ? You have visibly destroyed Nero, Domitian, and others. But did you destroy Trajan and Marcus in the same way? They certainly deserved destruction, for they failed to apprehend the miracles of Your grace when they had these miracles before their eyes. In addition, they persecuted Your servants. Yet, they died in their beds, honored, revered, loved, and esteemed by all men." [37] He despised pagan Rome, and "he never dismisses a virtuous emperor without pronouncing his damnation." [38] Conversely, he lavished praise on men to the degree that they complement his

[36] Du Fossé picked exactly these episodes from Tillemont's work to celebrate. Thus does he (IV, 259) put it: "He discovered the secret, in dealing with the profane history of the emperors, of intensifying their sins by applying the vivid lights of Christianity to their actions."

[37] Tillemont, *Réflexions*, pp. 251-252.

[38] XV, 28, n. 72.

own views. St. Augustine's ravings against the Donatists are accepted as unimpeachable truth; Orosius' continuation of Augustine's work is highly praised. Tillemont even applauds Orosius'
account of a massacre of the Gothic king Radagaisus and his followers by Christian treachery. The uneven work of Lactantius
is valued more than the masterpieces of Tacitus.

These are serious shortcomings in a historian, and they place
Tillemont in a long, if not honored, tradition of confessional historians. His is the official Jansenist history of early Christianity,
and as such it expresses the most passionate tenets of that persecuted sect. But far more serious than these confessional blind spots
is Tillemont's celebration of the loss of evidence uncongenial to
his views. For the period from the reign of Carus to Diocletian's retirement there is no reliable contemporary account.[39] Instead of
lamenting this gap, Tillemont, *incredible dictu*, praises God for
His wisdom in allowing all the contemporary materials to perish:
"God, who opposes the proud, has thus permitted the loss of these
works in order to confound the vanity of this insolent usurper
(the emperor Diocletian) of His divine name: the usurper of the
adoration which is due only to God Himself." [40] It is but another
manifestation of God's wonderful providence that He "has almost
erased the memory of this adversary of the Church; an adversary
who wanted to abolish His Holy Scriptures." [41]

There is in all Tillemont's work a tinge of naïveté which separates him from the more distasteful religous zealots of the seventeenth century. The level of violence, of hatred, of intolerance in
Tillemont is, if not lower than that of many contemporaries, at
least less vicious. This is not something that easily lends itself to
demonstration, but there is the testimony of at least two men who
admired Tillemont and were not friends to religious zeal or enthusiasm: Pierre Bayle and Edward Gibbon. Bayle was capable of
considerable sharpness in dealing with religious fanaticism, yet
when he discusses Tillemont's work he is quite mild: "Never has
such a complete collection of facts been seen, nor a work so amply

[39] Even the text of the Byzantine epitomizer, Zosimus, has been lost for this
crucial period.
[40] *Histoire des empereurs*, IV, 62.   [41] *Histoire des empereurs*, IV, 62.

provided with citations . . ." [42] is Bayle's cool but accurate description. He goes on to criticize the lame style of the work, and adds: "it would be well to get rid of many of the devout reflections which are scattered throughout the work, and which would be best saved for sermons or books of piety." [43] This is fair enough, and harmless enough: especially when one contrasts it with what Bayle said about Louis Maimbourg or Florimond de Remond.[44] Gibbon, too, is unusually generous to Tillemont. At one point he even says that Tillemont's "bigotry" [45] "is overbalanced by the merits of erudition, diligence, veracity, and scrupulous minuteness." [46]

However useful Tillemont's histories are, they are also quite dull:

[I do not know if it is necessary to report regarding the defeat of Achilleus] what can be read in the Greek and Latin editions of Eusebius. He says that the cities of Coptos and Busiris, in the Thebaid, having revolted against the Romans, were destroyed and razed almost to their foundations. The Greek text attributes this action to Diocletian and Hercules [Maximian], which account also appears in Theophanes: [however the Panegyrists do not say that Hercules was even in Egypt]. . . . Father Petau fixes the ruin of Coptos and Busiris in A.D. 298. Zonoras places it before the revolt of Achilleus, and reports that only Diocletian participated in the action.[47]

[42] Pierre Bayle, *Continuation des pensées diverses, Oeuvres diverses* (4 vols., Rotterdam, 1721), III, 8.

[43] Bayle, *Continuation des pensées diverses*, III, 9.

[44] Louis Maimbourg, a Jesuit historian of Calvinism in the seventeenth century, was the target—and deservedly so—of Bayle's extended and brilliant attack on confessional historiography. Bayle's *Critique générale de l'histoire du Calvinisme de M. Maimbourg* appeared in 1682. Remond, the sixteenth-century author of a history of heresy, is roughly handled by Bayle in his article in the *Dictionnaire historique et critique*.

[45] This is Gibbon's word. It is often used by him when he means no more than intolerance or radical deviation from his own ideas. For Gibbon a "bigot" need never act on his conviction, and he even at one point accuses Voltaire of bigotry because he favored a Moslem account over a Christian account. It is one of the few words Gibbon uses primarily in an emotive sense, and without his usual precision.

[46] XLVII, 141, n. 81.

[47] Diocletian recovered Egypt from the usurper Achilleus in A.D. 296. *Histoire des empereurs*, IV, 34-35.

The historian, in his role as creator—and even Tillemont was a creator—often writes, in the guise of some historical character, his own biography. The words Tillemont uses to describe Aper, the friend of St. Paulinus, admirably fit the author himself: "in applying himself to the study of Holy Letters for which nothing is more important than solitude, he formed within himself, so to speak, the spirit of Jesus Christ, which gave him strength for all his days. . . . He thus lived in peace and quiet, beyond the cares and the storms of his century, seeing himself in the Church as in a safe harbor in which he could constantly apply himself to meditation and to the practice of holy things." [48]

That Gibbon should have been drawn to Tillemont's work is not surprising. The very nature of that work, and Gibbon's own habits of composition, made the two men ideally suited to their needs. Gibbon had all the art, the powers of synthesis, a superb constructive vision of Roman civilization, and a literary mission to fulfill, which Tillemont lacked. He found in Tillemont the ideal "guide." With the folios of Tillemont Gibbon patiently worked his way through the first centuries of the Roman empire. At first his steps were tentative, but once he was convinced of the genius and reliability of his guide he used Tillemont as a handbook for Roman history. In the pages of the Jansenist he could follow the complex history of Rome in chronological order; from his notes he could find instantly the source of a quotation; from the longer technical notes he could study the state of scholarship on almost any given problem. In a word, Tillemont's histories were seemingly tailormade for a historian of Gibbon's synthetic interests and work habits.

As usual, Gibbon has left the most eloquent statement of his reliance on Tillemont: "I applied the collections of Tillemont, whose inimitable accuracy almost assumes the character of genius, to fix and arrange within my reach the loose and scattered atoms of historical information." [49] The best indication of Gibbon's debt to Tillemont is the fact, noticed by a contemporary critic, that Gibbon's step falters at precisely the point—around the middle of

[48] Quoted in Neveu, p. 76.
[49] *Memoirs*, p. 147.

the sixth century—when Tillemont's work breaks off.[50] At almost every point Gibbon's interpretations diverge radically from those of his guide, but he doggedly followed the lead of his "sure-footed mule" over the rough terrain of the first six centuries of the empire. He was content to mine the riches of Tillemont's volumes and weave them into the narrative of the *Decline and Fall:* in the notes he snapped at the Jansenist's heels for religious enthusiasm.

These attacks against "Jansenist fanaticism" are usually mild, frequently witty, and always entertaining. Gibbon describes the *Mémoires ecclésiastiques* as "an immense repertory of truth and fable, of almost all that the Fathers have preserved, or invented, or believed." [51] "Tillemont has" Gibbon writes "raked together all the dirt of the fathers; an useful scavenger!" [52] Or: "the life of St. Augustin [*sic*], by Tillemont, fills a quarto volume . . . of more than one thousand pages; and the diligence of that learned Jansenist was excited on this occasion by factious and devout zeal for the founder of his sect." [53] He even finds Tillemont's naïveté amusing. When he "swallows like a child" the "scandalous calumnies of Augustin, Pope Leo, &c." [54] Gibbon only smiles. It is only when the Jansenist ventures into the sacred grove of pagan antiquity and condemns Roman civilization because it fails to measure up to the Jansenist ideal, that Gibbon becomes more heated. He lashes out at his guide with the authority and diction only he could command: "The condemnation of the wisest and most virtuous of the Pagans, on account of their ignorance or disbelief of the divine truth, seems to offend the reason and the humanity of the present age." [55] And to all those who (like Tillemont) "still delight in recording the wonderful deaths of the persecutors," Gibbon recommends "to their perusal an admirable passage of

[50] See the anonymous and excellent review of the first volumes of the *Decline and Fall* in *Goettingische gelehrte Anzeigen*, band 3 (December 25, 1788), pp. 2051-52. This same charge is later repeated by J. B. Bury in his introduction to his edition of Gibbon's history. Gibbon, who refused to learn German, did not read these reviews, which were clearly the most intelligent of the day.

[51] Gibbon, *A Vindication of Some Passages in the XVth and XVIth Chapters of the History of the Decline and Fall of the Roman Empire* (1779), *MW*, IV, 591. Hereafter cited as *Vindication.*

[52] XXXVII, 161, n. 52.   [53] XXXIII, 430, n. 29.   [54] XXVII, 162, n. 57.
[55] XV, 28.

Grotius concerning the last illness of Philip II of Spain." [56] Gibbon's spiritual home was pagan Rome. He had little sympathy with things alien to his values. The invidious comparison between classical culture and Christianity is one of the minor themes in the *Decline and Fall*: "If it be possible to measure the interval between the philosophic writings of Cicero and the sacred legend of Theodoret, between the character of Cato and that of Simeon, we may appreciate the memorable revolution which was accomplished in the Roman empire within a period of five hundred years." [57]

Gibbon found not only Tillemont's general views on paganism and Rome anathema, but also his individual judgments on individual historians. Gibbon had no hierarchical conception of historical truth. Proximity to God had nothing to do with historical reliability. Gibbon found Orosius a "piously inhuman" character, and he adds: "how many interesting facts might Orosius have inserted in the vacant space which is devoted to pious nonsense!" [58] Lactantius, another Jansenist favorite, Gibbon dismissed as unreliable: he may "*sometimes* be admitted as an evidence of public facts, though very seldom of private anecdotes." [59] Tillemont described Constantine the Great as a man almost worthy of sainthood. Gibbon paints the first Christian emperor as a vulgar, power-mad hypocrite who pursued his path to domination of the Roman world through blood, and who must assume a large share of the blame for Rome's fall.

A study of Gibbon's citations of Tillemont reveals an obvious pattern. For the first six centuries of the empire Gibbon relies almost exclusively on Tillemont for fixing the dates of documents and events. A few examples will suffice. Maximin's elevation to Caesar and then to Augustus has "given occasion to a great deal of learned wrangling": "I have followed M. de Tillemont . . . who has weighed the several reasons and difficulties with his scrupulous accuracy." [60] "The difficulties as well as mistakes" concerning Diocletian's retirement have been cleared up by Tillemont.[61] And the problem of whether it took "a few years" or "a few months"

[56] XIV, 411, n. 44.   [57] XXXVII, 81.   [58] XXX, 280, n. 77.
[59] XIII, 386, n. 114.   [60] XIII, 352, n. 7.   [61] XIII, 387, n. 116.

to complete the walls of Constantinople, is solved by Tillemont.[62] Whenever Gibbon encountered some difficulty about what happened or when it happened, he did not resort to prayer, he consulted Tillemont; and he was seldom disappointed. On at least one occasion he even preferred Tillemont's account to that of the original source. The work in question is the *Historia Augusta,* that perpetual headache for all students of the late empire. Gibbon found the original impossible, and turned to Tillemont: "I read several chapters of M. de Tillemont's *Histoire des Empereurs* in relation to Longinus's Patrons Odoenathus and Zenobia. . . . It is much better to read this part of the Augustan history in so learned and exact a compilation than in the originals, who have neither method, accuracy, eloquence, or chronology. I think them below the worst monkish Chroniclers we have extant." [63] But the area in which Gibbon most needed guidance was church history. Again, Tillemont was the ideal guide.

None of Gibbon's numerous contemporary critics was able to catch him out in an error of fact; and no group of critics were more anxious to excoriate "the historian of the Roman empire." [64] And the reason for the high degree of accuracy is that Gibbon slavishly followed Tillemont. The complex history of Arianism was written with constant reference to the "indefatigable Tillemont." He used Tillemont to straighten out the confused chronology of the period and to disentangle the acts of the several councils of the church (Chalcedon, Ephesus, Constantinople), and to mediate between the surviving accounts of these councils (those of Evagrius and Liberatus).[65] "Tillemont, whom I follow and abridge" was a reliable guide to the eighteen different creeds which found adherents after the council of Nicaea.[66] And, finally, Tillemont was the biographer of the great religious figures of the age. The career of the mercurial Cyril, Bishop of Jerusalem, is extracted mostly from Tillemont, "who treats his memory with

[62] XVII, n. 65.   [63] *Jour. A.,* p. 163.

[64] Chapters XV and XVI occasioned a flood of pamphlets from the outraged divines of the English church. For a study of this pamphlet literature and Gibbon's response to it, see Shelby T. McCloy, *Gibbon's Antagonism to Christianity* (London, 1933), which includes a comprehensive list of the various pamphlets.

[65] XLVII, 132, n. 63.   [66] XXI, 370, n. 63.

tenderness and respect, has thrown his virtues into the text, and
his faults into the notes, in decent obscurity, at the end of the
volume." [67] Gibbon's portrait of the great Athanasius, which he
considered "one of the passages of my history with which I am
the least dissatisfied," [68] rests firmly on the evidence collected by
Tillemont: "the diligence of Tillemont . . . has collected every fact
and examined every difficulty." [69]

Examples of Gibbon's reliance on Tillemont could be multiplied, but there is no need. There is Gibbon's own affidavit that
he owes his accuracy in church history to Tillemont. In 1779 he
published *A Vindication of Some Passages in the XVth and XVIth
Chapters of the History of the Decline and Fall of the Roman
Empire.* Gibbon does not attempt to justify his conclusions about
Christianity, but rather to vindicate himself from the charges of mis-
representation and inaccuracy: "Had he [Davis] confined himself to the ordinary, and indeed obsolete charges of impious principles, I should have acknowledged with readiness and pleasure
that the religion of Mr. Davis appeared different from mine." [70]
But Davis attacked Gibbon's competence as a historian: "The
different misrepresentations, of which he has drawn out the ignominious catalogue, would materially affect my credit as an
historian, my reputation as a scholar and even my honour and
veracity as a gentleman." [71] Gibbon, of course, demolished the
foolish Mr. Davis, and it is important to note that he was proud
to stake his reputation as an accurate historian on the works of
Tillemont, which he regularly followed in ecclesiastical history.[72]

It is not coincidental that two of the men who had a profound
influence on Gibbon were Jansenist zealots. A sizable part of the
Decline and Fall is directly concerned with ecclesiastical history.
Gibbon's view is idiosyncratic, but it is not as hostile as has generally been assumed. However one views Gibbon's attitudes
toward Christianity, his account remains of considerable interest.
He was the first historian to treat both the ecclesiastical and secular
history of Rome together. Tillemont had intended to do this but
had been dissuaded by friends. For the first six centuries of the

[67] XXIII, 482, n. 70.   [68] LVI, 212, n. 101.   [69] XXI, 361, n. 97.
[70] *Vindication*, p. 519.   [71] *Vindication*, p. 520.   [72] *Vindication*, pp. 589-591.

empire, Gibbon's treatment of Christianity rests, almost exclusively, on Tillemont's sixteen volumes, his *Mémoires ecclésiastiques*. It is not Gibbon's want of accuracy that makes his treatment of Christianity so distasteful to devout men. Gibbon would never play fast and loose with the facts. What makes his classic account so Gibbonian is the withering irony with which he treats the subject. And as is well known, Gibbon says he learned to handle the weapon of irony, "even on subjects of Ecclesiastical solemnity,"[73] from Pascal.

It is possible to argue that Gibbon's reliance on Tillemont has nothing to do with Jansenism. Tillemont was a great historian and a superb source for a historian of Gibbon's interests and temperament. With magisterial ease he swept away the pious foundations and assumptions of Tillemont's work, and used him merely as an exceptionally reliable guide. That Tillemont was a Jansenist fanatic is merely coincidental so far as Gibbon is concerned. This would be a perfectly adequate explanation of Gibbon's numerous references to Tillemont and his respect for the work of his predecessor. It would be a perfectly adequate explanation, that is, were it not for the fact that Gibbon was fascinated with Jansenism throughout his life, and that another Jansenist fanatic, Blaise Pascal, was singled out by Gibbon himself as central to his intellectual development.

Pascal was no historian and he is not once directly mentioned or cited in the *Decline and Fall*. Yet Gibbon considered him one of the most important influences on his own mind, and thought the *Lettres provinciales* a book of extraordinary importance: "But I cannot forbear to mention three particular books, since they may have remotely contributed to form the historian of the Roman Empire. 1. From the provincial letters of Pascal which, almost every year I have perused with new pleasure, I learned to manage the weapon of grave and temperate irony even on subjects of Ecclesiastical solemnity."[74] The *Lettres provinciales* is the only book Gibbon "perused with new pleasure" almost every year; and when the supreme ironist in English credits his achievment to the ex-

[73] *Memoirs*, p. 79.
[74] *Memoirs*, p. 79.

ample of Pascal some idea of his importance for "the historian of the Roman empire" is seen.

Students of Gibbon—except for G. M. Young—have not troubled to explain how or why Gibbon became devoted to Pascal. They dutifully quote Gibbon's panegyric on Pascal, cited above, and pass on to other things. Perhaps they take the statement at face value, and readily assume that Gibbon was interested in Pascal only as a master of French prose, especially irony. This assumption creates problems instead of solving them. Gibbon, unlike many moderns, made no distinction between form and content. T. S. Eliot's dictum, for example, that Milton should be read for his "music" would have been incomprehensible to Gibbon. There is not a single example, in any of his writings, that Gibbon appreciated a writer for his artistry while ignoring his ideas. Gibbon was no aesthete, and his discussions of literature never deal only with form. Language, for Gibbon, was a tool of thought; style was the image of a man's mind.

Gibbon was a devoted reader of Pascal and Milton not merely because he appreciated their music. Remember, these two men in particular were far more interested in ideas than in art for its own sake. The aesthetic notions of the nineteenth or twentieth centuries must not be read back into the prosaic eighteenth century. Gibbon reread *Lettres provinciales* practically every year because he enjoyed it, and men seldom enjoy books that outrage their reason or their beliefs.

It would be useful to know precisely when Gibbon first read Pascal. Alas, as with almost all Gibbon's reading, this is impossible. He is seldom precise about when he read a book, and this makes any attempt to sketch his intellectual growth only tentative. Nevertheless approximately when he read the *Lettres provinciales* is known. The earliest mention of Pascal is in his journal entry for October 1, 1762, and there he suggests that Pascal was already a familiar author: "In this attack he [Erasmus] employs every arm both of argument and pleasantry. It may be divided into three parts; in the first, *Nosoponus* the Ciceronian is introduced; and with that exquisite species of humor, of which the *Lettres Provinciales* offers so fine a specimen, ridicules his own party by a bare exposition of those maxims which he himself venerated and practiced." [75] Long before the *Decline and Fall* Gibbon had learned to appreciate "the weapon of grave and temperate irony even on subjects of Ecclesiastical solemnity."

Whatever the initial impact of Pascal, his influence was continuous. This is precisely the problem: why did Gibbon find the Jansenists in general, and Pascal in particular, so fascinating? Gibbon had long been interested in religious problems, and in the *Memoirs* he sketches that slightly ludicrous scene of the young boy, with an oversized head, disputing earnestly on the mysteries of the trinity, or reincarnation, with his kind, loving, and limited Aunt Porten. This fascination lasted a lifetime, and besides the classics, the two species of books best represented in Gibbon's library are travel books and books on religion and theology. He was forever reading tracts and treatises on the most arcane and arid subjects of theology and church history. His careful and detailed histories of Arians, Monophysites, Gnostics, Armenians, and a dozen other Christian splinter groups, are ample proof of his interest. Perhaps no other man outside holy orders, indeed almost outside the church, knew as much of these things as did Gibbon. And what most fascinated him was fanaticism. The pathological side of religion provided an endless source of study for this sceptical rationalist.

Most of Gibbon's interest in fanatical religions and religious experience were confined to the chronological block covered by the *Decline and Fall*. But he also kept abreast of contemporary religious enthusiasm. The notes of his *History* make constant reference to modern fanatical groups, and he was especially interested in the Jansenists. He studied, for example, the series of miracles that followed the promulgation of the Bull Unigenitus, and concluded, "Ce fanatisme des Jansenistes est une de ces maladies Epidemiques de l'Esprit humain qui meritent beaucoup d'attention." [76]

There were, for Gibbon, several species of fanatics. The desert saint, the hermit, the inquisitor, the chiliast, none of these inter-

[75] *Jour. A.*, p. 151.
[76] *Jour. B.*, p. 30 (September 13, 1763).

ested him very much. Scorn and ridicule are Gibbon's usual weapons against such fanatics. Mysticism did not interest him, and he refused to credit visions. Yet those religious fanatics who remained rational, like Athanasius, or Augustine, or Bernard, or Pascal, were much admired by Gibbon. Whatever the temperamental or intellectual differences between these men, they all held in common a pessimistic view of human nature and human history. Pascal is full of good fun and broad humor, but *Lettres provinciales* and the *Pensées* are not light, entertaining reading. It is curious that Gibbon should have experienced new delight, almost every year, in the somber, pessimistic, and passionate pages of *Lettres Provinciales*.

In one of those frequent autobiographical digressions of the *Decline and Fall* Gibbon transcribes "an authentic memorial which was found in the closet of the deceased caliph [Abdalrahman]" in a discussion of human happiness: "I have now reigned above fifty years in victory or peace; beloved by my subjects, dreaded by my enemies, and respected by my allies. Riches and honours, power and pleasure, have waited on my call, nor does any earthly blessing appear to have been wanting to my felicity. In this situation I have diligently numbered the days of pure and genuine happiness which have fallen to my lot: they amount to FOURTEEN: —O man! place not thy confidence in this present world!" [77] To this passage Gibbon adds a long note:

This confession, the complaints of Solomon of the vanity of this world (read Prior's verbose but eloquent poem), and the happy ten days of the emperor Seghed (Rambler, No. 204, 205), will be triumphantly quoted by the detractors of human life. Their expectations are commonly immoderate, their estimates are seldom impartial. If I may speak of myself (the only person of whom I can speak with certainty), *my* happy hours have far exceeded, and far exceed, the scanty numbers of the Caliph of Spain; and I shall not scruple to add that many of them are due to the pleasing labour of the present composition.[78]

[77] LII, 26.   [78] LII, 26, n. 60.

These are certainly not the sentiments of the Jansenist community, let alone Pascal, who doubtless would have considered the caliph's happy days an excessive number.

On the basis of evidence like this, Gibbon should have been the least likely reader of Pascal and actively hostile to rigorist views of life. In fact this is not the case. Gibbon never tried to live like Pascal or Tillemont; he was too fond of creature comforts. Yet the quality of his devotion to writing and scholarship is not different from Tillemont's monastic regimen. Gibbon seldom put in an eighteen-hour day, but ten or twelve hours of uninterrupted work was not unusual for him. His work came first, and his delight in his own genius and fame was never tempered by the religious scruples of the Jansenists. He sacrificed everything for the *Decline and Fall,* and if his ambitions and his lifestyle were radically different from the Jansenist intellectuals, he could nevertheless appreciate the discipline and devotion that informed their lives. It was far easier for Gibbon to identify with these intellectual recluses than with the witty men of the Enlightenment who delighted in the public forum of the salon. Gibbon was never comfortable in the high-powered society of the *philosophes,* and he gratefully retired from the salons of Paris to the scholarly privacy of Lausanne. His dictum that the author himself is the best judge of his own work is but another aspect of this feeling that intellectual work is a private and lonely undertaking. Gibbon was temperamentally incapable of leading the life of a recluse, but as the "historian of the Roman empire" he did exactly that. His days were consecrated to his *History,* and only his evenings were deliberately given over to social intercourse. As he came closer to finishing the *Decline and Fall* even these periods of relaxation were sacrificed. The final volume was written in virtual seclusion, and Gibbon labored long into the night.

However much he wanted to be a gentleman scholar, he was willing to sacrifice the gentleman for the scholar. Gibbon was an intellectual voluptuary but he never suffered remorse over the delight he took in scholarship. He always admired the stoic virtues of the Romans—what he called the "manly virtues"—and perhaps he saw in himself, and in his Jansenist mentors, an intellectual stoicism. He was sympathetic to the Jansenists as men; he was also sympathetic to their view of life and human nature.

For a man to believe in the vanity of human wishes, the ceaseless march of time and the consequent obliteration of man's works, the inevitability of death, and the irrationality of most men, does not assume an acceptance of the Christian doctrine of original sin. Gibbon believed in all these things, yet denied, implicitly, original sin. He believed the creations of man's mind partially overcame the inherent evils of the human condition. He had little hope for the improvement of the species, but he believed that individuals might understand and create their own lives. As a historian he valued and celebrated those men of the past who had, through discipline and reason, escaped the dehumanizing pressures of their age. This belief he generalized to include all men in all times. The *Decline and Fall* would not make Gibbon live any longer, but its composition would give meaning and coherence to his life, and that huge image of his mind would be available to other men, despite the passage of time and the passions of men.

This humanistic faith drew Gibbon to Pascal and the Jansenists. He could accept Pascal's analysis of human nature without agreeing with him that it is to be explained by a perverse and fallen human nature, by a willfully obscure God, and by original sin. Gibbon could smile, with Pascal, at the accommodating morality of the Jesuits without insisting that all men are damned and the prisoners of their fallen nature. Gibbon could applaud Pascal's characterization of man as a thinking reed without following his mentor into despair and mysticism. Gibbon could find in Pascal not comfort, for he could not be comforted by Pascal's passionate religion, but satisfaction and intellectual pleasure. Gibbon had no illusions about human nature, and he consequently had little interest in the *philosophe* schemes for the improvement of society, or the quality of life. His was a completely secular mind and he could not leap, with Pascal, into the arms of a hidden, vengeful, and unknowable God, any more than he could leap, with the *philosophes*, into a bourgeois utopia.

Man's central problem, for Pascal, is his self-awareness. His bitter but magnificent celebration of this self-awareness is among the most memorable parts of his thought. The most spectacular features of nature—an infinite universe, the multitude of life, the geometry of the heavens—are all unconscious. Man, puny, fallen, fragile, alone knows himself. This view is not different from Gibbon's. Where the two men diverge is in the fate of this puny creature. Pascal sees no hope. The curse of original sin has driven man to despair. Pascal, who was a great hater, has no love for man or his works. Gibbon, a more balanced personality, put his faith in the works of the mind. But both men begin from the same analysis of human nature.

In addition to these temperamental affinities between Gibbon and the Jansenists, especially Pascal, there is a remarkably similar sensitivity to words and to things. Pascal and Gibbon, although beginning from many of the same premises, diverge radically. Gibbon's emotional responses to the human condition and his literary expression of these responses share with Pascal an atmosphere of sadness and pessimism. That God was hidden from man angered and frustrated Pascal, and drove him to rationalize these mysteries. That God was hidden from man liberated Gibbon and justified his aesthetic appreciation of the world. Pascal contemptuously dismissed the works of the human mind; Gibbon embraced them. For the Jansenist, human creativity was a snare and a delusion; for Gibbon it was an article of humanistic faith. And nowhere is this faith more evident than in Gibbon's ironic understanding of man and his history.

Gibbon learned to write his native tongue, he recorded, from the study of the English Augustans: "The favourite companions of my leisure were our English writers since the Revolution: they breathe the spirit of reason and liberty, and they most seasonably contributed to restore the purity of my own language which had been corrupted by the long use of a foreign Idiom." [79] Swift and Addison were particular favorites, yet there is no mention of having learned to wield the weapon of irony from the Augustans, especially Swift. The reason is clear. Swift's irony, so brilliant and so distinct, was distasteful to Gibbon. Swiftian irony is based on ridicule and exaggeration. The reader is forced to laugh at himself,

[79] *Memoirs*, p. 98.

or rather to see himself, like all men, as ridiculous. Swift assumes that his readers, as men, share a common absurdity and irrationality. No man escapes his barbed wit, and none can take refuge in a superior enlightenment. Gibbon's irony is completely different, and this is why Pascal, not Swift, was his mentor.

Gibbon's irony has been characterized as "dismissive" and this is a useful notion.[80] Gibbon takes his readers into his confidence. He assumes that his audience shares with him a faith in rationality, a knowledge of history, and similar tastes. In a word Gibbon addresses himself to men of enlightenment. He has no didactic purpose. Unlike Swift he does not want to force men to behave differently. He is not a moralist preaching to the unconverted. With extraordinary self-assurance and confidence, Gibbon preaches only to the converted. He flatters his readers, he chats amicably with them, he assumes they see things as he does. He assumes, always, that his audience shares his values, and consequently shares his ironic dismissal of fools and fanatics. Never does he suggest that his readers are either fools or fanatics. This good-natured and optimistic assumption takes the sting and bitterness out of his irony.

Gibbon views Roman civilization from the eminence of eighteenth-century civilization. Part of the charm of the *Decline and Fall* is the easy familiarity Gibbon establishes with his readers. One is amused and flattered by Gibbon because one is treated as an equal. He may be occasionally pedantic, he may be egotistical, but he is always charming. His readers are invited to see the foibles, the fanaticism, and the foolishness of other men: they are never asked to see these same failings in themselves.

The effectiveness of Gibbon's irony depends upon the acceptance of a system of values and taste. The Romantics, for example, who had little interest in Gibbon's celebrations of rationality and order, found the *Decline and Fall* an insidious book. Gibbon's tentative assertions, and his rhetoric of relative judgment, offended the Romantics as much as it offended pious Christians. But Gibbon

---

[80] See A. E. Dyson, "The Technique of Debunking," *The Twentieth Century,* CLVII, no. 937 (March, 1955), 244-256. And the same author's "A Note on Dismissive Irony," *English,* XI, no. 66 (Autumn, 1957), 222-225.

was not writing for such an audience. He deliberately addressed himself to men of good will and enlightenment; and to all who valued and value the classical virtues of reason, order, and humanism, Gibbon is delightful.

It might appear perverse to argue that Gibbon learned these things from Pascal, but in fact this is partially true. The irony of *Lettres provinciales* is dismissive in the same sense as Gibbon's irony. Pascal assumes that his readers share with him similar notions about religion and the human condition. He assumes that his hatred of the easy and complicit morality of the Jesuits will be similarly hated by all men of reason and good will. Pascal's picture of the Jesuits is perverse, one of those brilliant caricatures which cannot be eradicated by careful scholarship. The scheming, supple, amoral Jesuit, the Jesuit created by Pascal, has become the model of a Jesuit. The Jesuit created in *Lettres provinciales*—like Shakespeare's Richard III— is testimony of the power of great art. And Pascal's Jesuits were created through irony. He smiles contemptuously, he smiles amusedly, he laughs broadly, at the foibles of the Jesuits. His reverend father prattles on about the grossest absurdities without being aware of what he is doing. Refinement upon refinement is patiently and carefully recorded by Pascal, as the Jesuit system of morality is unraveled. Every hair is split by rationality gone wild, and the amused Pascal, profoundly convinced that religion is being corrupted and destroyed, records for his readers these Jesuitical arguments. Misplaced enthusiasm, reason functioning without principles, over-intellectualization, these are the sins of the Jesuits. And they are ironic to Pascal only because he believes in an austere, rigorous, hidden, awe-inspiring God. All of the legalisms and syllogisms of the Jesuits are measured against Pascal's Old Testament faith; and all appear foolish.

Throughout *Lettres provinciales* Pascal assumes that he is talking to men with similar views. He does not lecture his readers, he does not insist that they convict themselves of sharing Jesuitical views. Rather he assumes that he and his readers agree on what religion is and should be. One laughs with Pascal at the Jesuits. They are the butt of his ironic humor because they are at one and the same time so deadly serious and so profoundly wrong. They are foolish because they have created, out of their own imaginations, a religion that has little in common with historical Christianity as Pascal understands it. They are absurd because they are unaware of how far they have strayed from reality, from common sense. They are trying to accommodate Christianity to a fallen world, a corrupt society. This, says Pascal, cannot be done. The genius of Christianity lies precisely in its austere morality, its refusal to accommodate itself to fallen human nature. The religious life means not finding ways of sneaking into heaven—an impossibility and a Jesuit delusion—but suffering humiliation and even pain in the quest for the hidden God. This is the yardstick Pascal uses for measuring Jesuit perversity, and only by accepting Pascal's standards can one appreciate the fun of *Lettres provinciales*.

Gibbon, of course, did not share Pascal's religious passion and fanaticism. But he did share his sense of humor. Gibbon's irony, like Pascal's, rests ultimately on the acceptance of a clear system of values—reason, order, lucidity, humanity. All the foibles of mankind are measured against this standard, and their deviation from this standard is what makes them ironic for Gibbon, and for his readers. For all his formality, Gibbon is a very personal author. He invites, he even requires, that his readers participate with him in surveying the past. The reader of the *Decline and Fall*, like the reader of *Lettres provinciales*, participates in the fun, for he is assumed to share the values and the views of the author.

In addition to this technical aspect to Gibbon's irony, there is also a philosophic aspect. Gibbon's hesitancy about making definitive statements, his deliberate avoidance of direct confrontation, his preference for tentative or hesitant statements, is characteristic of the *Decline and Fall*. And his irony, with its olympian detachment and assumption of similar values, serves the same purpose. His irony lacks the passion of Pascal for the simple reason that confusion about the Trinity, for example, was not a matter of life and death for Gibbon. Gibbon can laugh ironically at all attempts to rationalize God or religion. There is no confessional rancour in Gibbon, and he would have found a *Provinciales* directed against the Jansenists or the church of England equally entertaining. The fact of the matter is that Gibbon is even ironic about his own views. He believes in humanistic culture, yet this belief itself is treated ironically. Again, he is hesitant. He is able to wrap even his most cherished beliefs in a rhetoric of ambiguity. Rationalistic fanatics, like Voltaire, are not spared by "the historian of the Roman empire" any more than religious fanatics. Gibbon is unwilling, and temperamentally unable, to be definitive. His scepticism and his irony do not lead him to a passionate, Pascalian assertion of the truth.

Only by citing some examples of Gibbon's irony will it become clear just how masterful and flexible he is. And since Pascal and subjects of "ecclesiastical solemnity" are being considered, examples from those sections dealing with ecclesiastical topics have been chosen. Gibbon's character sketch of the unpleasant Cyril of Alexandria is a masterpiece. In a single paragraph he gives the salient features of his character, and makes it clear to the reader that a fanatic is being introduced:

> The name of Cyril of Alexandria is famous in controversial story, and the title of *saint* is a mark that his opinions and his party have finally prevailed. In the house of his uncle, the archbishop Theophilus, he imbibed the orthodox lessons of zeal and dominion, and five years of his youth were profitably spent in the adjacent monasteries of Nitria. . . . by the theory and practice of dispute, his faith was confirmed and his wit was sharpened; he extended round his cell the cobwebs of scholastic theology, and meditated the works of allegory and metaphysics, whose remains, in seven verbose folios, now peaceably slumber by the side of their rivals.[81]

He could dismiss the pretentions of a church council in a single sentence: "Ephesus, on all sides accessible by sea and land, was chosen for the place, the festival of Pentacost for the day, of the meeting; a writ of summons was despatched to each metropolitan, and a guard was stationed to protect and confine the fathers till they should settle the mysteries of heaven and the faith of the earth."[82]

Sometimes he is more obvious, more heavy-handed, but only

[81] XLVII, 107.   [82] XLVII, 114.

when the grossness of the situation demands it. The condemnation of the heresy of the two natures of Christ is first quoted, and then commented upon: " 'May those who divide Christ be divided with the sword, may they be hewn in pieces, may they be burnt alive!' were the charitable wishes of a Christian synod." [83] But Gibbon's finest ironies are more subtle: "The Roman theology, more positive and precise, adopted the term most offensive to the ears of the Egyptians, that Christ existed IN two natures; and this momentous particle (which the memory, rather than the understanding, must retain) had almost produced a schism among the Catholic bishops." [84] Or: "In the name of the fourth general council, the Christ in one person, but *in* two natures, was announced to the catholic world; an invisible line was drawn between the heresy of Apollinaris and the faith of St. Cyril; and the road to paradise, a bridge as sharp as a razor, was suspended over the abyss by the masterhand of the theological artist." [85]

Gibbon particularly delighted in fixing the character of a protagonist and annihilating him at the same time: "Whenever any resistance or danger was apprehended, the champion of the faith, whose lameness would not allow him either to fight or fly, placed himself at a convenient distance, beyond the reach of darts. But this prudence was the occasion of his death; he was surprised and slain by a body of exasperated rustics; and the synod of the province pronounced, without hesitation, that the holy Marcellus had sacrificed his life in the cause of God." [86] In this short note he expresses his contempt for monks and for the enthusiasm of St. Athanasius: "His expressions have an uncommon energy; and, as he was writing to Monks, there could not be any occasion for him to *affect* a rational language." [87] There is, in Gibbon's irony, a remarkable quality of compression. He manages to say, in brief compass, an enormous amount. Not only does he convey information, but he also introduces himself into the story and comments on the information: "But, as the degrees of the theological hatred depend on the spirit of the war rather than on the importance of the controversy, the heretics who degraded, were treated with

[83] XLVII, 122.   [84] XLVII, 125-126.   [85] XLVII, 126.
[86] XXVIII, 198.   [87] XXI, 340, n. 32.

more severity than those who anhihilated, the person of the Son." [88]
And in his best Pascalian manner: "The Greek word which was
chosen to express this Mysterious resemblance bears so close an
affinity to the orthodox symbol, that the profane of every age
have derided the furious contests which the difference of a single
diphthong excited between the Homoousians and the Hoiou-
sians." [89]

And, finally, an example singled out by G. M. Young: "In the last
and fatal siege of Syracuse, her citizens displayed some remnant of
the spirit which had formerly resisted the powers of Athens and
Carthage. They stood about twenty days against the battering-
rams and catapultae, the mines and tortoises of the besiegers, and
the place might have been relieved if the mariners of the Imperial
fleet had not been detained at Constantinople in building a church
to the Virgin Mary." [90] Pascal would have condemned the irrever-
ence, but he would have enjoyed the expression of it. Gibbon had
truly learned "to manage the weapon of grave and temperate
irony even on subjects of Ecclesiastical solemnity."

Gibbon was not merely hostile to Christianity, or rather to
Christianity in its fanatical form. He was drawn to religion as an
explanation of the world. He was a man who knew, from his own
conversion and reconversion, the power of religion. He could
both understand and respect the genius of religion, and he was
able to see, as perhaps few of his enlightened contemporaries could
see, that it was religious feeling which gave Pascal his genius, and
Tillemont his accuracy. Athanasius' mind was tainted by fanaticism, but this is precisely the source of his remarkable energy.
Bernard was a bigot, but from his very bigotry sprang his genius.
Gibbon considered Christianity an enemy, but an enemy of extraordinary stature.

In a sense the *Decline and Fall* may be considered the first
answer to St. Augustine's *City of God*. From the vantage point of
the high Enlightenment Gibbon is looking back across the centuries to that giant, and is attacking Augustine's explanation of
why Rome fell. It is not, Gibbon argues, God's providence that

[88] XXI, 349.   [89] XXI, 352.   [90] Young, pp. 17-18.

brought Rome down. It is the very real, earthly enemy, the early Christians, that canker in the breast of an already decaying empire. Gibbon's Rome is the work of men, and its fall is the work of men. Gibbon is in many ways a pagan gentleman of the late empire, surveying with sadness and passion the accumulated crimes of *lèse-majesté* against his beloved Rome. His is the first extensive and comprehensive response to St. Augustine; and as the *Decline and Fall* recapitulates many of the arguments used by Pagan apologists in the fifth century, so, too, does it plead for an earthly cause for Rome's fall.

Tillemont and the Jansenists are, for Gibbon, the modern-day representatives of Augustine's views. As such they are the enemy. Tillemont accepts, without apparent question or modification, Augustine's explanation for Rome's fall. His compilation of the sources, especially from the age of Constantine to the invasions, rests on an assumption of providential action. It might legitimately be argued that Tillemont's work is the scholarly gloss to the *City of God*. And there is in this perhaps an additional irony. Gibbon, the pagan champion of Rome, took as his guide a modern Augustinian; and through a mastery of irony, learned from Pascal, he used one Augustinian to confound another. Gibbon's "sure-footed mule" is not only the most important of Gibbon's many guides; he is also the incarnation of the Augustinian view. The Jansenists are opponents of genius and stature. It is through Tillemont and Pascal that Gibbon reaches back through the centuries to confront St. Augustine, and to attempt to topple the *City of God* and replace it with the *Decline and Fall*.

CHAPTER V

THREE MODELS OF EXCELLENCE

*"But I cannot forbear to mention three particular books,
since they may have remotely contributed to form the
historian of the Roman Empire."*

T HE *Decline and Fall* is a great *summa* of European culture.
There is scarcely a book, or a writer, or an idea of importance, from later antiquity to the Enlightenment, that does not
have a place in Gibbon's *History*. Gibbon is perhaps the last great
representative of the classical tradition, in its broadest sense. The
scope of his *History* and his astounding learning are precisely what
make it so difficult to speak of influences. Gibbon collects in the
Decline and Fall, as Suzanne Curchod Necker noticed, "the torrents of thought of all the ages." The men he celebrates in his
History and *Memoirs* seem to have little in common. Some are
religious fanatics, some are sceptics, some are great artists, some are
undistinguished writers. And the student of Gibbon's mind,
anxious to find some common ground for analysis, is reduced to a
vague formulation, like humanism.

In the preceding chapter Gibbon's relationship to Tillemont and
Pascal, two Jansenist fanatics, was examined. Here Gibbon's rela-
tionship to Tacitus, Montesquieu, and Bayle will be examined.
This triumvirate inspired Gibbon to write "philosophical" history.

Yet the only thing they seem to have in common is a profound scepticism about human nature and a sense of despair about human history. And although there is much pessimism in the *Decline and Fall*, the overall impression of Gibbon's great work is optimistic. Human nature will probably not change, and the crimes and follies of men will always outweigh their capacity for good. Nevertheless, the lesson of the *Decline and Fall* is that man has the capacity to give order, coherence, and reason to his life. It is this humanistic faith that underlies Gibbon's views of man and his history, and it is far more optimistic than the views of any of his mentors.

Despite his fundamental optimism, his rational faith, Gibbon saw himself as a part of the humanistic tradition that emphasized man's limited capacity for happiness and saw human history as a tragic story. All the men he most admired shared his assumptions. Most men choose compatible friends. But had Gibbon been merely interested in finding support for his ideas he might have picked, almost at random, dozens of humanists. In fact he did not. Gibbon's mentors all share his humanistic biases, in addition to being men deeply concerned with the problems of writing history. From Bayle, Gibbon learned the value of brute facts in history and especially in controversy, and he also learned the importance of a science of facts. From Montesquieu he learned how the facts might be used to generalize about the past, to give order to the apparent chaos of history. He learned the significance of impersonal causes in history, and he far surpassed his master in using climate, geography, and historical traditions and customs to characterize a civilization. From Tacitus, the supreme historian in Gibbon's pantheon, he learned to go behind appearances and explain the underlying human motives for historical events. He had always in mind the excellence of Tacitus, which he hoped to emulate, or at least imitate.

Half a dozen different men might be selected and assigned the role of mentor to "the historian of the Roman empire." Hume and Robertson, Fielding and Locke, Middleton and Giannone, Cicero and Livy, a good case could be made for any one of these men. Yet the five chosen have the distinction of being singled out by Gibbon in the *Memoirs* and quoted at crucial places in the *Decline and Fall.* Each of them represents a possible and probable source for an important aspect of the *Decline and Fall*, and hence an important role in the making of the "historian of the Roman empire."

Gibbon first read Pierre Bayle's *Dictionnaire historique et critique* during his exile in Lausanne. When he came to try out his ideas about history, in the *Essai*, he gratefully acknowledged his debt to Bayle. The *Dictionnaire*, Gibbon wrote, is "an eternal monument to the force and the fecundity of erudition combined with genius." [1] Bayle, the Huguenot polymath, was the favorite reading of the *philosophes*. He appeared to them an encyclopedist *avant la lettre*, a *philosophe* of an earlier generation. For Gibbon, however, who was more interested in writing history than polemics, Bayle was a philosophic mentor and the most persuasive and talented of the Pyrrhonist historians. Gibbon ultimately abandoned Bayle's historical Pyrrhonism and his despair that there could ever be written an accurate history. But not before learning from him the arts of controversy, the importance of facts, and the technique of assuming the *persona* of historical actors.

In addition to his intellectual admiration for Bayle, Gibbon was also drawn to him for more personal reasons. In February, 1669, Bayle, having exhausted the resources of the Académie de Puylaurens, entered the Jesuit university at Toulouse. For the benefits of education Protestant parents often risked their children in Catholic schools, praying that they would not be converted by the casuists. Prayers in this instance were of no avail; within a month of his arrival Bayle abjured Protestantism.

The reasons for Bayle's conversion, or at least the reasons given by his biographer, Pierre Des Maizeaux, are similar to Gibbon's own motives. Bayle was a serious and scholarly boy, fond of religious disputation, and cut off, by physical frailness, from the usual activities of boys. He became a Catholic because he was unable to counter the best arguments of the church. Des Maizeaux says he was already wavering in his Calvinist convictions when he went to Toulouse. There "his doubts were augmented . . . by the conversations he had with a priest who lived in the same house. He believed himself to be in error, because he was unable to

[1] *Essai*, VII, 22.

counter the arguments advanced on behalf of Catholicism by the casuists." [2] Within seventeen months Bayle returned to the reformed church, and left Toulouse. He finally became an exile in Rotterdam, where he died.

The circumstances of Bayle's conversion—which are as vague and unsatisfying as those Gibbon reports of his own fall—are remarkably similar to Gibbon's. So much so that Gibbon, in the *Memoirs*, uses the example of Bayle to explain partially his own conversion. Bayle is the only figure outside Gibbon's family who receives an extensive character sketch and appreciation in the *Memoirs*.[3] Gibbon writes Bayle's panegyric both to excuse and justify his own conversion. After all, Bayle was not sixteen when he converted, he was twenty-two, and his understanding was "acute and manly." He converted because at the time he believed the arguments of Catholicism. But he soon recognized his error, for "Nature had designed him to think as he pleased and to speak as he thought." [4] He discovered, as did Gibbon, "the impossibility of Transubstantiation, which is abundantly refuted by the testimony of our senses." His return "to the communion of a falling sect was a bold and disinterested step" which finally forced him into exile. His great genius, for Gibbon, was his ability to remain "a calm and lofty spectator of the religious tempest" and to condemn "with equal firmness the persecution of Lewis XIV; and the Republican maxims of the Calvinists." [5] Gibbon cites with approval Bayle's *mot:* "I am most truly a protestant; for I protest indifferently against all Systems, and all Sects." [6]

[2] Pierre Des Maizeaux, *Vie de M. Bayle*, in *Dictionnaire historique et critique de Pierre Bayle* (new ed., 16 vols., Paris, 1820), XVI, 44. Hereafter cited as Des Maizeaux, *Vie*.

[3] *Memoirs*, pp. 63-65.   [4] *Memoirs*, p. 63.   [5] *Memoirs*, p. 64.

[6] *Memoirs*, p. 65. Voltaire recounts the same story and questions its authenticity. Gibbon probably found the anecdote in Voltaire's *Lettre . . . sur Rabelais et d'autres auteurs accusés d'avoir mal parlé de la religion chrétienne* (1767), but neglected to indicate his source. In Lettre VII, *Sur les Français*, Voltaire writes of Bayle: "il est rapporté dans un de ces dictionnaires historique où la vérité est si souvent mêlée avec le mensonge que le cardinal de Polignac, eu passant à Rotterdam, demanda à Bayle, s'il était anglican, ou luthérain, ou calviniste, et qu'il répondit: 'Je suis protestant; car je proteste contre toutes les religions.'" Voltaire gives several reasons for doubting the story, but adds: "Il est vrai que Bayle avait dit quelquefois ce qu'on lui fait dire: il ajoutait qu'il était comme Jupiter assemble-nuages d'Homère." See Voltaire, *Oeuvres*, ed. Beuchot, XLIII, 518.

Gibbon is here celebrating his own views, with Bayle as his mouthpiece. But his admiration for Bayle's work was a part of his admiration for the man, for whom he felt genuine friendship. Gibbon had the capacity to embrace, across the years, historical characters and treat them as personal friends. He would have understood Petrarch's motives in writing letters to ancient authors.

The two men were indeed very similar, but not for the reasons usually given. Bayle the *philosophe*, if such he was, held little interest for Gibbon. Almost all Gibbon's references to Bayle are to the *Dictionnaire*, and not to such clearly polemical works as the *Pensées diverses* and the *Addition aux Pensées diverses*. Bayle's masterful destruction of the superstitions and legends surrounding the appearance of a comet entertained Gibbon, but his interest was centered on the philosophical and historical arguments of the *Dictionnaire*. Gibbon liked Bayle's views of human nature, which in his case are those of a seventeeth-century Calvinist. They are not different in kind from the views of Pascal or Tillemont, which is another bit of evidence to support my contention that Gibbon's was a democratic mind: he took intellectual sustenance from any man who held views congenial to his own, whatever his confessional (or lack of confessional) bias.

Bayle's view of human nature is somber and pessimistic, and his historical studies only reinforced this view. History was, for Bayle, a laboratory experiment in the baseness of human nature. Like all students of the past he found what he was looking for, and the accumulation of the evidence of irrationality, destructiveness, and wickedness is impressive. Bayle took the "ancient paradox of Plutarch, that Atheism is less pernicious than superstition" and gave it, in Gibbon's words, "a tenfold vigour." It is superstition, not religion, that is the enemy. The great crimes of antiquity were committed not by atheists, but by idolators. Nero, in the midst of his crimes, venerated the image of a child; Cataline prepared himself to commit murder by worshiping in his chapel; Heliogabalus, the most infamous of the emperors, was a high priest of an idolatrous mystery cult.[7]

[7] See *Pensées diverses sur la comète*, edition critique avec une introduction et des notes publiée par A. Prat, Société des textes français modernes (2 vols., Paris, 1939), I, 338-340. Hereafter cited as *PD*.

The end of religion for Bayle, as for Gibbon, is to function as a system of social morality and personal ethics. The truly religious man is the man who lives a useful and good life; and Gibbon agreed with Bayle that the test of a man's virtue lies not in the punctiliousness of religious observation, but in how he behaves toward his fellow man. Bayle saw in the crimes of Christians demonstration of the failure of religion to change human nature. Bayle's survey of human history is an unalleviated scene of fallen nature. Only the rare individual manages to survive the corruptions of his own nature and the consequent corruption of his times. Bayle, like Gibbon, puts his faith in the few men in each generation who manage to rise above their condition. But Bayle, unlike Gibbon, had little faith in human reason as a source of liberation. Men act, thought Bayle, "only through prejudice, instinct, *amour-propre* and by the springs of a thousand passions, which seduce us and twist our reason to their own ends. One can very justly define the principle which rules us as a mass of prejudices and passions. . . ." [8] Prejudice and passion were the motors of history for Bayle, and thus history became a catalog of wicked deeds and wicked men: "This proposition, 'man is incomparably more attracted to evil than to good, and that he performs incomparably more bad actions than good ones' is as certain as any principle of metaphysics." [9] Whatever the historical setting, the motives of men are unchanging: "The Jew and the Mohammedan, the Turk and the Moor, the Christian and the Infidel, the Indian and the Tartar, the inhabitant of the continents and the inhabitant of an island, the noble and the plebian, in short all manner of men who, with regard to all else, can only be considered under the general category of "men," are so similar with regard to these passions that one might say that they copied each other." [10] "The life of man," Bayle argues, "is nothing but a scene of vicissitudes," [11] and "history is the mirror of human life; the condition of human life

---

[8] Quoted in Elisabeth Labrousse, *Pierre Bayle: hétérodoxie et rigorisme* (The Hague, 1964), p. 94. Hereafter cited as Labrousse.

[9] Quoted in Labrousse, p. 82.   [10] Quoted in Labrousse, p. 87.

[11] Pierre Bayle, *Dictionnaire historique et critique*, article *Nestorius*, remark N. For convenience all references to the *Dictionnaire* are hereafter cited by title of article and remark.

is such that the number of wicked and impious men, as well as the number of fools, is infinite. History is nothing else but a picture of the misery of mankind." [12] Contrast this with Gibbon's definition of history as "little more than the register of the crimes, follies, and misfortunes of mankind." [13]

It is not surprising that Bayle was a historical Pyrrhonist. He could not have much faith in men in general, and he had had enough experience of individual wickedness in his own lifetime to make him distrust men in particular. He concluded, naturally enough, that true histories could not be written. It is characteristic that Bayle, who was exceptionally gifted as a historian and a philosopher, left as his life's work neither a history nor a philosophy, but a diffuse *Dictionnaire historique et critique*. That great work is primarily concerned with criticism. But underlying his Augustinian pessimism about mankind there is a passion for the truth, and especially historical truth.

Bayle knew an enormous number of things about a wide range of topics. Practically nothing, except the natural sciences, was outside his interest. All of this information he threw into the *Dictionnaire*. Bayle's mind was stuffed with details and facts, and as he himself stated, he was "more interested in knowing the history of books and their authors than knowing the books themselves." [14] He well knew that this arcane knowledge might bore his readers. But he insisted there was a method to this madness: "The reader may reproach me with concerning myself too much with minutiae. I only hope that he realizes that I do it not because it is believed that these things are important in themselves, but rather to show by these examples that it is necessary to be distrustful of what one reads, and to employ one's genius in the proper discernment of facts." [15]

Bayle believed that if the facts could be discovered—and he developed like his contemporaries Tillemont, the Maurists, the Bollandists, a science of facts—all the false, extravagant, absurd systems and ideas could be destroyed. Like Tillemont he had no ambition to construct a great narrative history. He wanted only

[12] *Orose*, rem. G. [13] III, 77. [14] Quoted in Labrousse, p. 6.
[15] *Cappadocé*, rem. K.

to destroy the accumulated falsehoods of the centuries. "Does not," he rhetorically asked, "a factual truth destroy a hundred volumes of speculative reasoning?" [16] Bayle's mania for facts had a salutary effect on the study of history.[17] He liked facts because, like the Pyrrhonist's medals and inscriptions, they were more reliable because less subject to human corruption. Bayle believed he could establish the facts of history with something approaching the precision of scientific laws. Speculation is usually only supported by vague "vraisemblances": facts can be proved.[18]

The first law for discovering true facts is Cartesian doubt: "It is essential, in some ways, to follow, with regard to matters of fact, the advice M. Descartes gives regarding philosophical speculation: to examine each thing anew, without any regard for what others have written about it." [19] Having isolated the fact, and having rejected all authority, Bayle then proceeds to date the fact. It is crucial for his science that the earliest possible date be discovered. The reason for this is clear. Many, perhaps even most, of the facts Bayle studied, rested on a tradition. This long string of authorities tended to give a fact undeserved importance. If the fact derived from a single source then no matter how many men repeated it, it was not necessarily true. The testimony of the ages, however venerable, is meaningless if the original fact is false.[20]

Once the fact has been properly dated, Bayle can then indulge his favorite passion: writing the history of facts, tracing their corruption and perversion in the hands of men. Facts are the raw material of history, and nothing so pleased Bayle as demonstrating how a fact might be twisted and tortured to suit religious, national, or human vanity.

Bayle's interests were more those of a historiographer than a historian. He is far more interested in what men have said about the past—and this means how they perverted the truth—than in the past itself. He thought historical composition the most difficult of crafts:

[16] *Epicure*, rem. D.

[17] Ernst Cassirer, *The Philosophy of the Enlightenment*, trans. Fritz C. A. Koelln and James Pettigrove (Princeton, 1951), p. 161, sees Bayle as a positivist. There is some dispute on this point. Nevertheless, Cassirer's thesis that Bayle gave the Enlightenment an appreciation of facts as crucial to historical writing is valid.

[18] *Saducéens*, rem. G.   [19] *Goulu*, rem. F.   [20] See Labrousse, p. 62.

History, generally speaking, if not the most difficult form of composition is one of the most difficult. It requires great judgment, a noble, clear, and concise style, a good conscience, perfect probity, an abundance of excellent materials, and the art of placing them in good order. Above all, historical composition requires the power of resisting the instinct of religious zeal, which prompts one to cry down what one finds to be false, and to embellish what one thinks to be true.[21]

The difficulty comes from the nature of man himself, for all of these talents cataloged above might be possessed by a single individual, a Gibbon for example: "And a historian can never be too much on his guard; and it is almost impossible for him to be altogether free of prejudices. There are some forms of government and some moral and political maxims which he likes or dislikes."[22] "History," Bayle believed, "ought not to be handled except with clean hands." Only those who "have not embued their hands in the combat, either in the figurative or literal sense"[23] are qualified to write about the past. And so rare is Bayle's ideal historian that he "never can be found, and exists only as an idea."[24] His definition of a perfect history is one which is "unacceptable to all sects and nations; for it is a sign that the writer neither flatters nor spares any of them."[25]

Bayle's historical Pyrrhonism results from his pessimistic view of human nature and his intense interest in factual accuracy. The article on Calvin is a good example of his Pyrrhonist attack on history. Bayle read dozens of histories of Calvin and Calvinism, and he found them all wanting. But the study by M. Varillas he cites as especially defective. His errors "are so gross that they are enough to make one renounce the study of history."[26] This is especially disturbing since there is an enormous amount of information available on Calvin, and his works are complete and extant. The falsification of the history of the sixteenth century is symptomatic: "So many historians in former ages have labored

[21] *Remond*, rem. D. [22] *Remond*, rem. D. [23] *Remond*, rem. D.
[24] *Capriata*, rem. C.
[25] Pierre Bayle, *An Explanation Concerning Obscenities*, in *Historical and Critical Dictionary* (5 vols., London, 1734-38), V, 846.
[26] *Calvin*, rem. A.

under prejudices as strong as those of M. Varillas. How can one be sure that what they have related is any more to be credited than his falsehoods?" [27] And if the histories of contemporary events are false, despite the availability of evidence, what of ancient history? Bayle takes the famous story of Horatius' defense of the bridge as a case in point:

> If we have reason to wonder that even an event so noteworthy as the heroism of Horatius, and whether or not he was wounded, has partisans and supporters—even among the most famous writers— for both accounts, what shall we say of Polybius who reports that this brave and undaunted Roman lost his life in the Tiber? Shall we conclude from this that there is no way of knowing which side to take in an issue of this sort? And if two versions of this famous episode exist—an episode in which it was the easiest thing in the world to know the truth—we may well doubt the truth of less notable events which the historians have mentioned.[28]

Reason, and here he differs profoundly from Gibbon, is no help in historical writing. Reason is "a desultory, wavering, and supple instrument, which turns every way, like a weathercock." [29] It is like "certain powers so very corrosive that having consumed the proud and spongy flesh of a wound, then corrode even the quick and sound flesh, rot the bones, and penetrate to the very marrow." [30] All that can be hoped for is precision in discovering facts: true history is impossible. Gibbon accepted the validity of Bayle's historical pessimism, based on his analysis of human nature, but he believed history could be written. It is in Bayle's *Dictionnaire* that Gibbon confronted the arguments of the Pyrrhonists, and overcame them. He took from Bayle the imperative for a science of facts, indeed he took many of his own facts from Bayle.

Bayle's influence on Gibbon was considerable, but before assaying this intellectual debt, a survey of Gibbon's use of the *Dictionnaire* is in order. First and foremost Gibbon used the *Dictionnaire*,

---

[27] *Calvin*, rem. A.
[28] *Horatius*, rem. A. See on the same subject, *Adrastus*, rem. G.
[29] *Hipparchia*, rem. D.
[30] *Acosta*, rem. G. The same image is used in *Euclid*, rem. E.

as he used all his "guides," for information. There are twenty-two references to Bayle in the *Decline and Fall,* and all are favorable. The article *Balbus* helped him distinguish the several important Romans of that name, and Bayle "rectifies, with his usual accuracy, the mistakes of former writers." [31] Gibbon accepts, on Bayle's authority, the story of the emperor Tacitus, who claimed descent from the historian and reportedly ordered copies of his famous ancestor's works transcribed and deposited in libraries.[32] Bayle's article *Averroës* is the main authority for that subject in the *Decline and Fall.*[33] And there are many other examples where Bayle was Gibbon's authority.[34] Gibbon was always annoyed when he could not get *ad fons* and had to rely on the scholarship of others, but with Bayle, as with Tillemont, he felt confident. Gibbon found the *Dictionnaire* indispensable, and as a young man he developed the habit of beginning each project by first reading Bayle's article: "I formed a design, (but I doubt whether I shall find time to execute it) to give part of my day to Homer and part to Quintillian, that is to unite the example with the precept. Accordingly I began with Quintillian, in Burman's edition, read his article in Bayle's dictionnary [*sic*]. . . ."[35]

Gibbon respected and relied upon Bayle, but as with all his "guides" he was often critical. Bayle's rambling style, his discursive notes, and his passion for facts, however trivial, annoyed the historian: "How could such a genius employ three or four pages and a great apparatus of learning to examine whether Achilles was fed with marrow only; whether it was the marrow of lions and stags,

---

[31] VII, 181, n. 36.

[32] XII, 320, n. 10. Alas, the story is not true. Bayle himself would have been delighted to have his error pointed out. According to Ronald Syme, *Tacitus* (2 vols., Oxford, 1958), I, 59, the source of the story is the *Historia Augusta,* a notoriously unreliable source. The fiction passed through the ages without being questioned. For the evidence of the falsehood see Syme, *Tacitus,* II, appendix 88.

[33] LII, 35, n. 83. This article remained, until the nineteenth century, the standard authority on the life and works of the Muslim philosopher.

[34] *Mahomet II* (LXVIII, 166, n. 1); *Abélard, Foulques* and *Heloise* (LXIX, 229, n. 30); *Bonfinius* (LXVII, 153, n. 32); *Jodelle* (LXVI, 136, n. 20); *Grégoire VII* (LVI, 212, n. 101); *Papesse, Polonu* and *Blondel* (LXIX, 318, n. 120); *Valla* (LXIX, 294, n. 72); *Grégoire I* (XLV, 34, n. 71); *Nestorius* (XLVII, 120, n. 36); *Scamandre* (XXVIII, 212, n. 55); and *Simonide* (XXI, 361, n. 34).

[35] *Jour. A.,* p. 115 (August 15, 1762). In *Jour. B.,* p. 280 (February 5, 1764), he records that he walked to the Lausanne library to consult Bayle.

or that of lions only, &c?" [36] Bayle was indeed a philosopher, yet
he constantly violated Gibbon's own insistence that the trivial be
winnowed from the significant: "I read the articles of Jupiter
and Juno, in Bayle's dictionnary. That of Jupiter is very superficial. Juno takes up seventeen pages; but the great part of it, as
usual, very foreign to the purpose. A long inquiry when horns
began to be an emblem of cuckoldom; numberless reflections, some
original, and some very trivial." [37] Gibbon chose his authors for
reasons of taste and not doctrine, and he did not feel obliged to
subject Bayle to the hectoring he reserved for other equally trivial
and pedantic guides. Gibbon liked Bayle: he had genius, and that
was enough for Gibbon.

Finally, there is the question of technique. Bayle, who was not
a great French prose stylist, taught Gibbon nothing about literary
art. Bayle and Tillemont, among Gibbon's mentors, are almost the
only men who have no claim to art. But one thing Gibbon did
learn from Bayle was the technique of controversy, especially on
subjects of "Ecclesiastical solemnity." Bayle was the last, and one
of the greatest, in a long line of religious controversialists. He had
throughout life an insatiable appetite for controversialist literature,
and he brought to his own polemics superb gifts. He had studied
under the Jesuits, and had mastered the art of logic. "The art of
scholastic disputation is the foundation of Bayle's dialectic." [38] In
addition to this he knew more about more things than any of his
opponents. He was also ironic, witty, deliberately malicious, and
humorously salacious. Gibbon thus characterizes Bayle's method of
argument: "His critical Dictionary is a vast repository of facts and
opinions; and he balances the *false* Religions in his sceptical scales,
till the opposite quantities, (if I may use the language of Algebra)
annihilate each other." [39]

Bayle's technique was always to build his dialectical arguments
by taking the virtues from a man's enemies and the vices from his
friends. This habit, familiar to readers of the *Decline and Fall*, Gib-

---

[36] *Jour. A.*, p. 115.   [37] *Jour. A.*, p. 105 (July 18, 1762).
[38] Paul Dibon, "Redécouverte de Bayle," in Paul Dibon, ed., *Pierre Bayle, le
philosophe de Rotterdam* (Amsterdam, 1959), p. xiii.
[39] *Memoirs*, pp. 64-65.

bon probably learned from Bayle. When Bayle attacked Louis Maimbourg in his *Critique générale de l'histoire du Calvinisme de M. Maimbourg* (1682) he was careful to answer the attacks on Calvin's character not by quoting Calvin's followers, but by quoting his enemies. In the *Dictionnaire* this same technique is used: "That no one may complain that I have extenuated or amplified the matter, I will use the animadverter's own words." [40] This technique Gibbon adopted and perfected. He was especially proud of his chapters on Julian the Apostate, where he carefully avoided special pleading. "My impartial balance," he wrote, "of the virtues and vices of Julian was generously praised." [41] And this "impartial balance" was achieved by means of the Baylian technique. In all highly controversial matters Gibbon resorted to the technique learned from Bayle. Constantine the Great was another difficult character. "Even in the present age . . . [he is] an object either of satire or panegyric." [42] Gibbon wanted to achieve a *juste milieu*: "By the impartial union of those defects which are confessed by his warmest admirers and of those virtues which are acknowledged by his most implacable enemies, we might hope to delineate a just portrait of that most extraordinary man, which the truth and candour of history should adopt without a blush." [43] This is a recurring pattern in the *Decline and Fall*. When he draws Justinian's character Gibbon says "the confessions of an enemy may be received as the safest evidence of his virtues" [44] and he considered it the particular advantage of the historian, as opposed to a contemporary, to "enjoy the singular advantage of comparing the pictures which have been delineated by his [he is here speaking of Julian] fondest admirers and his implacable enemies." [45]

The influence of Bayle on Gibbon's mind and on the *Decline and Fall* is neither so direct and obvious as that of Tillemont, nor as oblique as that of Pascal. As with all his mentors, Gibbon felt a direct personal affection for Bayle, especially since he saw the

---

[40] *Grégoire I*, rem. C.   [41] *Memoirs*, p. 162.   [42] XVIII, 214.

[43] XVIII, 214. In his note for this sentence Gibbon adds: "Eusebius and Zosimus form indeed the two extremes of flattery and invective. The intermediate shades are expressed by those writers whose character or situation variously tempered the influence of their religious zeal."

[44] XLIII, 459.   [45] XXIII, 456.

Huguenot as a fellow convert who came to see his error. And as with all his mentors, Gibbon shared with Bayle a pessimistic view of human nature. The importance of facts in historical writing, and the techniques of controversy, also were lessons learned from Bayle. But Bayle was, first and foremost, for Gibbon, a philosopher, not a philosophic historian. The *Dictionnaire* was too verbose, too poorly organized, too pedantic and trivial, to be a model for "the historian of the Roman empire." Bayle was Gibbon's model of the philosopher. In the *Essai* he had, with Bayle in mind, defined the philosopher as a man capable of assuming the *persona* of historical characters, and Bayle was the supreme master: "No man has known as well as Bayle how to put himself in the place of his adversary, to enter fully into his system and to see all the advantages of which it is capable. This is one of the most precious powers of the philosophic sceptic." [46] But Bayle's profound scepticism about the possibility of writing history did not make an impact on Gibbon, largely because Gibbon's conception of history was different from Bayle's. Bayle demanded only superhuman accuracy and complete impartiality. Gibbon demanded accuracy and impartiality only with regard to what actually happened. He saw history in a much more personal way, and he saw the historian as something more than a dispassionate, objective, narrative voice recording events. This is why Gibbon turned to those great "philosophic" historians, Montesquieu and Tacitus, for his models. Neither would have met Bayle's criteria of ideal historian; but for Gibbon they were the masters of his craft. The philosopher of Rotterdam, to echo Gibbon, had not been useless to "the historian of the Roman empire," but there were other influences in the making of the historian of Rome.

Gibbon admired, without reservation, only one historian: Tacitus. The greatest of Roman historians occupies a unique place in the *Decline and Fall*, and Tacitus is perhaps the dominant influence on Gibbon the historian.

Neglected by the Romans,[47] Tacitus has, since the Renaissance,

---

[46] *Jour. B.*, pp. 256-257 (April 4, 1764).
[47] Until the end of the fourth century, when an Antiochene Greek, Ammianus Marcellinus, undertook to write a continuation of Tacitus' histories, the greatest

been considered Rome's greatest historian. For Gibbon he was "the first of historians who applied the science of philosophy to the study of facts." [48] Tacitus had imposed upon history, the history of his own times, the indelible imprint of his mind. He had created the history of the early principate, and the events of that time are seen almost exclusively through the eyes of Tacitus. This was Gibbon's own conception of the historian's task, and until the appearance of the histories of Hume and Robertson—not to mention the *Decline and Fall* itself—Gibbon found few historians deserving of praise. Gibbon celebrates the work of Montesquieu, Hume, Robertson, and several other of his contemporaries or near contemporaries, but he reached back across the centuries to Tacitus for his model and inspiration.

The spirit and the example of Tacitus inform the whole of the *Decline and Fall,* yet few have recognized the importance of Gibbon's debt. Mme Necker, one of Gibbon's shrewdest contemporary readers, was among the first to put her finger on the relationship between the senator and "the historian of the Roman empire": "I see that he [Tacitus] was the model and perhaps the source of your work, but the source has been enlarged by the torrents of thought of all the ages: you show what a fetile and sensitive imagination can add to depth and breadth of intellect." [49]

Tacitus' historical works lie outside the chronological scope of the *Decline and Fall.*[50] Yet he is frequently cited and always with

---

of Rome's historians is mentioned by no one but his friend and contemporary, Pliny.

[48] IX, 213. Gibbon had read Thucydides, or at least he makes a brief reference to him in the *Essai.* But apparently he was not impressed. It is interesting that Gibbon shared the eighteenth-century view of the Greek writers as less instructive, perhaps even inferior, to the Roman writers. Xenophon is the only Greek historian Gibbon makes reference to.

[49] Quoted by Young, pp. 136-137 (his translation). The entire letter is printed in *MW,* III, 176-180. It concerns only the first volume of the *Decline and Fall.*

[50] The *Annals* is a history of Rome from A.D. 14 (the accession of Tiberius) to A.D. 66 (toward the end of Nero's reign). Almost the complete narrative of Tiberius' reign is preserved (books 1-6); a portion of Claudius' reign and most of Nero's (books 11-16). The *History* covers the period from A.D. 69 (the year of the three emperors) to the death of Domitian (A.D. 96). From the *History,* the narratives of the civil wars, the revolt of Civilis, and the beginning of the seige of Jerusalem are preserved (books 1-5). The three early monographs, the *Germany,* the *Agricola,* and the Dialogue on *Oratory,* fill out the Tacitean canon.

reverence bordering on panegyric. The affinity between the two men is very complex. Gibbon was far more optimistic and cheerful than his mentor, and there is scarcely a hint in Gibbon of the smoldering anger and passion that is characteristic of Tacitus. Tacitus' capacity for hatred and his neurotic drive to villify his enemies is absent in Gibbon. Gibbon's anger at even the most unenlightened religious fanatics dissolves into polite and civilized irony, and the passionate invective of the Roman senator finds no place in the *Decline and Fall*. But as with Pascal, these temperamental differences did not mitigate Gibbon's admiration.

Sixteen hundred years before Gibbon's birth Tacitus created the model for the *Decline and Fall*. The somber, sceptical, disillusioned senator who mercilessly dissected the diseased body of the early empire was Gibbon's mentor in all facets of historical composition, from the choice of his subject to his literary art. The great themes of corruption and decline, of despotism and tyranny, of military oppression and moral degeneracy, which are the core of the *Decline and Fall,* are also Tacitus' themes. "I have," wrote Gibbon, "devoted myself to write the annals of a declining monarchy." [51] This is an echo of Tacitus' lament: 'My labours are circumscribed and inglorious; peace wholly unbroken or but slightly disturbed, dismal misery in the capital, an emperor careless about the enlargement of the empire, such is my theme." [52] Gibbon, however, whose view of history reflects the broader concerns of the Enlightenment, could alleviate the misery of the scene by turning his attention to more gratifying subjects: "From the paths of blood, and such is the history of nations, I cannot refuse to turn aside to gather some flowers of science or virtue." [53] But Tacitus must pursue the relentless story of corruption: "I have to present in succession the merciless biddings of a tyrant, incessant prosecutions, faithless friendships, the ruin of innocence, the same causes issuing

[51] LXIV, 471.

[52] *Annals*, 4:32, translated Church and Brodribb.

[53] LVIII, 236. Such interruptions of the narrative "will be censured only by those readers who are insensible to the importance of laws and manners, while they peruse, with eager curiosity, the transient intrigues of a court, or the accidental event of a battle," (XVII, 168-169).

in the same results, and I am everywhere confronted by a wearisome monotony in my subject matter." [54]

Not only do the two men develop the same themes, but they are products of the same social background. Tacitus was a senator and a republican, a proud member of the Roman aristocracy. The enduring feature of Roman history, like that of eighteenth-century England, was oligarchy. Sir Ronald Syme's brilliant *Roman Revolution* is a demonstration of the fruitfulness of Namier's methods and assumptions applied to an ancient oligarchy. Gibbon, although he made no abstract statement of the similarities between eighteenth-century England and Rome, was aware of the correspondence.[55] He, too, was a member of the governing class, but the services of his class had not been dispensed with by a tyrant. This fact, Gibbon believed, qualified him, as it had qualified Tacitus, to write authoritatively about politics.

At Rome an accurate view of politics and the empire was closed to all those outside the oligarchy. Livy, for example, was a provincial, a scholar, and perhaps a schoolmaster. He was an outsider in Roman politics and his history suffers accordingly.[56] Livy could no more write with authority about Roman politics than could an obscure country parson in eighteenth-century England describe the springs of parliamentary government. Gibbon understood this: "The eight sessions that I sat in Parliament were a school of civil prudence, the first and most essential virtue of an historian." [57] Tillemont and the great ecclesiastical historians of the seventeenth century had believed that the person and the pen must be conse-

---

[54] *Annals*, 4:32.

[55] See L. P. Curtis, "Gibbon's 'Paradise Lost'," in Frederick W. Hilles, ed., *The Age of Johnson: Essays Presented to Chauncy B. Tinker* (New Haven, 1949), for a discussion of the relationship between Gibbon's social status and his *History*.

[56] This is fully argued by Syme when he discusses Livy, see *Tacitus*, I, 136-137. Livy was not an aristocrat but a scholar. His accounts of politics and policies under the late republic suffer from this detachment from the springs of power. Gibbon, too, pointed out this difference between the two men (*Essai*, LII, 66-67). Livy, for Gibbon, is the great narrator. He "paints for me the abuses of power, a severity at which Nature both trembles and approves; he shows vengeance and love uniting with liberty, while tyranny falls before their blows. But the laws of the decemvirs, their character, their defects, their relationship with the genius of the Roman people . . . are all totally ignored by Livy." For these things one must go to Tacitus.

[57] *Memoirs*, p. 156.

crated in order to write the history of sacred things. For Gibbon secular consecration was necessary. There were things one could not learn from books. Gibbon had mastered—to give another example of this attitude—most of the literature on Roman warfare before he served in the militia. Yet he wrote that he never understood the movement of troops in battle until he had drilled the Hampshire militia himself. "The Captain of the Hampshire grenadiers . . . has not been useless to the historian of the Roman empire" [58] is Gibbon's famous judgment of his years of service. The same is true of his years in politics. Historians who had experience only of books were not, for Gibbon, reliable authorities for politics.

Gibbon admired in Tacitus what he admired in himself. Tacitus' social position permitted him to speak with authority of politics. His social position also permitted him to speak with authority of the obligations of the governing class.[59] A central theme in Tacitus, echoed by Gibbon, is the civic and moral responsibility of those who rule. Tacitus is the great chronicler of the destruction of the Roman aristocracy,[60] an aristocracy which gradually lost, or surrendered, its right to rule the Roman world.

Tacitus viewed politics *en philosophe*. The developments in Rome, at least since Augustus, had removed Tacitus and his class from power and influence. He stood above the fray, just as Bayle stood outside the religious fanaticism of his age. But if the times of the principate were corrupt and corrupting, Tacitus, almost alone, escaped this corruption. He found a model of excellence in the republic and he held contemporary affairs up to this standard. His social position gave to his work a moral—Gibbon would have called it a philosophic—vigor: 'Something much stronger is conveyed by Tacitus—that authority of rank, weight, and maturity which pronounced a consular verdict upon men and affairs, peremptory and incorruptible." [61] His horror at the servility of the senatorial class struck Gibbon as the classic analysis of the loss of civic pride and virtue. When Gibbon comes to write the history of the last years of Constantinople he returns, with disgust, to the theme of civic corruption and to the model of Tacitus. Thus did

[58] *Memoirs*, p. 117.   [59] Syme, *Tacitus*, II, 583.   [60] Syme, *Tacitus*, II, 574.
[61] Syme, *Tacitus*, I, 299.

Tacitus describe the reign of Tiberius: "Tradition says that Tiberius as often as he left the Senate-House used to exclaim in Greek, 'how ready these men are to be slaves.' Clearly, even he, with his dislike of public freedom, was disgusted with the abject abasement of his creatures." [62]

Tacitus despised the principate, toward which "he is harsh and malicious." [63] Augustus' settlement was nothing but a sham republic where naked tyranny was thinly masked by the forms of republicanism. Tacitus idealized, or romanticized, the republic, and a note of yearning for those happier republican days runs through his histories. Gibbon, too, preferred the republic to the empire, at least in his early volumes. He echoed Tacitus when he wrote of the "pure, invigorating air of the Republic." The principate he considered, with his mentor, an elaborate hypocrisy: "It may be defined an absolute monarchy disguised by the forms of a commonwealth. The masters of the Roman world surrounded their thrones with darkness, concealed their irresistible strength, and humbly professed themselves the accountable ministers of the senate, whose supreme decrees they dictated and obeyed." [64]

Not only does Gibbon view the principate through Tacitus' eyes, but the tone and the thesis of Gibbon's original conception of the *Decline and Fall* comes from Tacitus. The seeds of final decay are planted in the early empire, and it was Tacitus' unique genius to see the inevitability of Rome's fall long before it was clearly visible. The first thirty-eight chapters of Gibbon's *History*, that is the first half, are a splendid elaboration of Tacitus. The *Decline and Fall* begins, ostensively, with the death of Marcus Aurelius, but Gibbon devotes three chapters to the statement of his thesis by surveying the empire before A.D. 180. It is clear from these introductory chapters that Gibbon intends to follow Tacitus, and he even laments the fact that his mentor never wrote the history of Augustus' reign. Only Tacitus, Gibbon says, could have done justice to Augustan Rome. Only Tacitus could have analyzed the motives behind the Augustan settlement. Only Tacitus could have dissected

[62] *Annals*, 4:65.
[63] Syme, *Tacitus*, I, 420. See book four of the *Annals* for Tacitus' views on the republic.
[64] III, 63.

the character of the first Roman emperor. But Tacitus did not write
about Augustus, and Gibbon takes it upon himself to fulfill Tacitus'
original design—for he had contemplated such a work—and carry
the story back to the establishment of imperial government.

The moment when the princeps receives the supreme power in
the Roman world from the hands of a cowardly senate cries out
for a Tacitus: "It would require the pen of Tacitus (if Tacitus had
assisted at this assembly) to describe the various emotions of the
senate; those that were suppressed, and those that were affected." [65]
From this dramatic moment Gibbon believes, as did Tacitus, the
decline of the Roman empire can be said to begin. There can be no
doubt in the reader's mind that the history of Rome's decline and
fall is to be a slow, agonizing process, the inexorable development
of the principles of decay created by the Augustan settlement.
Even the relatively happy interlude of the Antonine emperors,
usually seen as Gibbon's golden age of Roman history, is an illu-
sion. The Antonines, for all their virtues, are unable to return Rome
to a republican constitution, and it is only their personal talents
which delay the inevitable process for a century. The attractive
exterior of the empire and the attractive characters of the emperors
mask a diseased constitution. The genius of Rome—civic virtue,
a citizen army, a healthy state paganism, a senate with *auctoritas*,
a ruling class bred for responsibility, a series of laws and customs
honored by every citizen—has been corrupted by the imperial
settlement of Augustus. A great man might hold together the dying
state, but sooner or later Rome would, and must, fall. Such is Gibbon's thesis in the first half of his *History*, and he learned it from
Tacitus.

Even the architecture of the *Decline and Fall* reflects the influence of Tacitus. The *Historiae* opens with a survey of the armies
and provinces of the Roman empire, setting the stage for the civil
wars of A.D. 69. This is unprecedented in ancient historiography.[66]
It reveals immediately the historian's concern with the sources of
power in the empire rather than a concern with a straight narrative

---

[65] III, 61. Gibbon's footnote to this sentence is Tacitean: "It was dangerous to
trust the sincerity of Augustus; to seem to distrust it was still more dangerous."
[66] Syme, *Tacitus*, I, 147.

of events. Gibbon declares to his readers that he, too, is interested in explaining not only what happened, but why it happened. The *Decline and Fall* begins with a similar survey.

After these introductory chapters, Gibbon leaves behind him the period covered by Tacitus' histories, and references to the Roman historian become rarer. Chapter IX is an exception. It is a historical survey of Germany, and Tacitus' monograph, *Germania*, is closely followed and often cited. In the remainder of the *Decline and Fall* references to Tacitus appear irregularly, but not infrequently. When describing the defeat and death of the emperor Decius at the hands of the Goths, Gibbon quotes verbatim from the *Annals:* "I have ventured to copy from Tacitus the picture of a similar engagement between a Roman army and a German tribe." [67] The Tacitean account dates from the first century, but Gibbon is not troubled by the anachronism. This is one of the very few instances when Gibbon transcribes a noncontemporary document. He argues that Tacitus is unsurpassed as a literary artist, that human nature being what it is the same passions are released by the same situations, and that technically the battles of the third century do not differ from those of the first. He considers Tacitus' description valid for all times. When he recounts the sack of Rome and the death of Anthemius, in A.D. 472, Gibbon again transcribes Tacitus. This time to prove that "stern cruelty and dissolute intemperance" are always the same: "Such has been the saevae deformis urbe tota facies, when Rome was assaulted and stormed by the troops of Vespasian (see Tacit. Hist. iii. 82, 83); and every cause of mischief has since acquired much additional energy." [68] And the master of compliment then adds one of the most graceful compliments in the *Decline and Fall:* "The revolution of ages may bring round the same calamities; but the ages may revolve without producing a Tacitus to describe them." [69]

When Gibbon is unable to find in Tacitus an analogous situation, when he is forced to rely on the contemporary historians of an event, he bemoans their inadequacy compared to the genius of

[67] X, 149, n. 50. The account is from *Annals*, 1:64.
[68] XXXVI, 49, n. 119.
[69] XXXVI, 49, n. 119.

Tacitus: "We are forced to content ourselves with the popular rumours of Josephus, and the imperfect hints of Dion and Suetonius." [70] Other historians are, for Gibbon, merely accurate (at best): Tacitus was a genius and a literary artist. He had a capacity to describe and to characterize men and events in an unforgettable and timeless manner: "When Tacitus describes the deaths of the innocent and illustrious Romans, who were sacrified to the cruelty of the first Caesars, the art of the historian, or the merit of the sufferers, excites in our breasts the most lively sensations of terror, of admiration, and of pity." [71] No other Roman historian, indeed no other historian, is in the same class. Even Ammianus Marcellinus, who modeled his history on Tacitus, and whom Gibbon admires, falls far short of Tacitean brilliance: "The coarse and undistinguished pencil of Ammianus has delineated his bloody figures with tedious and disgusting accuracy." [72] Notice that Gibbon does not praise Tacitus for accuracy. Rather he asks more of a great historian, and is consequently able to rank Ammianus below his hero.

The uniqueness of Tacitus is due not only to his philosophic understanding of motivation, his penetrating portraits, his grasp of politics, and his vision of Rome, but also to his literary art. He is the philosophic historian *par excellence* for Gibbon; and no historian was admitted to that charmed circle who was not also a literary artist: "The conciseness of Tacitus . . . avoids everything extraneous and captures the major idea in a phrase which is at once powerful and precise." [73] Just as Gibbon modeled his conception of Rome, of politics, and of human motivation on Tacitus, so, too, did he imitate the master's style. Gibbon's prose, at first glance, seems to owe far more to the ornate and elaborate style of Cicero,

---

[70] III, 72, n. 35.   [71] XXV, 20.

[72] XXV, 20. Ammianus is much praised by Gibbon: "It is not without the most sincere regrets that I must now take leave of an accurate and faithful guide, who has composed the history of his own times without indulging the prejudices and passions which usually affect the mind of a contemporary" (XXVI, 128). But Ammianus was not a literary artist. If he attempted to imitate the style of his model, Tacitus, he failed: "Ammianus is so eloquent that he writes nonsense" (XXV, 69, n. 161). In another place Gibbon speaks of "those turgid metaphors, those false ornaments, that perpetually disfigure the style of Ammianus" (XXVI, 109, n. 83).

[73] *Jour. B.*, p. 33. For an assessment of Tacitus' literary art see Syme, *Tacitus,* I, 191, 306, 358, and the references given there.

yet there is much of Tacitus here. Gibbon's sentences are unique, but he has successfully carried over into English prose the oracular brevity, power, and precision of the Tacitean style. There are too many echoes of Tacitus for accident. Gibbon often rounds off his balanced sentences with those pungent aphorisms familiar to readers of Tacitus. Thus does he characterize the contrast between the accomplished father and his weak offspring: "The sons of Constantine trod in the footsteps of their father, with more zeal and with less discretion." [74] When Maximus and Balbinus, two senatorial aspirants for the purple, were trapped on the capitol by "the seditious multitude" Gibbon observes: "It is prudent to yield, when the contest, whatever may be the issue of it, must be fatal to both parties." [75] The elevation of Macrinus, after the murder of Caracalla, put an unworthy man on the throne: "His rash ambition had climbed to a height where it was difficult to stand with firmness, and impossible to fall without instant destruction." [76] Alexander Severus' reformation of the government is thus described: "Learning, and the love of justice, became the only recommendations for civil office; valour, and the love of discipline, the only qualifications for military employments." [77] And a final example: "Revenge is profitable, gratitude is expensive." [78]

Selected at random, these examples echo the Tacitean style. They reveal a similar love of conciseness, antithesis, and aphorism. It is a style peculiarly suited to oratory, and both men wrote orally. Tacitus began his career as an orator,[79] and according to Pliny he was the greatest orator of his day.[80] The future historian can already be discerned in the *Dialogue on Oratory*.[81] He soon deserted the "eloquence of Senate and law courts" to devote himself exclusively to history, but he continued to test his prose against his ear [82] and occasionally read his history aloud. These habits left an indelible mark on his style. The striking phrase, the memorable aphorism, these are the hallmarks of Tacitus' art.

Gibbon, too, wrote orally, testing each phrase, each paragraph,

[74] XXI, 415. [75] VII, 182. [76] VI, 140.
[77] VI, 150. [78] XI, 302. [79] Syme, *Tacitus*, I, 100.
[80] Syme, *Tacitus*, I, 116.
[81] Syme, *Tacitus*, I, 112-120, discusses this development.
[82] Syme, *Tacitus*, I, 322-339.

on his ear before writing.[83] "It has always been my practise to cast
a long paragraph in a single mould, to try it by my ear, to deposit
it in my memory; but to suspend the action of the pen, till I had
given the last polish to my work." [84] Gibbon's ear, if not trained
by oratory like Tacitus', was attuned to the eloquence of a great
age of oratory. He lacked the nerves and fortitude of a public
speaker, but he was a keen student of the art:

> I took my seat at the beginning of the memorable contest between
> Great Britain and America; and supported with many a sincere and
> *silent* vote the rights, though not, perhaps, the interest, of the
> mother country. After a fleeting illusive hope, prudence con-
> demned me to acquiesce in the humble station of a mute. I was not
> armed by Nature or education with the intrepid energy of mind
> and voice . . . timidity was fortified by pride; and even the suc-
> cess of my pen discouraged the tryal of my voice.[85]

The splendid oratorical style of the eighteenth century, nurtured
on the Latin classics, has a large place in the *Decline and Fall*. In
G. M. Young's happy phrase "the apophthegms and asides with
which he punctuates his narrative are charged with the sarcasm,
the moral dignity, and the urbanity of the senatorial style." [86] Syme
has characterized Tacitus' achievement as "the dramatic genius of
an historian who composed the annals of the Empire in the spirit
of the Republic." [87] The description would fit Gibbon equally
well.

Gibbon's profound debt to Tacitus can be cataloged much easier
than evaluated. The affinities between the two men—not temperamentally, but as historians and artists—are striking. But even more
than the obvious influences cited here, a complex relationship is
involved. Gibbon wrote the first half of the *Decline and Fall*
in conscious imitation of Tacitus; there is good reason to assert

---

[83] E. M. W. Tillyard, *English Epic and Its Background* (London, 1954), says he
read about half the *Decline and Fall* aloud. He does not indicate whether he had
an audience. But he argues that this is the test of the oral qualities of Gibbon's
prose and reveals his epic qualities. If Gibbon did not intend his *History* to be
read aloud, he certainly wrote it that way.
[84] *Memoirs*, p. 159.   [85] *Memoirs*, p. 156.   [86] Young, p. 86.
[87] Syme, *Tacitus*, II, 516.

that he saw his *History* as a continuation of his master's work. Certainly he was flattered by Mme Necker's suggestion that this was his motive. In the making of what Lytton Strachey has called a "master spirit" of the European Enlightenment many materials were used; but in the final analysis the most profound influences on "the historian of the Roman empire" were those of Roman antiquity. Gibbon's achievement was the unique one of creating for his age the Roman empire—summing up for European humanism its debt to the Roman world. He returned to the classics for his inspiration, but he added to them "the torrents of thought of all the ages."

Much is usually made of Gibbon's debt to the *philosophes*, yet he admired only Montesquieu, the least typical critic of the *ancien régime*, and the most conservative. Montesquieu is the only *philosophe* Gibbon acknowledged as a mentor, and the only contemporary author transcribed at length in the *Decline and Fall*.[88] There are fifty-one references to Montesquieu in Gibbon's *History:* even Hume and Robertson together cannot equal that number.[89] The references are equally divided between the *Considérations sur les causes de la grandeur des Romains et de leur décadence* (twenty-one), and *L'Esprit des lois* (twenty-four); the remaining six references are to other works. The majority of these references are favorable, and a couple are lavish in their praise. Those few instances where Gibbon is critical of Montesquieu are gentle rebuffs rather than the vigorous ironic assaults reserved for Voltaire. But this specific evidence of influence tells nothing of the importance of Montesquieu to "the historian of the Roman empire."

Once again a familiar pattern is found: important temperamental differences between the two men coupled with a deep intellectual

[88] VII, 192, n. 69. Gibbon transcribes an entire page of Montesquieu's *Romains* in his account of the emperor Philip. He points out that Montesquieu is mistaken in his analysis. There are other, shorter, transcriptions.

[89] There are forty-one references to Voltaire. D'Holbach, d'Alembert, Diderot, and Rousseau are scarcely mentioned. The *Encyclopédie* is cited twice. Taken together there are perhaps a dozen references to these *philosophes* in the *Decline and Fall*, except for the special case of Voltaire. Of his English contemporaries, Gibbon refers to Hume twenty-seven times, to Robertson seven times, and thrice to Adam Smith.

respect. Montesquieu, the cynical aristocrat, was an amateur scholar and historian. He was extremely well read, but had none of the passion for detail and correctness that distinguishes Gibbon's work. He was, in a word, much more of a gentleman scholar than was Gibbon, who self-consciously gloried in that name. Montesquieu's visit to Rome was not marked by serious study of the ruins of antiquity. He showed little interest in the remains of Rome. He spent most of his time in the salons of the great.[90] Montesquieu was also a great joiner of learned societies, and a frequent contributor of papers on arcane subjects. The two men were quite different.

Gibbon was first attracted to Montesquieu as a young man, early in his exile. He was astounded by his ideas, his bold flights of imagination, and his literary art. As is often the case with an early influence, maturity and knowledge did not dim Gibbon's appreciation, although it did take the edge off his enthusiasm. In the *Memoirs* Gibbon praises "the brilliant imagination" of the *philosophe* and says "my delight was in the frequent perusal of Montesquieu." As a literary artist Gibbon ranked Montesquieu with Tacitus.[91] So struck was he by Montesquieu's genius that in his first book, the *Essai*, Gibbon played the sedulous ape. "How fatal," he later confessed, "has been the imitation of Montesquieu!" [92]

Montesquieu's apprehension of the importance of impersonal causes in history was a momentous contribution to historical analysis, and Gibbon was the first historian to make use of this discovery. The theory of impersonal causes provided Gibbon, during his formative years, with a new way of seeing the past. With youthful enthusiasm he could dismiss the Pyrrhonists, the providentialists, and the political moralists. Montesquieu's notions of impersonal causes explained what had happened in the past without having to resort to transcendental causes. It was a theory that could account for such different phenomena as the end of the ancient world and the multiplication of armed castles in France at the end of the fifteenth century. The general characteristics of a civilization and the individual historical fact both fit into Mon-

---

[90] See Robert Shackleton, *Montesquieu: A Critical Biography* (Oxford, 1961), pp. 95ff., for a description of Montesquieu in Rome. Hereafter cited as Shackleton.
[91] *Jour. B.*, p. 33 (September 16, 1763). [92] *Memoirs*, p. 103.

tesquieu's system of analysis. Gibbon was later to modify his judgment of Montesquieu's genius, but he never lost his delight in the president, and marks of his early enthusiasm are obvious throughout the *Decline and Fall*.

Montesquieu's *Considérations sur les causes de la grandeur des Romains et de leur décadence* was the most important theoretical discussion of the reasons for Rome's fall in the Enlightenment. But the importance of this essay was not immediately recognized.[93] His style was considered odd, his scholarship slight, and his conclusions insulting to the Romans. But perhaps more than any of these faults, or supposed faults, is the fact that the *Considérations* represents the first, and partial, statement of Montesquieu's theories of government and society. It is a tentative, and basically confusing, statement of theories yet to be worked out in his *Esprit des lois*. It is easy to see how this slight and brilliant book bewildered his contemporaries. Only with the publication of *L'Esprit des lois* is there a renewed interest in the *Romains*. Indeed, read without any familiarity with the *Lois*, Montesquieu's essay on Rome is misleading. It is brilliantly written,[94] sharply perceptive, filled with ingenious hypotheses, and disfigured by numerous errors of fact. The central thesis, the corruption of the *esprit général* of the Romans, is not clear. Nevertheless, the *Romains* is an exciting work, and it might best be characterized by applying Montesquieu's description of Boulainvilliers to his own work: "He had more cleverness than enlightenment, more enlightenment than learning: yet his learning was not contemptible, for he knew well the important things about our history and our laws." [95]

The *Romains* begins with the earliest days of the Roman republic and ends with the age of Tamerlane—even a larger slice of Roman history than attempted by Gibbon. But Montesquieu does

[93] See Shackleton, pp. 255-257, for the contemporary reception of the book.

[94] Shackleton, p. 196: "The other thing which must be said about the *Considérations* is that in no other work, with the exception of the *Defense de l'Esprit des lois*, does the President handle the French language with such consummate skill."

[95] *Lois*, XXX, 10 (all references are to the book, in Roman numerals, and the chapter). Montesquieu is difficult to translate without losing the nuance of his thought. Here is the original: "Il avait plus d'esprit que de lumières, plus de lumières que de savoir; mais ce savoir n'etait point méprisable, parce que, de notre histoire et de nos lois, il savait très bien les grandes choses."

not carry the story down to the end of the empire in the East: "I have not the courage to speak of the calamities which followed. I will only say that, under the last emperors, the empire—reduced to the suburbs of Constantinople—ended like the Rhine, which is no more than a brook when it loses itself in the ocean." [96] Here speaks the voice of instinctive humanity, which informs all Montesquieu's work.

In his survey of Roman history Montesquieu enumerates several causes for Rome's decline and fall, and these immediate causes are eventually collected into one general, impersonal cause. Montesquieu sees Rome's history as a dilemma. Rome became great because the republic was constituted to encourage growth and expansion. Yet this inevitable growth and expansion is what destroyed Rome. Armies became too large and too scattered to be controlled; the conquered peoples formed a population no longer unanimous in its love of liberty, its hatred of tyranny, and its dependence on Rome. The healthy disagreements which gave republican Rome a vigorous and creative political life took the form of destructive civil wars; and the original laws of the senate were no longer appropriate to a world empire.

A republic, Montesquieu believed, was most effective when its territory was small and it adhered to the principle of virtue. Rome expanded too rapidly, and this rapid expansion outstripped the development of principles. "The corruption of each government generally begins with that of its principles," [97] and the physical expansion of Rome transformed republican virtues into imperial vices. The principate was the inevitable outcome of the republic, yet it was doomed: "just as the greatness of the republic was fatal to its republican government, so the greatness of the empire was fatal to the lives of the emperors." [98]

Montesquieu believed in a strict correspondence between the form of a government and its size. The limits of the empire were quickly achieved. All subsequent attempts to expand the empire

---

[96] *Romains*, XV, 139 (all references are to the chapter number, followed by the page number), in the edition of Camille Jullian of the *Romains* (10th ed., Paris, n.d.).

[97] *Lois*, VIII, 1.   [98] *Romains*, XV, 139.

were disastrous: "Nature has given states certain limits to mortify the ambition of men. When the Romans transgressed these limits, the Parthians almost always destroyed them; when the Parthians dared to transgress their own limits, they were forced back." [99] Thus does he sum up Roman history: "Here, in a word, is the history of the Romans. By means of their maxims they conquered all people, but when they had succeeded in doing so, their republic could not endure. It was necessary to change the government, and contrary maxims employed by the new government made their greatness collapse." [100]

The generalizations in the *Romains* seem only manifestations of Montesquieu's scepticism, indeed cynicism, about the ability of men to govern themselves well. Ambition, greed, pride, glory, the passions of men, lead them to activate, sometimes unintentionally, the impersonal forces of history which govern change and which cannot be controlled by men. A volcano, he argues, erupts when some foreign matter is introduced which stimulates its latent activity.[101] The ambition of men, acting for their own selfish ends, causes an eruption in history.[102] The theory is strikingly similar to Hegel's "cunning of reason." Indeed, it is strikingly similar to the Christian view of history.

Montesquieu's cynicism about human nature, when coupled to his theory of the *esprit général*, produces his theory of historical change. In the *Romains* he is clearly moving toward a comprehensive theory of the *esprit général:* "There exists in each nation a general spirit on which power itself is based, and when this spirit is betrayed it turns against itself and ceases to function normally." [103] In the *Lois* a more satisfactory explanation is given: "Mankind is influenced by various causes; by the climate, by religion, by the laws, by the maxims of government, by precedents, morals, and customs; whence is formed a general spirit of nations." [104] The

---

[99] *Romains*, V, 61. [100] *Romains*, XVIII, 169. [101] *Romains*, VIII, 83.

[102] *Romains*, XI, 107-108: "Finally the republic was crushed. We must not blame it on the ambition of certain individuals; we must blame it on man—a being whose greed for power increases the more he has of it, and who desires all because he already possesses much."

[103] *Romains*, XXII, 210.

[104] Montesquieu's theory of climate is one of his most original contributions to

ancient simplicity of manners, created by the climate, geography, and racial composition of the Romans, is the *esprit général* of the republic, Rome's natural form of government. The corruption of this *esprit général* through immoderate growth is the cause of her fall.

Gibbon saw in Montesquieu both a theoretical and analytical framework for writing history. Although he had little use for theoretical constructs, he seems to have accepted Montesquieu's metaphors and used them to good advantage. Nowhere in the *Decline and Fall*, or in any of Gibbon's writings, can one find criticism of the notion of an *esprit général*. Gibbon has much to say about Montesquieu's errors of fact, and he was unhappy with the lack of coherence in the *Lois*. His description of the Justinian code might apply equally well to Montesquieu: "The works of Justinian represent a tesselated pavement of antique and costly, but too often incoherent, fragments." [105]

Montesquieu was an enormously erudite man, yet the greatest scholar of Rome in the eighteenth century found little to praise in Montesquieu's scholarship. Montesquieu was no scholar, and in those rare instances when the president supported his hypotheses with precise and accurate historical data, Gibbon was surprised: "He illustrates the nature and use of the censorship with his usual ingenuity and with uncommon precision." [106] Or: "Montesquieu has delineated, with a bold easy pencil, some of the most striking circumstances of the pride of Attila, and the disgrace of the Romans. He deserves the praise of having read the fragments of Priscus, which have been too much disregarded." [107] On at least one occasion Gibbon even complains that Montesquieu abandons his usual speculative boldness and gets bogged down in the details of his legal profession. Montesquieu was "a lawyer as well as a philosopher" and "the philosopher is sometimes lost in the legal antiquarian." [108]

---

historical study. See Robert Shackleton, "The Evolution of Montesquieu's Theory of Climate," *Revue internationale de philosophie* (1955). *Lois*, XIX, 4, and this entire book.

[105] XLIV, 493.   [106] X, 247, n. 41.   [107] XXXIV, 457, n. 39.
[108] XXXVIII, 137, n. 86.

The philosopher and the antiquarian are seldom happily blended in Montesquieu's work. Throughout his *History* Gibbon snaps at the heels of his mentor for lack of precision. Montesquieu asserts that Constantius Chlorus, and Galerius, the successors of Diocletian and Maximin, first divided the empire.[109] No, says Gibbon: this was Diocletian's work.[110] Montesquieu asserts that "the senate, and the equestrian order, with their innumerable attendants" followed Constantine to his new city on the Propontus, leaving Rome without inhabitants.[111] This is hyperbole and "in the course of this history," says Gibbon, "such exaggerations will be reduced to their just value." [112] Montesquieu says that the Goths during the reign of Valens "ravaged everything, from the Danube to the Bosporus, exterminated Valens and his army" and then recrossed the Danube. Nonsense, says Gibbon: "The president Montesquieu seems ignorant that the Goths, after the defeat of Valens, *never* abandoned the Roman territory. . . . The error is inexcusable; since it disguises the principal and immediate cause of the fall of the Western Empire of Rome." [113]

The catalog of Montesquieu's failings as an accurate historian is long. He has "used and abused the relations of travellers" [114] and he always indulges his "lively fancy" by opting for the largest number of troops recorded in the sources.[115] He has "peopled, with flourishing cities and nations, the isthmus between the Euxine and the Caspian" but these imagined riches "shine only through the darkness of conjecture or tradition." The genuine history of the area "presents an uniform scene of rudeness and poverty." [116] These are serious shortcomings in a historian, but Montesquieu gets off lightly. Far more lightly than does Voltaire for similar errors. Gibbon's early enthusiasm for the author, and his recognition of his debt to Montesquieu, rendered his criticism mellow, even charitable. Montesquieu is one of those rare individuals whose faults Gibbon is willing to excuse because of his obvious virtues: "In the forty years since its publication, no work [he is speaking of the *Lois*] has been more read and criticized; and the spirit of

[109] *Romains*, XVII, 159.   [110] XIV, 394, n. 1.   [111] *Romains*, XVII, 159.
[112] XVII, 164, n. 55.   [113] XXVI, 139, n. 143.   [114] XXVI, 79, n. 11.
[115] XI, 188, n. 13.   [116] XLII, 399.

inquiry which it has excited is not the least of our obligations to its author." [117]

Gibbon's debt to Montesquieu is twofold. To the young man, wrestling with the problems of how to write history, Montesquieu was a great liberating influence. He demonstrated to the aspiring historian how one might write philosophic history without falling into the scepticism of Bayle or having to rely upon metaphysical schemes for meaning. Montesquieu, like Bayle, was instrumental in turning Gibbon's thought in fruitful directions. And he amply repaid this early debt in the *Essai*. Montesquieu's influence on "the historian of the Roman empire" was more substantial than that of Bayle. On the most obvious level Gibbon often cites Montesquieu. The "lively fancy" and "brilliant imagination" of Montesquieu are commemorated in the *Decline and Fall*. More important than this form of literary commemoration is Gibbon's refinement of Montesquieu's views. The remarkable analytic powers of Montesquieu's theories are nowhere more evident than in the *Decline and Fall*. Gibbon's magnificent deduction of the history of the nomads, for example, from their way of life is much finer than anything in Montesquieu. Montesquieu was the guide and the inspiration, but it was Gibbon's genius which gave to the theories genuine historical application. In Gibbon's *History* the potential of Montesquieu's thought is first fully realized. But without Montesquieu the chapters on Islam, on Roman law, on the society and government of the Germans, the Turks, and the Mongols, might not have been written.

[117] LVIII, 332, n. 147.

CHAPTER VI

GIBBON'S "AGE OF CONSTANTINE"

"It is difficult to arrange with order and perspicuity the various transactions of the age of Constantine."

G IBBON LAVISHED more space and energy—and experienced more frustration—on the age of Constantine than on any other period of Roman history. On his own testimony the composition of the *Decline and Fall* was incredibly smooth. Once he had fixed on a style, "the middle tone between a dull Chronicle and a Rhetorical declamation," he seldom suffered the painful drudgery of rewriting.[1] Only two sections of his *History* presented difficulties: the chapters on Christianity (XV and XVI) were "reduced by three successive revisals from a large volume to their present size"[2] and those on the age of Constantine. Gibbon burned his first essay on Constantine, and commemorates that singular event in his *Memoirs:* "It is difficult to arrange with order

---

[1] *Memoirs,* p. 159. Gibbon's description of composing his *History* orally while pacing back and forth in his study is familiar. The first three chapters were rewritten until Gibbon felt comfortable with his style; after this he suffered few delays. J. B. Bury, in his introduction to the ninth edition of the *Decline and Fall* (1925), has collected the variants between the first quarto edition of volume I (1776) and the second quarto edition of the same volume (1782). From these examples (see pp. xxxii-xxxviii) one can see how satisfied Gibbon was with his original version.

[2] *Memoirs,* p. 156.

and perspicuity the various transactions of the age of Constantine: and so much was I displeased with the first Essay, that I committed to the flames above fifty sheets." [3]

At least part of the frustration Gibbon experienced is that faced by any historian of this complex period. The smooth flow of Gibbon's narrative belies the difficulties, but a historian familiar with the period will appreciate his achievement. The problems presented by the third and fourth centuries of the empire are intricate, complex, and demand competence in half-a-dozen disciplines. And it is fair to say that not only is the general interpretation of the age of Constantine open to debate, even today, but also almost every major event and source is the subject of scholarly controversy.[4] The central figure of the age, the emperor Constantine, presents the first and perhaps most difficult hurdle. Much depends on the interpretation of Constantine's motives and character.

Not only did Gibbon have to contend with a set of difficult sources, not to mention the ambiguities of Constantine's character, but he also discovered that he needed a new organizing principle. The chronological arrangement of events, which had successfully carried him through the first two centuries of the empire, was no longer satisfactory. Gibbon abandoned a chronological schema and broke the age down into subjects or problems, each of which received a separate chapter: [5] "The age of the great Constantine and

---

[3] *Memoirs*, p.159.

[4] The best introduction to the problems presented by the age of Constantine is Norman H. Baynes, *Constantine the Great and the Christian Church* (London, 1930). More recent discussions, with elaborate bibliographical suggestions, are: E. Stein, *Histoire du bas-empire*, vol. I, trans. and ed. J.-R. Palanque (Paris, 1959), especially 95-130, and notes; volumes II and III of *Histoire de l'eglise depuis les origines jusqu'à nos jours*, ed. A. Fliche and V. Martin; *De la fin du 2e siècle à la paix constantinienne* (Paris, 1935), by J. Lebreton and J. Zeiller, and *De la paix constantinienne à la mort de Théodose* (Paris, 1936), by P. de Labriolle, G. Bardy, and J.-R. Palanque; André Piganiol, *Histoire de Rome*, in the "Clio" series (Paris, 1962), especially pp. 460-472; A. H. M. Jones, *The Later Roman Empire: 284-602* (2 vols., Norman, Oklahoma) is the most recent general history of the later empire. See for a fuller discussion of the problems faced by Gibbon my article, "Gibbon's 'Age of Constantine' and the Fall of Rome," *History and Theory*, VIII, no. 1 (1969), 71-96.

[5] The age of Constantine, for Gibbon, constitutes the period from Diocletian's accession (A.D. 285) to the death of Athanasius (A.D. 373). Gibbon devotes six complete chapters to this period, and major sections of three other chapters: chapter XIII (the reign of Diocletian); chapter XIV (from Diocletian's abdica-

his sons is filled with important events; but the historian must be impressed by their number unless he diligently separates from each other the scenes which are connected only by the order of time." [6] First, he will "describe the political institutions which gave strength to the empire, before he proceeds to relate the wars and revolutions which hastened its decline." [7] Furthermore, the emergence of Christianity as the state religion demands that the historian "adopt the division, unknown to the ancients, of civil and ecclesiastical affairs: the victory of the Christians and their intestine discord will supply copious and distinct materials both for edification and for scandal." [8]

Gibbon is aware that this departure from chronology is unorthodox, both for his own century and for the ancients. He had already criticized Voltaire for separating the past into distinct categories. Now he must follow suit, and argues that he is a philosophic historian, not a mere annalist. "Laws and manners" [9] will receive a prominent place in his account. The *Decline and Fall* is to be in the new style created by Montesquieu, Hume, and Robertson.

For a philosophic historian the age of Constantine is a crucial era in the history of European civilization. It is, for Gibbon, one of those ages when world history changed its direction; and the introduction of Christianity, officially, into the empire is the central event. Thus the age of Constantine occupies a central position in the structure of the *Decline and Fall*. During the early decades of the fourth century Gibbon could already discern clearly the causes for the decline and fall of the empire. And in his account of the age he moves gradually away from the fatalism of his first conception. So, too, does he move gradually away from the institutional cum constitutional view of his first chapters.

---

tion to Constantine's victory over Licinius); chapter XVII (foundation of Constantinople and Constantine's political system); chapter XVIII (character of Constantine, division of the empire, death of Constantine); chapter XX (conversion of Constantine and its effects); chapter XXI (the major heresies). Chapter XV and XVI (the progress of Christianity) contain much material on the first Christian emperor, as do chapters XIX, XXII, XXIII. No other period of Roman history receives such extensive treatment from Gibbon.

[6] XVII, 149.   [7] XVII, 149.   [8] XVII, 149.
[9] XVII, 168-169.

Gibbon saw in Constantine's adoption of Christianity the realization of his worst fears. And he thunders against the effeminacy, superstition, religiosity, corruption, and degeneracy of the age, for which he holds Constantine personally responsible. He sees nothing praiseworthy in Constantine's many reforms. The apparently sincere efforts of the first Christian emperor to save Rome are dismissed by Gibbon as manifestations of weakness, irrationality, or political manipulation. The new capital, founded by Constantine at Byzantium, is often regarded as the crowning political achievement of the age.[10] Gibbon considers it the work of a pusillanimous emperor willing to sacrifice the old Rome in order to erect a vain monument to his own glory. The separation of the military and civil services—again considered a much needed reform—"relaxed the vigour of the state, while it secured the tranquility of the monarch."[11] Constantine's distinction between the *borderers*, or frontier troops, and the *palatines*, or garrison troops, was, for Gibbon, the fatal undermining of the military discipline of the empire. All of these reforms, considered together, are "the mortal wound which had been so rashly or so weakly inflicted by the hand of Constantine." They sapped the strength and vitality of the empire, "til the last moment of its dissolution."[12]

Gibbon's view of the age of Constantine, at this point of his development, rests on his assumptions about Christianity. He is still convinced that Rome fell because of barbarism and Christianity, and he sees the age of Constantine as an important, perhaps the most important, link in this causal chain. The only two sections of the *Decline and Fall* that required extensive rewriting were the chapters on Christianity and on Constantine. They are closely related, for in both sections the author's purpose was the same. Gibbon, when he wrote these chapters, was "attached to the old Pagan establishment."[13] He was convinced that the growth of the new religion was a principal cause of Rome's fall. Obviously so important a series of events as the conversion of the Roman em-

---

[10] See for example, J. B. Bury, "Causes of the Survival of the Roman Empire in the East," *Selected Essays*, ed. Harold Temperley (Cambridge, 1930).
[11] XVII, 187.   [12] XVII, 188.
[13] Gibbon to Lord Sheffield, February 5, 1791, *Letters*, III, 216.

peror and the subsequent establishment of Christianity as the state religion called for the most careful treatment.

Gibbon had been warned by Hume that his free and ironic treatment of Christianity would not be taken lightly. But he knew what he was doing. He was acutely aware that even in an age of enlightenment the majority of mankind—even Whig mankind—held tenaciously to their religious "superstitions." The age of Constantine was, for him, a test of his thesis and his principles. He would destroy, through irony and erudition, this Christian hero. And his treatment of the age of Constantine and the Christianization of the empire was to be no mere tour de force of the historian's craft. The chapters on the trinitarian controversy or monasticism might amuse or offend a learned reader, but they could hardly be expected to stir the passions of the majority of men. But the age of Constantine was a more basic issue. Even for the benevolent Anglican church the conversion of the emperor and the empire was an article of some importance. This was not a subject for theological hair-splitting or recondite learning. It involved the palpable triumph of Christianity, the very proof of God's providence. Even those latitudinarian divines who refused to squabble over which miracles were true and which false drew the line at assailing the sincerity of Constantine and questioning the benefits of Christianity. Gibbon recognized this: "The victories and the civil policy of Constantine no longer influence the state of Europe; but a considerable portion of the globe still retains the impression which it received from the conversion of that monarch; and the ecclesiastical institutions of his reign are still connected, by an indissoluble chain, with the opinions, the passions, and the interests of the present generation."[14]

Gibbon took special pains in the composition of these chapters. There is in his treatment of the age of Constantine a passionate attention to detail. In the earlier and later parts of the *Decline and Fall* he was usually content to concentrate on his narrative line. He sought to present the contours of Roman history rather than monographic details.[15] Here there is more precision: "The suc-

---

[14] XX, 306.
[15] David Hume, after reading the first volume, wrote Gibbon that he found the

cessive steps of the elevation of Constantine, from his first assuming the purple at York to the resignation of Licinius at Nicodemia, have been related with some minuteness and precision." [16] This minuteness and precision is the result of Gibbon's awareness of the contemporary implications of the age and the probability that his critics would delight in catching him in errors of fact. It is also a result of Gibbon's perception of the age of Constantine as central to his thesis of the triumph of barbarism and Christianity.

Constantine absorbed Gibbon's attention as did few other men in Roman history. He is not one of the emperors Gibbon admired: he is one of the villians of the piece. But Gibbon saw in the career of Constantine a microcosm of the decline and fall of the Roman empire. In his treatment of Constantine Gibbon sought to paint the fate of Rome in miniature. The analysis of Constantine's character is one of the most ambitious in the *Decline and Fall*. For Gibbon Constantine's early career recapitulates the history of the empire before the fourth century: his later career is a study in the decay and degeneracy which would eventually destroy Rome. The young Constantine was a model prince: vital, talented, full of promise. His young manhood represents the partial fulfillment of this promise. But in his old age—an old age disgraced by religious fanaticism and dark and bloody deeds—Constantine reveals his true character, sacrifices his brilliant reputation, and fatally weakens the empire in a mad rush after personal glory.

Gibbon heightens the tragedy of Constantine's career by painting his early exploits in glowing colors. But after the defeat of Licinius (A.D. 324) Constantine sinks rapidly into degeneracy, and the decline of the empire quickens which each successive reign. The legacy of Constantine is the slow but effective poison of moral corruption, institutionalized in the Christian church and the new constitutions of the state. So well did he do his work that even Julian the Apostate, one of Gibbon's heroes and a noble Roman, could not save Rome by attempting to return her to the good old ways.

---

work "concise and superficial." Gibbon acknowledged the validity of the criticism (*Memoirs*, p. 156).

[16] XIV, 441.

Gibbon's Constantine is similar to Shakespeare's Julius Caesar: a man of splendid parts who degenerates into a somber tyrant in old age. Constantine is neither saint nor hero. He is a semiliterate barbarian, not different in kind from the Illyrian princes of the third century who "restored the empire, without restoring the sciences." He is a gifted man, "enriched by nature with her choicest endowments,"[17] but he deserves the epithet "great" only with regard to the rough and ready virtues of the military camp and the battlefield. He is, for Gibbon, one of the great soldiers of the empire, not one of its great statesmen.

Constantine began life with every advantage. He was tall, majestic-looking, and graceful. He was strong, active, and adept in all the military arts. He was chaste and temperate, and delighted "in the social intercourse of familiar conversation." He was courteous and liberal, and gained the confidence and admiration of all those close to him. Although semiliterate, he esteemed learning and protected the arts and sciences (despite the fact that he was devoid of taste).[18] He was a devoted and indefatigable civil servant. He had the "magnanimity to conceive, and patience to execute, the most arduous designs, without being checked either by the prejudices of education or by the clamours of the multitude." In the field he displayed the talents "of a consummate general" and "to his abilities, rather than to his fortune, we may ascribe the signal victories which he obtained over the foreign and domestic foes of the republic."[19] He was, or rather might have been, an ideal prince.

In building up his portrait of Constantine Gibbon used a technique familiar to the religious controversialists of the seventeenth century, and perfected by Bayle. He took Constantine's virtues from his enemies and his vices from friends: "The virtues of Constantine are collected for the most part from Eutropius and the younger Victor, two sincere pagans, who wrote after the extinction of his family. Even Zosimus and the *Emperor* Julian acknowledge his personal courage and military achievements."[20]

[17] XVIII, 215.
[18] XIV, 425: "The triumphal arch of Constantine still remains a melancholy proof of the decline of the arts, and a singular testimony of the meanest vanity." [19] XVIII, 215.   [20] XVIII, 216, n. 2.

Despite his exceptional promise and capacity—even on the testimony of his pagan enemies—he had a tragic flaw. "He loved glory, as the reward, perhaps as the motive, of his labours." [21] The "boundless ambition," which, "from the moment of his accepting the purple at York, appears as the ruling passion of his soul," is the key to his character and leads, inevitably, to his decline.[22]

Gibbon was remarkably subtle and sensitive in his analysis of character, but he did accept the assumption of his age, indeed of European humanism, that man had an identifiable essence. He saw, with other men of enlightenment, human nature as unchanged by history. The same causes would produce the same effects throughout all time and in all societies. The same passions, identified by the ancients and clearly understood by the Renaissance and the *Grand Siècle* and the Enlightenment, had always and would always motivate human behavior. Thus history was not the study of the evolution of human nature. History was the study of how and in what ways this human nature responded to different circumstances. The doctrine of a human essence accepted by the Enlightenment also implied that a man's character could not change. His psychological makeup remained static from birth to death. Change is only apparent, not real. The passage of time or the changing circumstances of life might reveal a man's true character, and this true character might be different from that usually attributed to him, but this is not fundamental change.

Men might, through supreme individual effort, rise above their historical circumstances, but even these exceptional men will reveal a consistency of motivation and character. Gibbon himself did not become, objectively, "the historian of the Roman empire" until he began work on his *History*. Yet he saw a consistency in his development, an inevitability. When Gibbon finally became the historian he had imagined, or created, as a young man, he merely realized the essence of his character. He was not radically transformed.

When Gibbon came to consider the character of Constantine

[21] XVIII, 215.   [22] XVIII, 215.

he accepted these psychological doctrines. Once he had isolated and analyzed the spring of Constantine's character—"boundless ambition"—he had only to demonstrate how this ambition dictated the emperor's actions and how, as Constantine grew older, his true character was revealed. The emperor's early years, when he acquired a reputation for benevolence and appeared to contemporaries as a good man, are only a period when he successfully masked his "boundless ambition." Constantine was, in Gibbon's view, always ambitious, but the peculiarities of his early history forced him, or taught him, to dissemble his true nature. Constantine's youth and early manhood were a theatrical representation. He was a hypocrite, and his true nature was exposed to public view and to history only after he achieved sole dominance of the Roman world.

It is important for Gibbon's notions that Constantine's duplicity be firmly established. His interpretation of Constantine's motives (especially his motives for converting to Christianity) rests on his ability to satisfy his "boundless ambition." It is equally important for Gibbon's philosophy that Constantine be a hypocrite when he converts to Christianity.

Constantine's conversion is the central event in the emperor's life, and Gibbon is anxious to prove that the conversion was a cynical, callous political move, dictated by overweening ambition. If this can be proved, Constantine is guilty of lèse-majesté against Rome. With this end in mind, Gibbon sets out to write the history of Constantine's life.

Gibbon accomplishes his anatomizing of Constantine's character by concentrating on the emperor's early years, spent at the court of Diocletian. These years were a school of duplicity for the future emperor. At Diocletian's court—he became a virtual prisoner when Galerius was raised to Augustus in A.D. 305—surrounded by enemies and jealous courtiers, Constantine learned the arts of dissimulation and deception at an early age. In this hostile atmosphere "he had learned to command his own passions, to encounter those of his equals, and to depend for his present safety and future greatness on the prudence and firmness of his personal conduct." [23]

[23] XVIII, 226.

When he escaped from Galerius' court to join his dying father in Britain, he was a master of duplicity. What had originally been a stratagem necessary for survival became, with the years, an unconscious habit. Hypocrisy is the essence of Constantine's character: only Augustus and Constantine are consistently referred to as "artful" in the *Decline and Fall*.

The next period in Constantine's life, his reign in Gaul (A.D. 306-312), "seems to have been the most innocent and even virtuous period of his life."[24] "Seems" is the operative word here. During these years the emperor successfully masked his "boundless ambition," using the techniques learned at the court of Diocletian. He appeared to his contemporaries the man most worthy to rule the empire, and doubtless the undisguised tyranny and cruelty of his rivals served to enhance Constantine's reputation.[25] He had, and seemingly deserved, the reputation of a benevolent despot. But at the end of this period, when he embarked on the series of civil wars that would eventually bring him sole possession of the empire, a hint of his true character is revealed. With the civil wars began the middle period of his career, from 312 to 324 (from the war against Maxentius to the final defeat of Licinius). During this period the virtues of benevolence, tolerance, and limited ambition were swept away by the impetuous and irresistible demands of Constantine's lust for power and glory. It is precisely during this period of his life that his military genius is most evident. In the long series of civil wars Constantine established his claim to military greatness, while sacrificing his reputation as a magnanimous and humane ruler: "Had Constantine fallen on the banks of the Tiber, or even in the plains of Hadrianople, such is the character [of the young ruler of Gaul] which, with a few exceptions, he might have transmitted to posterity."[26] But he achieved his dream of universal empire and "the conclusion of his reign . . . degraded him from the rank which he had acquired among the most deserving of the Roman princes."[27]

[24] XIV, 412.
[25] The complicated politics of this period, when Rome had six emperors, is outside the scope of this chapter. For a reliable and clear survey see Volume XII of the *Cambridge Ancient History*, chapters XIX and XX.
[26] XVIII, 216.   [27] XVIII, 216.

The victory over Licinius made Constantine sole ruler of the Roman world, "thirty-seven years after Diocletian had divided his power and provinces with his associate Maximian." [28] With his victory there vanished every necessity of disguising his passions and his true character. Slowly he let slip his duplicity. He degenerated into "a cruel and dissolute monarch, corrupted by his fortune, or raised by conquest above the necessity of dissimulation." [29] The last fourteen years of his reign "was a period of apparent splendour rather than of real prosperity; and the old age of Constantine was disgraced by the opposite yet reconcilable vices of rapaciousness and prodigality." [30] He now indulged his long-denied passions. He adopted and elaborated the ceremonial extravagance of his predecessor, and Gibbon sneeringly comments that the new system of government "might have been mistaken for a splendid theatre, filled with players of every character and degree, who repeated the language and imitated the passions, of their original model." [31] Under Constantine the Oriental pomp introduced by Diocletian "assumed an air of softness and effeminacy." [32] The aged emperor appeared in false hair "of various colours," an elaborate diadem, "a profusion of gems and pearls, of collars and bracelets, and a variegated flowing robe of silk, most curiously embroidered with flowers of gold." [33] Such prodigalities could scarcely be excused by the youth and folly of Heliogabalus; how account for them in the aged Roman veteran? Such superficial and costly luxury could not fail but take its toll on the character and the mind of the emperor: "A mind thus relaxed by prosperity and indulgence was incapable of rising to that magnanimity which disdains suspicion and dares to forgive." [34] It is precisely during this period of peace, security, moral turpitude, and oriental despotism that Constantine was converted to Christianity.

In any account of the age of Constantine it is crucial to fix precisely the date at which the emperor became a Christian. On this fact will hinge most of one's interpretation of the age. This is no easy task.[35] It is absolutely essential for Gibbon's view that Con-

[28] XIV, 441.   [29] XVIII, 216.   [30] XVIII, 216.
[31] XVII, 170.   [32] XVIII, 217.   [33] XVIII, 217.
[34] XVIII, 217.
[35] With regard to the date of Constantine's conversion, there are three schools

stantine be converted during his period of moral decay, that is, after A.D. 324. An earlier conversion would mitigate Gibbon's argument that self-intereset motivated all Constantine's acts, in addition to depriving him of the ironic implications of a conversion to Christianity during a period of moral degeneracy. A late conversion strengthens Gibbon's argument that Constantine acted as a hypocrite. An earlier conversion, before his final victory over Licinius, would have been the action of a religious fanatic (and Gibbon refuses to see Constantine in this light), and would have seriously compromised his chances of ruling the entire empire. If Constantine is to be one of the major destroyers of Roman civilization, it is important for Gibbon that the connection between moral decay and Christianity be established. There is some evidence supporting a conversion after 324, but the evidence for an earlier conversion (around 312) is much stronger. Gibbon's first task is to destroy the validity of this tradition and the evidence on which it rests.

The traditional Christian version of Constantine's conversion is compounded from the accounts of Eusebius and Lactantius.[36]

---

of interpretation, and each of them rest ultimately on assumptions about Constantine's character, or rather how the historian discerns Constantine as a man. (1) Those who deny the sincerity of Constantine's conversion and argue that it was motivated by purely political considerations are willing to accept an early conversion, but they reject the pious motives given by the Christian writers Lactantius and Eusebius. Among the champions of this view are: H. Grégoire, "La conversion de Constantin," *Revue de l'université de Bruxelles*, XXXVI (1930-31), 231-272; and subsequently argued in *Byzantion*, VI (1932), 645-661; XIII (1938), 561-583; and XIV (1939), 341-351. Burckhardt, H. von Schoenebeck and E. Schwartz also hold this view. (2) Those who admit the sincerity of Constantine's conversion, but argue that he turned to Christianity late in life, and only after adopting several pagan cults (among them the worship of the sun, hence the persistence of "Sol Invictus" on the emperor's coins) in his quest for a syncretic monotheism. The most persuasive defenders of this thesis are L. Salvatorelli, *Constantino il grande* (Rome, 1928), and André Piganiol, *L'empereur Constantin* (Paris, 1932). (3) Those who insist upon the reality and the sincerity of Constantine's conversion in 312, accepting the date and the testimony of Eusebius, if not all his miraculous details. Norman H. Baynes, *Constantine the Great and the Christian Church* (London, 1930); the *Cambridge Ancient History*, XII (1939) (Baynes is responsible for the relevant chapters); and A. H. M. Jones, *Constantine and the Conversion of Europe* (London, 1948) are the leading exponents of this view.

[36] The version of Lactantius is in *De mortibus persecutorum*, xlviii, 5. Eusebius' testimony comes from *De vita Constantini*, i, 28-30; but he also has vague indications of the conversion in his *Ecclesiastical History*, IX, ix, 10. Philostorgus gives

Before the battle of the Milvian Bridge, the tradition runs, the emperor saw a vision in the sky. This vision was repeated in a dream on the night before the battle, and the emperor was ordered to place the sign—the Labarum—on his banner and fight Maxentius under the protection and with the aid of the Christian God. Gibbon sets out to destroy this famous story.

First he attacks the validity of both the vision and the dream: "I shall endeavour to form a just estimate of the *standard,* the *dream,* and the *celestial sign;* by separating the historical, the natural, and the marvellous parts of this extraordinary story, which, in the composition of a specious argument, have been artfully confounded in one splendid and brittle mass." [37] But before exorcising the miraculous from history, Gibbon first questions the reliability of the sources, Eusebius and Lactantius. Gibbon disliked both men: they were religious enthusiasts and second-rate historians. Their testimony was automatically suspect for him. The account given by Lactantius is brief and gives only Constantine's dream on the eve of the battle.[38] Gibbon dismisses his testimony with contempt: "Some considerations might perhaps incline a sceptical mind to suspect the judgment or the veracity of the rhetorician, whose pen, either from zeal or interest, was devoted to the cause of the prevailing faction." [39] Lactantius' account was published "at Nicomedia about three years after the Roman victory" and the interval of "a thousand miles, and a thousand days" allows "ample latitude for the invention of declaimers, the credulity of party, and the tacit approbation of the emperor himself." [40] Besides, Gibbon argues, why accept a miraculous explanation when a reasonable one is available: "Whilst his anxiety for the approaching day, which must decide the fate of the empire, was suspended by a short and interrupted slumber, the venerable form of Christ, and the well-known symbol of his religion, might forcibly offer themselves to the active fancy of a prince." [41]

---

a narrative of a vision similar to that reported by Eusebius, but seen in the nighttime (*Fragm.* 6).

[37] XX, 317.

[38] Lactantius' account says that the emperor was warned in his sleep to carve upon his shield "the heavenly sign from God" and he did as commanded.

[39] XX, 320.   [40] XX, 321.   [41] XX, 321.

Having thus dismissed Lactantius, he turns to Eusebius. There is no circumstantial account of the miracle in the *Ecclesiastical History*—which fact Gibbon emphasizes—but the fullest account of the episode is in Eusebius' *De vita Constantini*.[42] Gibbon opens his attack on Eusebius with a general statement on miracles: "The philosopher, who with calm suspicion examines the dreams and omens, the miracles and prodigies, of profane, or even of ecclesiastical history, will probably conclude that, if the eyes of the spectators have sometimes been deceived by fraud, the understanding of the readers has much more frequently been insulted by fiction." [43] All accounts of miraculous events must be distrusted, but those from the pen of a polemicist like Eusebius, attached to the court and an adherent of Constantine, are especially suspect:

> Eusebius himself [in his account of the Great Persecution], indirectly confesses that he has related whatever might redound to the glory, and that he has suppressed all that could tend to the disgrace, of religion. Such an acknowledgement will naturally excite a suspicion that a writer who has so openly violated one of the fundamental laws of history has not paid a very strict regard to the observance of the others; and the suspicion will derive additional credit from the character of Eusebius, which was less tinctured with credulity, and more practiced in the arts of court, than that of almost any of his contemporaries.[44]

The reports of miracles are suspect on several grounds, and the occurrence of miracles is emphatically rejected. Gibbon triumphantly concludes that the entire episode is a fraud, deliberately perpetrated by the emperor and the Christian party. Eusebius' circumstantial account is a "Christian fable" approved by Constantine and written down some twenty-six years after the event.[45] For proof of this conclusion Gibbon cites the embarrassing fact that there is no mention of this remarkable episode in Eusebius' earlier

---

[42] Eusebius reports that before the battle, in the presence of the entire army, Constantine had a vision of a shining cross in the sky with the words 'In this sign thou shalt conquer." On the next night, in a dream, he was ordered to copy this sign on his banner. On the morrow these apparitions were explained to him by Christian priests, and a standard was made in accordance with the divine command.
[43] XX, 322.   [44] XVI, 144-145.   [45] XX, 323.

work: "The silence of the same Eusebius, in his Ecclesiastical History, is deeply felt by those advocates for the miracle who are not absolutely callous." [46] He drives home the point by arguing that "the advocates for the vision of Constantine are unable to produce a single testimony from the Fathers of the fourth and fifth centuries." In their voluminous writings they repeatedly celebrate the triumph of the church and of Constantine and "these venerable men had not any dislike of a miracle." [47] It would have been a simple matter to verify the truth of the episode by including the testimony of "so many living witnesses [Constantine's soldiers], who must have been spectators of this stupendous miracle." Such information about "the precise circumstances of time and place, which always serve to detect falsehood or establish truth" would have placed Eusebius' account beyond criticism. [48] Instead he preferred "a very singular testimony, that of the deceased Constantine, who, many years after the event, in the freedom of conversation, had related to him this extraordinary incident of his own life." [49] The only authority for the story is the emperor's solemn oath, and that cannot be verified.[50] The episode is a fraud, and "maintained an honourable place in the legend of superstition" until "the bold and sagacious spirit of criticism presumed to depreciate the triumph, and to arraign the truth of the first Christian emperor." [51]

Constantine was a superstitious man, [52] interested in mystery religions and intrigued by magic. In addition, the emperor was by temperament chaste and austere in his early years. Christianity, with its awful mysteries and its moral fervor, appealed to the emperor. As an added attraction, Christianity offered the promise of eternal salvation. But Gibbon is not satisfied to establish an inclination toward Christianity. He wants to prove that the conversion was a self-conscious, deliberate act, dictated by self-interest.

Gibbon's Constantine is neither a disillusioned sceptic nor a free-

[46] XX, 323, n. 48.   [47] XX, 324, n. 52.
[48] As a further critical dig at the defenders of Eusebius' marvelous account, Gibbon gleefully reports that "the pious Tillemont . . . rejects with a sigh the useful Acts of Artemius, a veteran and a martyr, who attests as an eye-witness the vision of Constantine" (XX, 324-325, n. 50).
[49] XX, 324.   [50] XX, 324.   [51] XX, 324.
[52] XX, 308-309.

thinker (the favorite explanations of the nineteenth century). He is, as one might expect, an eighteenth-century politician. Gibbon, in his function as creator, makes his characters after his own image. Constantine is endowed with reason, and the function of reason is to allow a man to calculate what is in his best interests. Constantine's best interests are, according to Gibbon, absolute control of the Roman empire. In addition, Constantine is, like all men, ruled by passions, which are directed by his reason. Gibbon's Constantine was converted to Christianity only after weighing the advantages and the disadvantages of the move. He desired the empire, and he was willing to do whatever was necessary to secure it.

Constantine did not fall victim to religious enthusiasm brought on by a miracle. This interpretation would make him a blind fanatic, not a greedy politician. He fell victim to the insidious arts of Lactantius and Eusebius, his own inclinations toward mystery religions, and a series of political calculations which convinced him that a new religion would support his new dynasty and his new state. Constantine was seduced, but as in all seductions he allowed himself to fall. Lactantius and Eusebius became the trusted advisers and friends of the emperor. They insinuated themselves into his confidence and poured into his ear Christian propaganda. Just as Gibbon himself had been seduced by the Catholic tracts he read at Oxford, Constantine was seduced by evil and shrewd advisers:

> Lactantius, who has adorned the precepts of the Gospel with the eloquence of Cicero, and Eusebius, who has consecrated the learning and philosophy of the Greeks to the service of religion, were both received into the friendship and familiarity of their sovereign; and those able ministers of controversy could patiently watch the soft and yielding moments of persuasion, and dextrously apply the arguments the best adapted to his character and understanding.[53]

An enlightened man need not be surprised "that the mind of an unlettered soldier should have yielded to the weight of evidence which, in a more enlightened age, has satisfied or subdued the reason of a Grotius, a Pascal, or a Locke." [54]

[53] XX, 326.   [54] XX, 326.

Constantine was ready, indeed anxious, to be seduced. He had calculated the numerous practical advantages of conversion. The church was rich and powerful, and had drawn to itself much of the brains and energy of the empire. The non-Christians were largely inert, like the nobility, or poor and uneducated. The intellectual vigor of the Christians was patent in the third century, especially in the second half. The emperors had, from Decius on, irregularly fought the new faith, and then gradually attached Christians to the government. Gibbon is careful to point out that although Christians represented a distinct minority in the empire, they were dedicated men who stood out from their degenerate contemporaries: "In the beginning of the fourth century the Christians still bore a very inadequate proportion of the inhabitants of the empire; but among a degenerate people, who viewed the change of masters with the indifference of slaves, the spirit and union of a religious party might assist the popular leader to whose service, from a principle of conscience, they had devoted their lives and fortunes." [55] In a footnote he reinforces his point: "In the beginning of the last century the Papists in England were only a *thirtieth* and the protestants of France only a *fifteenth* part of the respective nations, to whom their spirit and power were a constant object of apprehension." [56]

Constantine was not unaware of these advantages, and as he came ever closer to the realization of his dreams, his attitudes toward Christianity underwent a change. Until 312, when the civil wars began, he had no need to change his religion. He himself was satisfied with a vague paganism and he tolerated Christianity. But with his fight against Maxentius and the exposure of his true character, his overpowering ambition, a new religion became both appealing and useful: "Personal interest is often the standard of our belief, as well as of our practice; and the same motives of temporal advantage which might influence the public conduct and professions of Constantine would insensibly dispose his mind to embrace a religion so propitious to his fame and fortunes." [57] The emperor was flattered to consider himself the chosen representative of the

[55] XX, 316.   [56] XX, 316, n. 23.   [57] XX, 325.

Christian God, and his advisers did nothing to discourage this view. Whatever happened on the night before the battle of the Milvian Bridge—and it certainly was not a miracle—Constantine decided to fight as the representative of the Christian God against his pagan rival. This was the first tentative step. Victory under the banner of Christianity convinced Constantine that the new religion might be not only politically expedient, but potent as well: "His vanity was gratified by the flattering assurance that he had been chosen by Heaven to reign over the earth; success had justified his divine title to the throne, and that title was founded on the truth of the Christian revelation." [58]

The political uses to which Christianity might be put presented no problem to Constantine. At least since Augustus' establishment of the empire, and probably earlier, religion had been considered an integral part of state policy. The emperor himself was, traditionally, the head of the state religion. It was clear to Constantine that paganism was everywhere in decay, and "the cause of virtue derived very feeble support from the influence of the Pagan superstition." [59] Under these circumstances "a prudent magistrate might observe with pleasure the progress of a religion which diffused among the people a pure, benevolent, and universal system of ethics, adapted to every duty and every condition of life; recommended as the will and reason of the Supreme Deity, and enforced by the sanction of eternal rewards or punishments." [60]

Christianity proved irresistible to Constantine. His vanity was flattered, his political purposes were furthered, and he had no doubt that he could control Christianity once it became the state religion. He was well aware "that the care of religion was the right as well as the duty of the civil magistrate." [61] In fact, the control of the new religion would doubtless prove easier than the regulation of a moribund paganism. Christianity emphasized obedience: "But the Christians, when they depreciated the wrath of Diocletian, or solicited the favour of Constantine, could allege, with truth and confidence, that they held the principle of passive obedience, and that, in the space of three centuries, their conduct had always been

---

[58] XX, 325.   [59] XX, 312.   [60] XX, 312.
[61] XX, 333.

conformable to their principles." [62] The emperor's most important consideration at the end of the civil wars was peace. His dynasty was new and lacked solid support. The principles of Christianity were admirably suited to his needs: "The throne of the emperors would be established on a firm and permanent basis, if all their subjects, embracing the Christian doctrine, should learn to suffer and obey." [63]

Gibbon has thus far made a strong case, and his cynical conclusion that Constantine "used the altars of the church as a convenient footstool to the throne of the empire" [64] follows logically. But he has not yet established the date of Constantine's conversion. If his reading of the emperor's character is correct, and if the emperor's duplicity is to remain central to his character, then Gibbon must place the conversion after 312. Constantine had no need to change religions before that date. He had no reason to be converted until he had secured control of the empire. Any intemperate move before 324 might have jeopardized his career. In addition, Constantine's career after 324 is punctuated by bloody deeds and characterized by moral degeneracy. He is finally, in these last years of supreme power, revealed to history as a tyrant. His conversion to Christianity in the midst of his crimes and moral corruption gives to Gibbon's argument that touch of bitter irony so far lacking.

Why, asks Gibbon, did Constantine receive baptism only on his deathbed? Because, he answers, he was not a religious enthusiast but a crafty politician and a man terrified about the fate of his soul. Despite the outraged cries of the church fathers, baptism just before death was common in the early church: "by the delay of their baptism, they could venture freely to indulge their passions in the enjoyments of this world, while they still retained in their hands the means of a sure and easy absolution." [65] Imagine the appeal this expedient had for an emperor consumed by ambition and willing to pursue his goals "through the dark and bloody paths of war and policy." For Constantine baptism *in extremis* was more than an attraction: it was a necessity. After his victory over Licinius "he abandoned himself, without moderation, to the abuse of his

[62] XX, 314. [63] XX, 314. [64] XX, 325.
[65] XX, 329.

fortune." [66] Success had removed the need for dissimulation and the emperor's true character stood nakedly exposed. In 326 he murdered his son, Crispus, and soon afterwards, his wife, Fausta: "he could no longer be ignorant that the church was possessed of an infallible remedy," [67] Constantine's Christianity was a rough-and-ready, pragmatic faith. "The sublime theory of the gospel had made a much fainter impression on the heart than on the understanding of Constantine himself." [68] Whatever political advantages conversion to Christianity offered, the crimes and tyranny of his last years finally decided the issue. Constantine was baptized on his deathbed to "remove the temptation and the danger of a relapse" and in this act he declared to the public and to posterity the true and insidious nature of his conversion to Christianity.

Gibbon has no solid tradition for postponing Constantine's conversion.[69] There is some perplexity produced by the "discordant authorities" but it "is derived from the behaviour of Constantine himself." [70] But for Gibbon all perplexity vanishes once the character of the emperor is rightly understood. Once the emperor is seen as a man consumed by a lust for power and a "boundless ambition," his action (including the date of his conversion) becomes transparent. Gibbon's reading of Constantine's character, outlined above, allows no other interpretation than a late, insincere conversion.

Gibbon does not set a precise date for the conversion, but he rejects any date prior to 324. He favors 324-326, with a definitive public declaration coming only on his deathbed. Around this time the pagan symbolism disappears, or begins to disappear, from imperial coins; this is the period of Constantine's famous circular letter exhorting his subjects to "imitate, without delay, the example of their sovereign, and to embrace the divine truth of Christianity." [71] In 325 the emperor presided over the first ecumenical coun-

---

[66] XX, 329.   [67] XX, 329.   [68] XX, 329.

[69] The pagan Zosimus places the conversion in Rome in 326 (*Hist.* II, xxix), and attributes it to the influence of an Egyptian who went from Spain to Rome subsequent to the murders of Crispus and Fausta. So obviously unacceptable is this legend that Gibbon does not deign to discuss its possibilities, let alone rest his case on so mediocre an authority.

[70] XX, 307.   [71] XX, 315.

cil; he proscribed the pagan gods in his new capital soon afterwards, and he secured Christian tutors for his sons. These facts, coupled with the political and personal reasons for Constantine's conversion, satisfy Gibbon, and he rests his case. He has achieved his purpose: he has reduced the conversion to political expediency aided by seduction and moral corruption; he has blackened the name of the first Christian emperor; and he has suggested that Constantine's crimes and political reforms, both of which hastened the fall of Rome, occurred *after* he was a Christian.

Gibbon's age of Constantine is but one of many possible examples of Gibbon's remarkable ability to construct a narrative of consummate art, and at the same time impose a highly personal interpretation on events. And it should be obvious from this case study that Gibbon achieved his magic without any distortion of the facts. He does not do violence to the evidence, but—as shown here—he so arranges it that the reader is led, almost imperceptibly, to grant the validity of his interpretation. The age of Constantine is a particularly good example of "the historian of the Roman empire" at work, for, as suggested earlier, he saw in Constantine's career a microcosm of Rome's fall. Thus does he characterize the age: "The same timid policy, of dividing whatever is united, of reducing whatever is eminent, of dreading every active power, and expecting that the most feeble will prove the most obedient, seems to pervade the institutions of several princes, and particularly those of Constantine." [72]

Gibbon's age of Constantine also reveals his basic moral attitude toward Rome. All of the reasons for decline attributed to Constantine are forms of moral corruption—feebleness of purpose, lack of civic virtue, otherworldliness, official corruption. And Gibbon never tires of pointing out that these things are the work of a *Christian* emperor: "The religion of Constantine achieved, in less than a century, the final conquest of the Roman empire; but the victors themselves were insensibly subdued by the arts of their vanquished rivals." [73] In the character of the emperor as well as in the history of the age can be seen the disgusting pattern of corrup-

[72] XVII, 189.   [73] XVIII, 227.

tion and decay caused by Christianity: "As he [Constantine] gradually advanced in the knowledge of truth, he proportionably declined in the practice of virtue." [74] Gibbon would extend the same judgment to the entire empire.

Gibbon's age of Constantine is a unique creation. All the sources then known are examined, all the authorities are cited, yet the historian as creator has imposed himself on his materials. He has arranged his materials in such a way, and has told his story with such brilliance and cleverness, that the reader is led to see Constantine as personally responsible for many of the ills which ultimately destroyed Rome, especially the introduction of a new, foreign religion.

Gibbon was later to alter his views of the importance of individuals in history. But at this point in his development "the historian of the Roman empire" saw concentrated in Constantine all the fatal forces driving the empire to ruin. The treatment of the age of Constantine marks a transition in Gibbon's development. The first half of the *Decline and Fall* concentrates on indirect forces in history; the middle chapters, on Constantine and Julian the Apostate, tend to see history as the work of exceptional men, managing to overcome the apparent fatalism of time. It is only with the final two volumes that Gibbon reaches his final view: the active narrative voice of the historian controlling, ordering, creating the past. And this mature view is best seen in Gibbon's treatment of the problem of Rome's fall.

[74] XX, 329.

CHAPTER VII

GIBBON AND THE
FALL OF ROME

*"The greatest, perhaps, and most awful scene in the
history of mankind."*

To argue that Gibbon's explanation of Rome's fall is confusing
is merely to describe his *History.* In the first half of the *Decline and Fall* there are at least two dozen specific "causes" given
for the fall of Rome. These include personal indictments of individual emperors for political blunders, melancholy reflections on
the vanity of human wishes, an analysis of the anti-Roman nature
of Christianity, moral arguments on the corrupting nature of luxury, sociological discussions on the barbarians, and pessimistic reflections on the inevitable collapse of all human institutions. Sometimes one cause, sometimes another, is stressed. In his opening
chapters Gibbon describes the Augustan settlement as the deliberate
work of a single man, and carrying within itself the seeds of even-
tual destruction and corruption. In the chapters on Christianity he
argues that the "insensible" penetration of Christianity in the empire fatally undermined the genius of a great people. In the chapters
on Constantine he accuses that emperor of destroying Rome for
his own personal glory. The "causes" for Rome's fall march across
the pages of the *Decline and Fall,* seemingly without pattern, and
seemingly unrelated to each other.

Gibbon has no explanation for why Rome fell. Rather he has a moral, almost tragic, view of the stupendous history of Rome, a view familiar to readers of eighteenth-century literature. His great *History* is held together not by a consistent, closely argued thesis, but by his literary art, which is a faithful expression of his mind. Gibbon created the Roman empire, and his ideas of order and lucidity, human nature and motivation, indeed his prejudices and assumptions, give his *History* coherence. His Rome, like Burckhardt's Renaissance, or Clarendon's great rebellion, or Thucydides' Peloponnesian war, is unique and cannot be successfully pigeonholed. Like all great historians, Gibbon has imposed himself on his subject.

Gibbon was no *philosophe*, and consequently he had little interest in validating a principle through the study of history. In the *Essai* he had rejected the comprehensive analytical systems available in the eighteenth century. He wanted only to tell the story of Rome, to transform the facts of history into a great narrative. He was apparently untroubled by inconsistencies, and once he had found his narrative voice he marched steadily through a thousand years of history, describing everything he though important. Those sections of the *Decline and Fall* where he deliberately adopted an analytical approach (like chapter XXXVIII) are disappointing and unconvincing.

But if Gibbon had no thesis, or rather if he abandoned his original thesis about halfway through the *Decline and Fall,* he worked within the traditions of Renaissance historiography. His first answer to the question "why did Rome fall" is familiar to all readers of Gibbon, and it is usually assumed to be the thesis of his *History.* Rome fell through internal moral corruption. The barbarians, never more than a fraction of the population of the empire, merely toppled an already dying—and in some areas dead—government. In this view he was not the disciple of Voltaire, but the last of the humanists.[1] Yet even this thesis of moral corruption is ambiguously stated. He wavers between a fatalistic view of an overripe state collapsing under its own weight, and a state victimized by incom-

---

[1] Christopher Dawson, "Edward Gibbon and the Fall of Rome," in John H. Mulloy, ed., *The Dynamics of World History* (New York, 1956), p. 329.

petent or unscrupulous rulers. The two views receive almost equal expression in the *Decline and Fall*, and Gibbon neither reconciles them nor opts for one or the other. This fatalistic view, a faithful echo of Montesquieu, is best expressed in Gibbon's "general observations" on Roman history in the West: "But the decline of Rome was the natural and inevitable effect of immoderate greatness. Prosperity ripened the principle of decay; the causes of destruction multiplied with the extent of conquest; and, as soon as time or accident had removed the artificial supports, the stupendous fabric yielded to the pressure of its own weight." [2]

Had Gibbon rested his case here, had he terminated the *Decline and Fall* with the end of the empire in the West, as was his original plan, we might question the vagueness of his formulation, we might suggest that his analysis is almost identical to Montesquieu's, and yet we could accept this as a thesis. Such vague notions as "the artificial supports" or "the principle of decay"—which are nowhere clarified in the *Decline and Fall*—are not very satisfying. As a moral, literary view of Rome's fall, they are acceptable. But Gibbon was not content himself with this analysis, nor did he believe that Rome's fate could be understood without a study of the thousand years of the Eastern empire. He carried his *History* down to A.D. 1453, and in so doing was led to abandon even this thesis.

The *Decline and Fall* breaks clearly into two almost equal parts: the history of Rome until A.D. 476 (concluded with chapter XXXVIII), and the history of Rome until A.D. 1453. And before examining Gibbon's final view of Rome, it is useful here to recapitulate his first solution to the problem. A sketch of the argument of the first half of the *Decline and Fall* will make clear the ambiguity of Gibbon's thinking about Rome's fall.

The story of Rome's fall for Gibbon begins with the Golden Age of the empire, the age of the Antonines. The historical tradition supporting the age of the Antonines as a Golden Age is "not a very good one." [3] There are no surviving contemporary histories of the period, and the tradition rests, aside from jejune

[2] XXXVIII, 173-174.
[3] See A. H. M. Jones, *The Later Roman Empire*, I, 33.

chroniclers, on the *Historia Augusta*, which was probably compiled in the fourth century.[4] But if the historical tradition is weak,
the European literary tradition is very strong. By the eighteenth
century Gibbon's characterization of the age was accepted without
question by most educated men: "If a man were called to fix the
period in the history of the world during which the condition of
the human race was most happy and prosperous, he would, without hesitation, name that which elapsed from the death of Domitian to the accession of Commodus."[5] This tradition goes back at
least as far as Machiavelli[6] and enters English literature with
Francis Bacon.[7] Among Gibbon's English contemporaries Henry
Fielding parallels Gibbon's statement, and there is some evidence
that the notion was widely accepted.[8]

It was during the century of enlightenment, and the *Decline
and Fall* begins with an age of enlightenment and ends with the
dawning of learning in the Renaissance, that "the vast extent of
the Roman empire was governed by absolute power, under the
guidance of virtue and wisdom."[9] But even Gibbon's Golden Age
is ambiguous. The reigns of Pius and Marcus Aurelius might be
"possibly the only period in history in which the happiness of a

[4] Jones, *Later Roman Empire*, I, 33.   [5] III, 78.

[6] Machiavelli, *Discoursi*, I, 10.

[7] Bacon, *The Advancement of Learning*, in *Works*, ed. Spedding and Ellis, VI,
146-152.

[8] Fielding, in *Tom Jones* (Book XII, chapter xii), provides a statement whose
sentiment is exactly parallel to Gibbon's: "Mankind have never been so happy as
when the greatest part of the known world was under the dominion of a single
master, and this state of their felicity continued during the reign of five successive
princes [the footnote to this passage names Nerva, Trajan, Hadrian, and the two
Antonines]. This was the true era of the Golden Age, and the only Golden Age
which ever had any real existence, except in the warm imagination of the poets,
from the expulsion from Eden down to this day." L. P. Curtis pointed out the
interesting artistic parallel between Gibbon's statement about the age of the
Antonines and a statement in Robertson's *History of the Emperor Charles V*
(1769), *Works* (London, 1818), IV, 11: "If a man were called to fix upon the
period in the history of the world during which the condition of the human race
was most calamitous and afflicted, he would without hesitation name that which
elapsed from the death of Theodosius the Great to the establishment of the
Lombards in Italy." The parallels are almost word for word, although the purpose
of the two authors diverges sharply.

[9] III, 78. On Gibbon's understanding of "virtue," "wisdom," and "power," see L.
P. Curtis, "Gibbon's 'Paradise Lost,'" in Frederick W. Hilles, ed., *The Age of
Johnson* (New Haven, 1949).

great people was the sole object of government" [10] but this happy interlude was the work of two great men. The institutions of the empire, even under the Antonines, were corrupt. The happiness was apparent and not real. Beneath the attractive surface the historian can discern clearly the poison that would destroy Rome. Indeed, no contemporary left a record of universal happiness in the second century, and it should be noted that Gibbon is careful to say "if a man [not a philosopher] were called to fix the period . . . ," and so forth. To a philosopher, able to see more clearly than mere men, the Golden Age was not so golden.

The Antonines ruled with a "firm but gentle hand" and their "characters and authority demanded involuntary respect." They "were pleased with considering themselves the accountable ministers of the laws," [11] but the laws, or rather the constitution, had been created by Augustus. And the Augustan settlement, for Gibbon, is the beginning of Rome's decline. The Augustan settlement is not directly discussed by Gibbon, but it is clear from his introductory survey of the empire that he holds Augustus personally responsible for many of Rome's ills.

Like his mentor, Tacitus, Gibbon idealized the republic, and Augustus destroyed the republic. "The system of Imperial government, as it was instituted by Augustus" and maintained by his successors, "may be defined an absolute monarchy disguised by the forms of a commonwealth." Augustus was the first of the complete masters of the Roman world who "surrounded their throne with darkness, concealed their irresistible strength, and humbly expressed themselves accountable ministers of the senate, whose supreme decrees they dictated and obeyed." [12] The Augustan constitution made it inevitable that the fate of the Roman world depended on the character of the emperor. And in the Caesars one "may trace the utmost lines of vice and virtue; the most exalted perfection and the meanest degeneracy of our own species." [13]

Not only did the Augustan settlement fix irresistible power in the hands of one man, but it also made possible and necessary two

[10] III, 78.   [11] III, 78.   [12] III, 68.
[13] III, 79.

policies: the elimination of the great republican families and the creation of the Praetorian guards, "whose licentious fury was the first symptom and cause of the decline of the Roman empire." [14] When Tiberius established the Praetorians in a permanent camp in Rome itself, he "riveted the fetters of his country." [15] The Augustan settlement destroyed or corrupted the genius of the Romans. "Public courage," and the "long peace, and the uniform government of the Romans, introduced a slow and secret poison into the vitals of the empire." [16] The much celebrated Augustan peace brought the "languid indifference of private life" and "the minds of men were gradually reduced to the same level, the fire of genius was extinguished, and even the military spirit evaporated." [17]

The Roman world was peopled by "a race of pigmies" who were incapable of enjoying "a rational freedom." Gibbon shared with the *philosophes,* and indeed with the Whigs, a fear of despotism and governmental tyranny. He believed, as did all European liberals of the age, that the enemy of personal happiness was governmental tyranny and oppression. And the best safeguard against official oppression was a division of power within the state: "A martial nobility and stubborn commons, possessed of arms, tenacious of property, and collected into constitutional assemblies, form the only balance capable of preserving a free constitution against the enterprise of an aspiring prince." [18] Notice he does not argue that a benevolent despot, like the Antonine emperors, preserves a free constitution. Gibbon was too much of a whig to trust his freedom to the will, however enlightened, of a single man: "Unless public liberty is protected by intrepid and vigilant guardians, the authority of so formidable a magistrate will soon degenerate into despotism." [19] The Augustan constitution destroyed these traditional safeguards against tyranny. The elimination of the aristocracy, the checks on the senate, removed the machinery for control over despotism; only assassination and armed rebellion remained as checks on the emperor. The history of Rome

[14] V, 103.   [15] V, 104.   [16] II, 58.
[17] II, 56.   [18] III, 59.   [19] III, 59.

becomes, consequently, a disgusting repetition of assassination and rebellion.

Gibbon's major theme is internal decline. "The enemies of Rome were in her bosom—the tyrants and the soldiers." [20] Each emperor is to be trapped in this vicious circle. But some are more culpable than others, and Septimius Severus is the second emperor, after Tiberius, indicted for Rome's fall: "The contemporaries of Severus, in the enjoyment of the peace and glory of his reign, forgave the cruelties by which it had been introduced. Posterity, who experienced the fatal effect of his maxims and example, justly considered him as the principle author of the decline of the Roman empire." [21] Severus realized the logical potentialities of the Augustan settlement. He created an unabashed military despotism: "The rougher trade of arms was abandoned to the peasants and barbarians of the frontiers, who knew no country but their camp, no science but that of war, no civil laws, and scarcely those of military discipline. With bloody hands, savage manners, and desperate resolutions, they sometimes guarded, but much oftener subverted, the throne of the emperors." [22]

The rude, vulgar soldiers overawed the state, and the nobility sank into hopeless decay. The "stubborn commons" had been eliminated by the Augustan settlement: the "martial nobility" were either eliminated or reduced to elegant debauchery. "The corrupt and opulent nobles of Rome gratified every vice that could be collected from the mighty conflux of nations and manners." [23] The barriers to tyranny were thrown down, the citizens were corrupted. Neither a madman like Heliogabalus nor a saint like Alexander Severus could significantly transform the state. Degenerate and stoic alike were murdered by their own troops: "Such was the unhappy condition of the Roman empire that whatever might be their conduct, their fate was commonly the same. A life of pleasure or virtue, of severity or mildness, or indolence or glory,

---

[20] VIII, 195.

[21] V, 125. Altogether Gibbon specifically indicts six emperors as being the principal authors of Rome's fall. And each indictment is unrelated to the others. That is, he never summarizes the six together.

[22] VI, 165.   [23] VI, 147.

alike led to an untimely grave; and almost every reign is closed by the same disgusting repetition of treason and murder." [24]

One of the things that fascinated Gibbon about Rome's decline was the apparent insensitivity of contemporaries to what was happening. He was soon to generalize this observation into a theory, or rather a notion. In the *Essai* he had argued that the philosopher was a man who saw individual events in perspective. In the *Decline and Fall* this becomes his notion of "insensible" development. By "insensible" development Gibbon meant, simply, a complex of events so slow that they passed unrecognized by contemporaries. Contemporaries were, of course, aware of the events of their age, but they were unable to see any cause and effect relationships. These "insensible" developments are obvious only to a philosophic historian. Under the emperor Philip the Arab (A.D. 244-249), for example, Rome seemed as healthy as ever. Her borders "still extended from the Western Ocean to the Tigris, and from Mount Atlas to the Rhine and the Danube." The emperor himself appeared "no less powerful than Hadrian or Augustus had formerly been," but to the philosophic historian "the animating health and vigour are fled." The industry of the people was "discouraged and exhausted by a long series of oppression." The discipline of the legions, "which alone, after the extinction of every other virtue, had propped the greatness of the state, was corrupted," and the strength of the frontiers "was insensibly undermined." The fairest provinces were "left exposed to the rapaciousness and ambition of the barbarians, who soon discovered the decline of the Roman empire."

The Illyrian emperors of the late third century, unable to see and understand the moral rot of the state, sought only to restore the traditional institutions and discipline of Rome. They assumed that a resurrection of the old forms would restore the old vigor. The reforms of Diocletian rigidified the state without treating the disease. Rome was indeed saved from immediate extinction, but the process of decline was not stopped. Rome's fate still depended on the character of the emperor, and Constantine insured Rome's collapse by extending Diocletian's reforms to their logical con-

[24] XII, 317.

clusion: "The emperor Diocletian was, indeed, the author of that system; but during his reign the growing evil was confined within the bounds of modesty and discretion, and he deserves the reproach of establishing pernicious precedents, rather than of exercising actual oppression." [25]

It is at this point that Gibbon adds Christianity to the causes of Rome's fall. It is clear that he is already confused. Apparently he has abandoned his original thesis of Christianity and barbarism as the causes of Rome's fall, for the entire argument has been centered on the internal corruption of the empire, caused by the Augustan settlement. Christianity and barbarism play little or no part in the story of Rome until the fourth century. And Gibbon has already argued that Rome was doomed to fall, given the nature of her constitution. Christianity thus becomes not a necessary, but an additional, cause of Rome's fall. At any rate, he here begins arguing (with the age of Constantine) the direct responsibility of Christianity for Rome's fall. Theological controversy, ecclesiastical corruption and internecine war tear the demoralized empire apart. The otherworldliness of the new religion, monasticism, and the celibacy of the Christians fatally undermine what little remains of the traditional Roman virtues.

Christianity is another of Gibbon's "insensible" developments. To contemporaries, certainly to Constantine and his sons, a savior of the sick empire, it is for Gibbon the final insidious poison introduced into the empire. So thoroughly does Christianity undermine Rome that even the virtuous Julian the Apostate cannot reverse the process. His death in Persia leaves the empire to Jovian. The ignominious peace concluded with Sapor "has justly been considered as a memorable era in the decline and fall of the Roman empire." [26] It is the first time in Roman history that "the god Terminus, who guarded the boundaries of the republic, had . . . retired before the sword of a victorious enemy." [27] It would not be the last time.

---

[25] XIII, 385. This judgment had little support in Gibbon's day, and is today dismissed by historians as mistaken. For a more judicious appraisal of the work of Diocletian, see M. I. Rostovtzeff, *The Social and Economic History of the Roman Empire* (Oxford, 1926), chapter XII.

[26] XXIV, 556.   [27] XXIV, 556.

From Augustus to Jovian is the period of Rome's decline. With the reign of Valens begins Rome's fall.[28] From this time on "the happiness and security of each individual were personally attacked; and the arts and labours of ages were rudely defaced by the Barbarians of Scythia and Germany."[29] Valens and his army were cut to pieces at the battle of Adrianople (A.D. 378), and the Goths remained permanently in the empire. They were soon joined by the Suevi, the Vandals, the Alani, and the Burgundians, who crossed the Rhine in A.D. 406: "The memorable passage . . . may be considered as the fall of the Roman empire in the countries beyond the Alps; and the barriers, which had so long separated the savage and the civilized nations of the earth, were from that fatal moment levelled with the ground."[30] Only Italy and Rome itself remained intact, and four years later (410) Alaric entered the Eternal City: "Eleven hundred and sixty-three years after the foundation of Rome, the Imperial city, which had subdued and civilized so considerable a part of mankind, was delivered to the licentious fury of the tribes of Germany and Scythia."[31] By the sixth century the Roman empire in the West was no more, and Gibbon's original plan for the *Decline and Fall* is complete:

> At that unhappy period, the Saxons fiercely struggled with the natives for the possession of Britain; Gaul and Spain were divided between the powerful monarchies of the Franks and Visigoths, and the dependent kingdom of the Suevi and Burgundians; Africa was exposed to the cruel persecution of the Vandals and the savage insults of the Moors; Rome and Italy as far as the banks of the Danube, were afflicted by an army of Barbarian mercenaries, whose lawless tyranny was succeeded by the reign of Theodoric the Ostrogoth.[32]

The "victorious nations of Germany established a new system of manners and government in the Western countries of Europe"[33] and the narrative of the *Decline and Fall* is ended.[34]

Except for the indictment of Christianity there is nothing very

[28] XXVI, 73.   [29] XXVI, 73.   [30] XXX, 284.
[31] XXXVI, 339.   [32] XXXVIII, 170-171.   [33] XXXVIII, 171.
[34] For Gibbon's explanation of why he decided to carry the story down to 1453 see his several prefaces, and the opening paragraph of chapter XLVIII.

original about this account of Rome's fall. Gibbon closely follows
the traditions of Renaissance historiography and Montesquieu,
especially Montesquieu. He does not speak explicitly of the corruption of Rome's *esprit général*, but at the core of his argument
is the assumption that imperial Rome, through the Augustan settlement, and Christianity, betrayed the genius of the Roman people.
But he wavers between Montesquieu's impersonal causes and his
own predilection for a biographical approach. Gibbon is uncom-
fortable with the fatalistic implications of impersonal causes, and
he tries to avoid the problem by singling out individuals as instrumental in Rome's fall. The vulgarity of Severus, the ambition of
Constantine, the artfulness of Augustus, these accidents of personal
character represent for Gibbon some mitigation of the fatalism of
impersonal causes. But in the first half of the *Decline and Fall* he
is unable to strike a balance between the two explanations, and
the reader is left suspended, wondering what is Gibbon's real explanation. Doubtless Gibbon himself was also uneasy about the
explanation, for in the second half of his *History* he alters the
argument. At any rate, the incomplete synthesis between impersonal causes and personal causes is but another indication of
Gibbon's quest for a consistent explanation of why Rome fell.

The problem is further complicated by Gibbon's insistence on
seeing Roman history in moral terms. He dutifully discusses the
specific causes for Rome's decline—excessive taxation, military li-
cense, economic crisis, civil war, assassination—but he returns, always, to a moral explanation. Human happiness, vice, luxury,
misery, civic virtue, these are the terms in which he views the
tragedy of Roman history. And like so many of the men of enlightenment, his humanitarian instincts often divert the rigor of
his analysis. Gibbon frequently sacrifices consistency to humanity.
His view of society and history is essentially pluralistic. The individual is the point of intersection of many influences. The state,
the church, the family, politics, and economics are all judged in
terms of their impact on the individual. His original thesis, the
triumph of barbarism and Christianity, is slowly sacrificed to his
concern for the individual. Not only was Gibbon not interested in
validating a principle through the study of history, but he was

seemingly not especially interested in sustaining his original thesis. He returns, time and again, to the moral concerns of Enlightenment humanism. But it is Enlightenment humanism in a Roman toga.

Gibbon's attachment to the civilization of Rome needs no demonstration. As he worked on the *Decline and Fall* he came increasingly to identify himself with his subject. And as he worked on the *Decline and Fall* he assumed more and more obviously the toga of a Roman censor, exercising that office with the vigor and stubbornness of Cato the Elder. He views Christianity just as Cato had viewed the mystery cults of an earlier age: a foreign and degenerate influence corrupting Roman morals.

Gibbon sees Christianity as it might have been seen by a Roman senator of the second or third century. From the vantage point of the Roman aristocracy, at least, Gibbon's view of Christianity is historically accurate. His sneering dismissal of the obscure events in Palestine would have been comprehensible to any senator. And this is precisely what so offended his eighteenth-century contemporaries. James Boswell, who was no friend to Gibbon, put the complaint very well. Reporting a conversation he and Dr. Johnson had about Gibbon, Boswell says: "We talked of a work much in vogue at that time, written in a very mellifluous style, but which, under pretext of another subject, contained much artful infidelity. I said it was not fair to attack us thus unexpectedly; he should have warned us of our danger, before we entered his garden of flowery eloquence, by advertising, 'Spring-guns and men-traps set here.'"[35] Boswell is angered by the devotion of an elegant style to insidious arguments. But Gibbon's arguments against Christianity are essentially those of the Romans themselves. Boswell considered Gibbon an infidel, and this characterization is not wide of the mark.

There is much else in the *Decline and Fall* besides Christianity that is seen from the perspective of an old Roman. Gibbon was convinced, for example, that the heavy infantry represented the genius of Roman military development. He scorned the evolution

[35] *Boswell's Life of Johnson*, ed. George Birkbeck Hill, rev. ed. L. F. Powell (6 vols., Oxford, 1934-50), II, 512-513.

of a new style of fighting and accused the innovators, especially
Constantine, of betraying the Roman genius. This led him into
absurdities. He lamented the passing of "the short sword and the
formidable *pilum*, which had subdued the world." And when the
soldiers put aside their heavy body armor to increase their mobil-
ity, Gibbon accused them of "effiminate luxury" and concluded
that "their pusillanimous indolence may be considered as the immediate cause of the downfall of the empire." [36] This is nonsense.
It is indeed an accurate representation of the views of Cato the
Elder and the conservative aristocratic position at Rome, but it is
also the analysis—if it is analysis at all—of a man unable to find a
consistent and coherent explanation for Rome's fall. This cast of
mind, so evident in the *Decline and Fall*, is distinctly Roman. The
Romans habitually saw political and social issues as moral issues,
and viewed change as a potential corruption of public morality.
Gibbon was perfectly at home in this world.

Gibbon's instinctive identification with the values of the Roman
aristocracy was only partly conscious. Certainly he knew that he
was not living in the late empire, and certainly he knew that his
Roman view of Christianity would offend his contemporaries. But
he made few concessions to such modern feelings. His arguments
against Christianity are preeminently the arguments of the pagan
apologists of later antiquity. And the burden of responsibility he
lays on Christianity is a faithful echo of the pagan writers who
tried to explain the sack of Rome by Alaric as a catastrophe caused
by Christianity, caused by the desertion of the pagan gods who
made Rome great. Gibbon fixes on the psychological impact of
Christianity on the Roman, and leaves the realm of historical argument for the rhetorical world of pagan apologetics: "The active
virtues of society were discouraged; and the last remains of the
military spirit were buried in the cloister." [37] What wealth there
remained in the empire was "consecrated to the specious demands of
charity and devotion" and "was lavished on the useless multitudes
of both sexes, who could only plead the merits of abstinence and
chastity." [38] There is not sufficient evidence to support either con-

[36] XXXVIII, 179.   [37] XXXVIII, 175.   [38] XXXVIII, 175.

tention, and Gibbon would have pilloried any Christian writer who made a similar argument against paganism.

The specific causes for Rome's fall march across the pages of the *Decline and Fall;* emperors are excoriated, Christianity is indicted, famous battles take their place in the long series of decline. Yet "the historian of the Roman empire" returns always to the theme of the corruption of the ruling classes of Rome. Gibbon's theme is Tacitus' theme. Whether or not Gibbon intended his *History* to be a moral lecture directed at the ruling classes of his own day—which was at least part of Tacitus' motive—cannot be easily proved. A perceptive critic has argued this thesis [39] and concluded "his entire history revolves around a formula, around three words . . . virtue, wisdom, and power." [40] The loss of virtue, wisdom, and power by the Roman aristocracy caused Rome's fall— and let the British ruling classes beware. Perhaps Gibbon was being consciously didactic; at any rate his thesis is moral decay, and not the triumph of Christianity and barbarism.

After 1782, after he had destroyed the Western empire, Gibbon turned his attention to the East. Insensibly, as he would have it, his *History* swelled from a history of Rome to a truly universal history. Not only Europe, but Asia, Africa, the Middle East, and the Far East became the concern of "the historian of the Roman empire." And as his *History* took on universal proportions, his theme of aristocratic moral decay is abandoned. The thesis was scarcely adequate to account for Roman history until A.D. 476; it could explain nothing about the history of the Byzantine empire.

It is sometimes argued that Gibbon's treatment of the Eastern empire is weak because the scholarship of his day was inadequate for a great synthesis. This is partially true. The Eastern empire had been less thoroughly studied than the Western, and even

---

[39] See Curtis, "Gibbon's 'Paradise Lost.'" Joseph Ward Swain, *Edward Gibbon the Historian* (London, 1966), makes somewhat the same argument, although at much greater length and with much less subtlety. Swain does not argue specifically that the *Decline and Fall* is a moral treatise addressed to the ruling class of England, but he does try to explain much that is in Gibbon's *History* in terms of his political experiences, especially during the American rebellion. His case is tendentious.

[40] Curtis, "Gibbon's 'Paradise Lost,'" p. 79.

many of the literary sources were not available to Gibbon, not to mention nonliterary evidence. But this is only a partial explanation for his disappointing treatment of the Eastern empire. Gibbon neither liked nor understood the Byzantine world. He dismissed the history of Byzantium as "a tedious and uniform tale of weakness and misery." [41] The Eastern Romans, "who dishonour the names of both Greeks and Romans, present a dead uniformity of abject vices, which are neither softened by the weakness of humanity nor animated by the vigour of memorable crimes." [42] J. B. Bury has characterized this statement as "one of the most untrue, and most effective, judgments ever uttered by a thoughtful historian." [43]

The genius of Byzantine civilization was its synthesis of the Greek and Christian heritages. It is precisely this unique blend which escaped Gibbon. He considered the Eastern Romans merely inferior Romans. He had never mastered Greek as thoroughly as Latin, he was relatively unfamiliar with Greek culture—the *Iliad*, alone among the Greek classics, is consistently mentioned—and he had little sympathy with the abstract speculation of Eastern theologians. The Western church, with its emphasis on politics and organization, was more congenial to Gibbon, and he always preferred the Latin to the Greek fathers. In a word, the two components of Byzantine civilization were both uncongenial and unfamiliar to him. In place of the sensitive empathy that served him so well in the history of the West, Gibbon could offer little more than scholarly diligence. He read all that was then available, but his imagination never caught fire. He hopelessly compressed his materials[44] and subjected the Byzantine empire to the standards of Cato and Tacitus.

[41] XLVIII, 180.   [42] XLVIII, 181.
[43] See Bury's introduction to the *Decline and Fall*, p. liv.
[44] The thousand years of Byzantine history occupy less than half the space given to the Western empire. The age of Justinian is fully treated, as are the last years of Constantinople. The rest is neglected, or rather merely sketched. As Gibbon himself explained in his preface of 1782: "At our entrance into this period, the reign of Justinian and the conquests of the Mahometans will deserve and detain our attention, and the last age of Constantinople (the Crusades and the Turks) is connected with the revolutions of Modern Europe. From the seventh to the eleventh century, the obscure interval will be supplied by a concise narrative of such facts as may still appear either interesting or important." Gibbon, reportedly, told Horace Walpole, that "elegant triffler," when he asked Gibbon why he had given

The history of Byzantium is almost an intrusion into Gibbon's vision of Rome's fall. The seeds of decay and corruption are already present in Roman civilization, and when Constantine moved his capital to the East and shifted the gravitational center of the empire, he merely transplanted those seeds. Gibbon's treatment of the decline and fall of the East is a survey of the ripening of these seeds. The same causes which brought down the West are at work in the East. Gibbon finds no new causes, and he is apparently not troubled by the ability of the East to endure, with the same disease, for another thousand years after the fall of the West.

Gibbon did not alter his moral scheme when his *History* became universal, but he did change his mind about the relative importance of impersonal and personal forces in history. He had been troubled by the fatalistic implications of the first half of his *History*, and in the second half he tried to escape the fatalism of his title and of his creation. He came increasingly to identify himself with Rome, and this change is most apparent in the increasing frequency of the pronoun "I." The narrative voice of the historian, implicitly the ordering instrument of the *Decline and Fall*, now becomes explicit. In the second half of his *History* Gibbon shows us his secret: order and coherence are the creation of the historian, not the natural result of his materials or imposed by a theoretical scheme.

Gibbon abandons the façade of objectivity and now sees history as the creation of the historian. And as he moves toward his mature position his emphasis shifts from institutions, classes, and impersonal forces to individuals. His character sketches become longer, and at the same time more tentative. Instead of seeking the characters who might illustrate the age in which they live, Gibbon seeks the individuals who define their age and at the same time stand out from it. He concentrates on those characters in the past who were not overcome by circumstances. He does not return to the sceptic's position that history can be understood only as accident, but he does move in this direction. The relationship between the individual and impersonal causes becomes the dominant theme. And the exceptional individual, able to understand his cir-

---

so much space to the worthless and dull history of the Eastern empire, that "it had never been done" before.

cumstances, able to order his life despite historical forces working against him, becomes the hero of the *Decline and Fall*. Gibbon comes to see history not so much as a study of cause and effect, but rather as a dialectical process in which men struggle to over-come, through reason and energy, the forces of history. The man who does not struggle to impose an order on his own life is in-variably overwhelmed by history.

Gibbon comes to believe that, within limits, man can make what he will of his life. In writing the history of himself Gibbon at-tributed much to chance, but certainly not all:

> When I contemplate the common lot of mortality, I must ac-knowledge that I have drawn a high prize in the lottery of life. The far greater part of the globe is overspread with barbarism or slavery: in the civilized world the most numerous class is con-demned to ignorance and poverty; and the double fortune of my birth in a free and enlightened country in an honourable and wealthy family is the lucky chance of an unit against millions.[45]

Such are the impersonal forces of history. The vast majority of men in the world, now and in the past, are almost from birth trapped by their circumstances and forced to live according to the dictates of historical necessity. The majority of men are fatalis-tically trapped by history, and fail to realize their humanity. Even among the minority, who are fortunate enough, like Gibbon him-self, to be free of material want and to have the option of intel-lectual development, there are few who rise above their historical situation. It is these few who interest "the historian of the Roman empire." It is precisely those men who, through sheer intellectual effort, impose an order on their lives that Gibbon admires. Man is everywhere and at all times born into circumstances over which he has no control. But there are always a handful of men in every generation who overcome, through superior gifts or hard work, their circumstances. Man, for Gibbon, can create his own life out of the inherited materials. In writing the history of his own life Gibbon is most interested in understanding how he imposed an order on events, how he himself created his own life. How he

[45] *Memoirs*, p. 186.

made himself something unique: "the historian of the Roman empire."

In the *Decline and Fall* and the *Memoirs* this mature attitude is apparent. It is small wonder that the thesis of barbarism and Christianity scarcely appears in the second half of the *Decline and Fall*. And it is small wonder that once Gibbon came to see that the Roman empire was his own creation, he should suggest more than two dozen specific reasons, or causes, for Rome's fall. The point is not to explain the cause and effect relationships in the past. Gibbon abandoned this task when he decided to carry his history down to A.D. 1453. The task set for the "historian of the Roman empire," a task set by himself, is to understand and explain that man is not trapped by history, he does not live in a haunted house. He can emancipate himself through reason. And just as man can order and understand his own life, so "the historian of the Roman empire" can order and understand the past.

Gibbon's view of Rome is profoundly moral, profoundly Roman. But his thesis is an expression of the rational optimism of the Enlightenment. Gibbon's thesis is not that barbarism and Christianity triumphed over the Roman virtues fallen into decay. Rather his thesis is the supreme importance of order, lucidity, precision, and reason—what he called the "profane virtues." This is not strictly a thesis, yet this is precisely what Gibbon did with the *Decline and Fall*. He did not explain the causes of Rome's fall, but he did, for the first time in European history, establish "the miracle of order . . . over the chaos of a thousand years." [46] Gibbon's thesis is not to be found in the *Decline and Fall*. His thesis *is* the *Decline and Fall* itself, a self-contained artistic creation.

The "miracle of order" is the essence of Gibbon's achievement, and it is, as Lytton Strachey noticed, extremely improbable that "the gigantic ruin of Europe through a thousand years" should have been "mirrored in the mind of an eighteenth-century English gentleman." [47] It is indeed extremely improbable, and quite wonderful, that Edward Gibbon should have created the most memorable of all Roman empires: his Roman empire.

[46] Lytton Strachey, "Edward Gibbon," *Portraits in Miniature and Other Essays* (London, 1931), p. 159.
[47] Strachey, "Edward Gibbon," p. 157.

BIBLIOGRAPHY

THIS IS NOT a definitive bibliography of works on Gibbon and his *History*, but a list of books and articles (with short comments) which I have used.

The best edition of the *Decline and Fall* to date is J. B. Bury's fifth edition, *The History of the Decline and Fall of the Roman Empire* (7 vols., London, 1909). The fifth edition contains a number of notes which are not included in earlier editions, and the index is expanded. The ninth edition (7 vols., London, 1925) has an expanded introduction by Bury, including some of Gibbon's marginalia from the first quarto edition of volume I (1776). There are several other editions of Gibbon's *History*, and J. E. Norton, *A Bibliography of the Works of Edward Gibbon* (London, 1940) is a useful guide.

Gibbon's manuscript of the *Decline and Fall* has not survived, so a definitive text cannot be established, but Frank Brady has compared and analyzed the various editions of chapter XV (Frank Brady and Martin Price, eds., *English Prose and Poetry, 1660-1800, A Selection* [New York, 1961]). It would be an enormous task, but Brady's edited chapter suggests that a new edition of the *Decline and Fall* would be very useful.

Gibbon's *Miscellaneous Works* were published in two editions by Lord Sheffield, Gibbon's literary executor. The first edition (2 vols., London, 1796) was issued as soon after the author's death as possible. The second edition (5 vols., London, 1814) contains much additional material plus Sheffield's second version of the *Autobiography*.

Gibbon's *Memoirs of My Life*, usually called the *Autobiography*, has a complicated history. First published from Gibbon's unfinished manuscripts in 1796, it was revised by Sheffield in 1814. The 1814 edition has become the "official" version. There is a good presentation of this "official" version by J. B. Bury, *The Autobiography of Edward Gibbon as Originally Edited by Lord Sheffield* (London, 1907). This version is readily available in "The World's Classics" series, most recently reissued in 1959.

Until the opening of the Gibbon papers in 1894, Sheffield's 1814 version was accepted as definitive. Only Dean H. H. Milman, Gibbon's most famous nineteenth-century editor, had seen the manuscripts, and he curiously did not call for a new, critical, edition. In fact Sheffield's "editing" of the manuscripts is downright haphazard by modern standards. The first complete version of the six-and-one-half autobiographical fragments left by Gibbon at his death was published and edited by John Murray, *The Autobiographies of Edward Gibbon, Printed Verbatim from Hitherto Unpublished MSS* (London, 1896).

For a fascinating picture of Sheffield at work on his edition of the *Memoirs*, see J. H. Adeane, ed., *The Girlhood of Maria Josepha Holroyd* (London, 1896). Maria Josepha helped her father with the task of putting Gibbon's papers in some kind of order, and her pencil comments are still visible on the original drafts of the *Memoirs*. There is, in the Yale University Library, an interesting copy of the *Memoirs*. It is Lord Sheffield's copy of the 1796 edition, which he apparently used to prepare the 1814 edition, and contains his notes and interleavings. The edition of the *Memoirs* by G. B. Hill (London, 1900) is a collation of the 1796 and 1814 editions, and contains excellent notes.

There are two modern reconstructions of Gibbon's *Memoirs*, both of which are more readable than Murray's verbatim edition. Georges A. Bonnard, Gibbon's best modern edition, has minutely edited the manuscripts and given us the definitive scholarly edition of the work: Edward Gibbon, *Memoirs of My Life*, edited from the manuscripts by Georges A. Bonnard (London, 1966). His detailed introduction explains the problems involved, and the footnotes and backnotes provide all the variant readings. A more readily accessible (and readable) edition which takes textual problems into account is Dero A. Saunders, ed., *The Autobiography of Edward Gibbon* (New York, 1961). Saunders's article, "Six-and-a-Half Autobiographies of Edward Gibbon," *History*, III (1960), 143-53, explains in less cumbersome fashion than Bonnard the problems facing any editor of Gibbon's *Memoirs*.

The French original of the *Essai sur l'étude de la littérature* is reprinted by Sheffield in the *Miscellaneous Works* (1814). There was a contemporary hack translation: *An Essay on the Study of Literature, Written Originally in French, by Edward Gibbon, Jun. Esq.* (London, 1764). It is notoriously inaccurate, and includes the howler "buffoon" for "Buffon."

All of Gibbon's diaries have now been published, and they contain a fascinating commentary on his intellectual development up to 1764. *Miscellanea Gibboniana*, ed. Georges Bonnard, G. R. de Beer, and L. Junod (Lausanne, 1952), is the earliest of the diaries. *Le Journal de Gibbon à Lausanne*, ed. Georges Bonnard (Lausanne, 1945), is the record of Gibbon's preparations for his Italian journey. *Gibbon's Journal to January 28th, 1763: My Journal, I, II, & III and Ephemerides*, ed. D. M. Low (New York, 1929), is the record of Gibbon's militia service. *Gibbon's Journey from Geneva to Rome: His Journal from 20 April to 2 October 1764*, ed. Georges Bonnard (London, 1961), is the last of the diaries.

Gibbon's letters have been edited by J. E. Norton, *The Letters of Edward Gibbon* (3 vols., New York, 1956), and Geoffrey Keynes has compiled an invaluable reference source with his reconstruction of the contents of Gibbon's library: *The Library of Edward Gibbon* (London, 1950).

BIOGRAPHICAL AND CRITICAL WORKS

Africa, Thomas W. "Gibbon and the Golden Age," *Centennial Review*, VII (1963), 273-81.
  Critical of Gibbon's treatment of the age of the Antonines, which becomes in Gibbon's hands a "Tory Utopia."
Bagehot, Walter. *Estimates of Some Englishmen and Scotsmen*. London, 1858.
  Contains an interesting essay on Gibbon.
Black, J. B. *The Art of History*. London, 1926.
  Essays on Gibbon, Hume, Voltaire, and Robertson. Stresses Gibbon's narrative powers and his Enlightenment biases.

Bond, Harold L. *The Literary Art of Edward Gibbon*. Oxford, 1960.
The only full-length study of Gibbon the writer. Sees a unity of style and conception throughout the *Decline and Fall*, and takes a belletristic view of Gibbon.

Bonnard, Georges A. "Gibbon's *Essai sur l'étude de la littérature* as Judged by Contemporary Reviewers and by Gibbon Himself," *English Studies*, XXXII (1951), 145-53.
A straightforward essay dealing with the response to Gibbon's first published work. No attempt is made to deal with the content of the *Essai*.

————. "L'importance du deuxième séjour de Gibbon à Lausanne dans la formation de l'historien," *Mélanges d'histoire et de littérature offerts à M. Charles Gilliard*. Lausanne, 1944.
A study of Gibbon's preparations for his Italian journey. Contains a good assessment of the place of Gibbon's historical geography in his intellectual development.

Braudy, Leo. *Narrative Form in History and Fiction: Hume, Fielding and Gibbon*. Princeton, 1970.
The best study of Gibbon's narrative stance, and the only study that takes into account his development, in the *Decline and Fall*, as an artist and a historian.

Cochrane, C. N. "The Mind of Edward Gibbon," *University of Toronto Quarterly*, XII (1942), 1-17; XIII (1943), 146-66.
A highly personal interpretation of Gibbon by a historian not temperamentally attracted to the *Decline and Fall*.

Curtis, Lewis P. "Gibbon's 'Paradise Lost'," in *The Age of Johnson*, ed. F. W. Hilles. New Haven, 1949.
An elegant essay which sees the *Decline and Fall* as a kind of Bolingbrokian handbook offering instruction in political power, and addressed to the English ruling classes.

Dawson, Christopher. "Edward Gibbon and the Fall of Rome," in *The Dynamics of World History*, ed. John J. Mulloy. New York, 1956.
An outstanding essay by a master historian. Especially good on Gibbon's seventeenth-century predecessors and his place in the humanistic tradition. Perhaps the best criticism of Gibbon from a Roman Catholic point of view.

de Beer, Sir Gavin. *Gibbon and His World*. New York, 1968.
A handsome book, full of carefully selected illustrations. The text is carefully written and, except for some medical information on the nature of Gibbon's malady, offers no new judgments.

———. "The Malady of Edward Gibbon," *Notes and Records of the Royal Society*, VII (1950).

Dyson, A. E. "The Technique of Debunking," *The Twentieth Century*, CLVII (1955), 244-56.
    An attack on Lytton Strachey, but Gibbon's form of irony is discussed and used for comparison.

———. "A Note on Dismissive Irony," *English*, XI (1957), 222-25.
    A continuation of Dyson's analysis of "dismissive" irony.

Fuglum, Per. *Edward Gibbon*. Oslo, 1953.
    A rather wooden essay, repeating all the conventional judgments on Gibbon and his work.

Fussell, Paul. *The Rhetorical World of Augustan Humanism: Ethics and Imagery from Swift to Burke*. Oxford, 1965.
    Very good on the rhetorical patterns used by Gibbon to evoke the importance of culture and civilization, and the metaphors and conceits used for describing man's relationship to history itself.

Giarrizzo, G. *Edward Gibbon et la cultura europea del settecento*. Naples, 1954.
    An immensely learned book. Full of information on the seventeenth century and Gibbon's debt to this tradition, but often repetitive.

Geanakoplos, Deno J. "Edward Gibbon and Byzantine Ecclesiastical History," *Church History*, XXXV (1966), 170-85.
    The only detailed study of Gibbon's treatment of the Eastern church. Concludes that when Gibbon did not have reliable guides to follow he went directly to the sources. His treatment of the Eastern church is praised.

Gruman, Gerald J. " 'Balance' and 'Excess' as Gibbon's Explanation of the Decline and Fall," *History and Theory*, I (1960), 75-85.
    Interesting but overly intellectualized explanation of Gibbon's explanation of Rome's fall. Gruman argues that Gibbon explains Rome's fall as a lost of the *juste milieu*.

Guizot, François. *Mélanges biographiques et littéraires*. Paris, 1868.
    Contains an interesting essay on Gibbon by another great historian.

Helming, V. P. "Edward Gibbon and Georges Deyverdun," *Publications of the Modern Language Association*, XLVII (1932), 1028-49.
    Contains information on the *Mémoires Littéraires* written jointly by the two friends.

Hutton, E. "The Conversion of Edward Gibbon," *Nineteenth Century*, CXI (1932), 362-75.

Jordan, David P. "Gibbon's 'Age of Constantine' and the Fall of Rome," *History and Theory*, VIII (1969), 71-96.

———. "LeNain de Tillemont: Gibbon's 'Sure-Footed Mule'," *Church History*, XXXIX (1970), 483-502.

Joyce, Michael. *Edward Gibbon*. London, 1953.
  A readable and shrewd biography.

Keast, W. R. "The Element of Art in Gibbon's *History*," *English Literary History*, XXIII (1956), 153-62.
  A belletristic approach which sees no development in Gibbon's literary art and confines itself to a description of his style.

Low, D. M. *Edward Gibbon, 1737-1794*. London, 1937.
  The standard modern biography, thoroughly admirable.

Machin, I. W. J. "Gibbon's Debt to Contemporary Scholarship," *Review of English Studies*, XV (1939), 84-88.
  Useful for the tables which analyze Gibbon's use of secondary authorities in the *Decline and Fall*.

MacRobert, T. M. "Gibbon's *Autobiography*," *Review of English Literature*, V (1964), 78-83.

McCloy, Shelby T. *Gibbon's Antagonism to Christianity*. London, 1933.
  A thorough study of the contemporary reaction to Gibbon's chapters on Christianity. A useful supplement to Gibbon's account in the *Memoirs* which plays down the extent and character of the attack from the church.

Momigliano, Arnaldo. "Ancient History and the Antiquarian," in *Contributo alla storia degli studi classici*. Rome, 1955. Reprinted in *Studies in Historiography* (London, 1966).
  An important essay which traces the history of antiquarian studies from antiquity to the nineteenth century. Places Gibbon in the context of the antiquarian tradition.

———. "Gibbon's Contribution to Historical Method," *Contributo alla storia degli studi classici*. Rome, 1955. Reprinted in *Studies in Historiography* (London, 1966).
  Analyzes Gibbon's achievement as a unique combination or synthesis of the erudition of the seventeenth century and the philosophy of the eighteenth century. Gibbon is taken as the central figure in developing this synthesis, so important to the subsequent development of historical studies.

Morison, J. Cotter. *Gibbon*. London, 1880.
  An old but still interesting study. Written before the opening of

the Gibbon papers, but especially sensitive to Gibbon's painful education after his exile from England.

Morris, John N. *Versions of Self*. New York, 1966.
Has some interesting suggestions on Gibbon's *Memoirs*.

Mowat, Robert. *Gibbon*. London, 1936.

Offler, H. S. "Gibbon and the Making of His Swiss History," *The Durham University Journal*, XLI, n.s. (1949), 64-75.
The only study of Gibbon's Swiss history.

Oliver, E. J. *Gibbon and Rome*. London, 1958.
Not sympathetic to Gibbon, especially on his attitudes toward Christianity and the Middle Ages, but good on his response to the French Revolution.

Oliver, J. W. "William Robertson and Edward Gibbon," *Scottish Historical Review*, XXVI (1947), 86.
A short note pointing out the parallel between Gibbon's celebration of the "five good emperors" and Robertson's *History of Charles V.*

Quennell, Peter. *Four Portraits*. London, 1945.
A popular and sympathetic portrait of Gibbon and his contemporaries, Boswell, Sterne, and Wilkes.

Robertson, J. M. *Gibbon*. London, 1925.

Sarton, George. "The Missing Factor in Gibbon's Concept of History," *Harvard Library Bulletin*, XI (1957), 277-95.
Sarton's last essay and a spirited criticism of Gibbon for his neglect of the history of science and technology. This blind spot, Sarton argues, led Gibbon to a fundamentally pessimistic view of the past.

Saunders, J. J. "Gibbon and *The Decline and Fall*," *History*, XXIII (1939), 346-55.
Points out Gibbon's weaknesses, especially on the history of the Byzantine empire and the development of the Slav kingdoms, but essentially favorable in judgment.

———. "Gibbon in Rome, 1764," *History Today*, XIV (September 1964), 608-15.
The model of a popular article. Describes the Rome Gibbon saw, and points out a couple of faulty recollections of the historian/ autobiographer.

———. "The Debate on the Fall of Rome," *History*, XLVIII (1963), 1-17.
A general discussion of the theories of Rome's fall, which gives

some attention to Gibbon's explanation. The author himself stresses the importance of the barbarians rather than moral corruption.

Strachey, Lytton. "Edward Gibbon," in *Portraits in Miniature, and Other Essays*. London, 1931.

A brilliant portrait by a master essayist who was particularly sympathetic to the eighteenth century.

Stephen, Sir Leslie. *History of English Thought in the Eighteenth Century* (2 vols., London, 1903), I, 448-50.

A famous description of Gibbon as one of the "infidels" of the English enlightenment. Considers Gibbon too intellectual and abstract in his treatment of Christianity, and dismisses him as a man temperamentally incapable of understanding the religious mind.

Swain, Joseph Ward. "Edward Gibbon and the Fall of Rome," *South Atlantic Quarterly*, XXXIX (1940), 77-93.

An attempt to relate the political judgments in the *Decline and Fall* to Gibbon's political career. Thus sees some development in Gibbon as historian.

———. *Edward Gibbon the Historian*. London, 1966.

An expansion, and consequent dilution, of the ideas adumbrated in his earlier essay. Swain's Gibbon is a relatively uncomplicated character whose political and emotional life is faithfully reflected in the *Decline and Fall*.

Thompson, David. "Edward Gibbon the Master Builder," *Contemporary Review*, CLI (1937), 583-91.

Thompson, J. A. K. *Classical Influences on English Prose*. London, 1956.

Has some discussion of Gibbon's debt to Latin writers.

Thompson, James W. "The Library of Gibbon the Historian," *Library Quarterly*, VII (1937), 343-53.

A short essay, superseded by Keynes's splendid catalogue.

Tillyard, E. M. W. *The English Epic and Its Background*. Oxford, 1954.

Has a chapter on the *Decline and Fall* as epic.

Trevor-Roper, H. R. "Edward Gibbon after 200 Years," *The Listener*, LXXIV (1964), 617-19; 657-59.

A brilliant appreciation of Gibbon by his shrewdest contemporary admirer.

———. "The Historical Philosophy of the Enlightenment," in *Studies on Voltaire and the Eighteenth Century*, ed. T. Besterman, XXVII (1963).

Places Gibbon in the tradition of Montesquieu and Giannone and describes his achievement.

Wedgwood, C. V. *Edward Gibbon*. London, 1955.

An elegant essay by a contemporary historian self-consciously working in the tradition created by Gibbon.

White, Lynn, Jr., ed. *The Transformation of the Roman World: Gibbon's Problems after Two Centuries*. Los Angeles, 1966.

Contains an essay on Gibbon, by Andrew Lossky, which stresses Gibbon's devotion to the leading ideas of the Enlightenment. Interesting as a survey of the most recent historical thought on Rome's fall.

Winks, Robin. "Hume and Gibbon: A View from a Vantage," *Dalhousie Review*, XLI (1961), 496-504.

A popular essay presenting the conventional views on Gibbon.

Woolf, Virginia. "The Historian and 'The Gibbon'," in *The Death of the Moth and Other Essays*. New York, 1942.

A sensitive and intelligent essay by a brilliant critic.

———. "Reflections at Sheffield Place," in *The Death of the Moth and Other Essays*. New York, 1942.

A moving evocation of Sheffield Place during Gibbon's lifetime, with a portrait of Maria Josepha Holroyd, the daughter of Gibbon's dearest friend.

Young, G. M. *Gibbon*. London, 1932.

A brilliant essay, full of suggestions.

INDEX

A NOTE ON THE AUTHOR

David P. Jordan is assistant professor of history at the University of Illinois at Chicago Circle. He received his B.A. from the University of Michigan and worked as a violist and a newspaperman before earning his M.A. and Ph.D. at Yale University. *Gibbon and His Roman Empire* is his first book.

UNIVERSITY OF ILLINOIS PRESS

DATE DUE